A Way That's Mighty Sweet

A Mother's Legacy of Faith and Family

Linda Aurelia B. Blackmon

Copyright © 2022 Linda Aurelia B. Blackmon.

All rights reserved. No part of this book may be used or reproduced by any means, graphic, electronic, or mechanical, including photocopying, recording, taping or by any information storage retrieval system without the written permission of the author except in the case of brief quotations embodied in critical articles and reviews.

This book is a work of non-fiction. Unless otherwise noted, the author and the publisher make no explicit guarantees as to the accuracy of the information contained in this book and in some cases, names of people and places have been altered to protect their privacy.

WestBow Press books may be ordered through booksellers or by contacting:

WestBow Press
A Division of Thomas Nelson & Zondervan
1663 Liberty Drive
Bloomington, IN 47403
www.westbowpress.com
844-714-3454

Because of the dynamic nature of the Internet, any web addresses or links contained in this book may have changed since publication and may no longer be valid. The views expressed in this work are solely those of the author and do not necessarily reflect the views of the publisher, and the publisher hereby disclaims any responsibility for them.

Any people depicted in stock imagery provided by Getty Images are models, and such images are being used for illustrative purposes only. Certain stock imagery © Getty Images.

ISBN: 978-1-6642-6182-2 (sc)
ISBN: 978-1-6642-6183-9 (hc)
ISBN: 978-1-6642-6181-5 (e)

Library of Congress Control Number: 2022905632

Print information available on the last page.

WestBow Press rev. date: 03/30/2022

Acknowledgments

I thank God for salvation and for my parents, Berkeley Herbert Brown and Willie Elizabeth Long Brown who birthed, nourished and taught me right from wrong through the lens of God's word. I thank my family; husband, James W. Blackmon Jr and my children Jaminda F. Blackmon, Jaime Elizabeth Blackmon and James W. Blackmon, III. Without them I would not have experienced the most important role of my life; being a mother.

    I thank God for my siblings who through them, I was able to experience sisterhood and friend. I extend a special thanks to my sister Edna who gave me a listening ear throughout my years of parenting. To Harris and Tucker's Daycare (New Haven Connecticut) for providing my children with enriched learning while in their care. To Mrs. Mozelle Gethers for the mentoring and support she provided throughout my career and freeing me up to have some extra time with my children. And to my precious granddaughter, Jodie A. Blackmon, who is the beginning of the third generation of the legacy I leave with my children.

Introduction

> I have no greater joy than to hear that
> my children walk in the truth.
> —3 John 1:4 (KJV)

How many times have we heard the saying, or cliché, "A child lives what he learns"? He or she is a "product of his or her environment." Dorothy Nolte's famous poem says if a child lives with criticism, he learns to condemn, if he lives with hostility, he learns to fight (New York Times, mobile *NYTimes.com*). Her poem speaks about fear causing apprehensiveness, and living with pity causes children to feel sorry for themselves. On the other hand, when children are encouraged, they are confident, they learn patience when they've lived with tolerance, when they're praised, they learn to appreciate and most of all, when they live acceptance, they learn to love!

The world is full of distractions; there are so many that can easily influence how children see the world and most importantly, how they see themselves. The foundation where love, appreciation, acceptance and tolerance are first introduced is often at home. Can that foundation support the weight and the pressure of society's message of acceptance? A child's life is integrated in the community which includes his/her neighbors, families, friends, school, teachers, classmates as well as his church and other people and places. These people and places are important and contribute to how that child develops and grows. All of these people and places help shape and mold children. It truly takes a village to raise a child.

Although life provides much experiences that contributes to the growth and development of children, the home is the place that provides the core learning and understanding of life and of one's self. It is there where those experiences and understanding is lived. Teaching a child to love is by example; nurturing, forgiving, giving, taking and acceptance is where love begins. Teaching a child to trust is by exemplifying honesty, following up on promises, teaching children to talk and express their feelings. Teaching them respect by allowing them to make mistakes so that they can understand and forgive others when mistakes are made. Help them to respect themselves by teaching them values of life, encouraging them to do well by reminding them of who they are and their capabilities. Let them know that their purpose is to do well in life so that they can be of service to others.

What exactly does "do well" means? The basics as I understood it as a child was to listen to my parents first. Understand what they were teaching; go to school; education is important and it is to prepare us for work later in life. Be honest and respectful to everyone and be an upstanding citizen; have goals and work towards accomplishing those goals, and to know and love God. Learning to overcome the scrapes and bruises that are physically present prepares children to overcome the emotional bruises that life presents. The key to this, (as I was taught) was to walk in truth. Knowing right from wrong and making the right choices through truth and accountability will make you free. This foundation is laid when God is the center of the family. In my parents' house, God was first and we were in church every Sunday. I was constantly reminded to remember who I am. It took me a while before I understood what that meant. To walk in truth is to know who you are; know that you are a child of God and to never forget it. A child does live what he/she learns. It's up to us to teach them so that their learning allows them to walk in truth and live a life that will never forget who they are.

- 1 -

There's No Place like Home

Train up a child in the way he should go: and
when he is old, he will not depart from it.
—Proverbs 22:6 (KJV)

HOME IS CERTAINLY WHERE THE HEART IS! LIFE HAS taken me on several journeys and adventures, and as time goes by, I'm constantly reminded of the life I had at home with my parents. These are memories that strengthen me, as I learned at an early age that all things are possible when God is involved. My parents, Berkeley Herbert and Willie Elizabeth Long Brown, had a strong faith in our Lord and Savior. Although I did not truly understand the words, I often heard about the Lord while growing up, and I've learned that it was those words that has kept me over the years. The heart is the pulse of life; home is that pulse for me. It is where I learned to love, to live, to grow, and to accept what life offers while deciding how I could participate in positive change. I thank God for the parents he gave me.

I was the sixth child born to the two most important people in my life: my parents. I loved hearing from my mother the story of my birth! She talked to me often about the day I was born. It was the year of 1955. I don't know if it was the practice in those days or if I was just privileged. Mama told me about how the doctor came to the house to deliver me. I felt extremely special because the doctor came to me. I was born in the house where we lived. I was not delivered by a midwife like most but by a doctor! It was on a fall day with temperature in the seventies.

Between September 18 and the early morning of September 20, Hurricane Ione was expected to land in North Carolina and would be the first hurricane to be observed by the newly installed Cape Hatteras Radar. The hurricane did not reach my parents' home. It was a typical beautiful fall day, and my birth would add to the family history of five children before me. My parents behaved as if I were the first born all over again. My oldest sister described the scene during my birth. She was only eleven at the time but played a role in the delivery. She talked about how she was excited to assist by bringing fresh water for the delivery when needed.

After the delivery, the doctor assured my parents that everything was OK; the delivery went well, and both mother and baby were fine. This was the beginning of a life where I would learn that social issues would not interfere with family values.

Hearing Mama talk about me as a child gave me a warm sense of importance. Her conversations were so real and full of pride. She often told me that I was peculiar. She said it so often that I would look up the word to gain an understanding of what the word *peculiar* meant. She talked about how "busy" I was as a baby. She described a time when she left me on the bed for a few minutes and wasn't concerned in regard to me moving or falling because I wasn't walking or crawling at the time. To her surprise, when she returned to her bedroom, I was sitting on top of her sewing machine, which was sitting next to the bed. She said she never could figure out how I was able to get off that bed. She shared other stories about my behavior that may have seemed peculiar. She remarked about how she couldn't figure out why I always smelled my food before eating and how I was the only child she didn't nurse as long as she wanted because I often indicated that I was ready for solid food. I bit her too often while feeding. I enjoyed hearing those stories and mostly because it was a time that she and I shared alone—just the two of us.

Knowing Who I Am

Although I don't remember every moment I lived in my childhood, I have snapshots of endearing moments that I shared with Mama and Daddy. I recall my mama often saying, "Be who you are," and Daddy reminding me that I'm just as important as anyone and I could not allow anyone or anything to convince me differently. It was clearly communicated by Mama and Daddy that God came first and then family. We were to behave a certain way; as Daddy often said, we must have proper manners. It was mandatory that we treated each other with respect and dignity; cursing and swearing were not heard in our home. Name-calling was prohibited. Honoring my mother and father was clearly understood as this was not only a house rule and expectation but was a commandment. We had to show love for each other at home first, as it was only then that we could demonstrate brotherly love outside the home.

We had to do what we were told by our parents as well as the adult neighbors. I certainly grew up in a "village that raised the children." I was watched by all the neighbors, and any behavior observed by the neighbors was immediately communicated to our parents. Education was a must! Yes, I had to attend school regularly and produce grades that supported my attendance. I always felt important because of them, and being a child was an important place in the household. They taught me on a daily basis the importance of parents and what it meant to be blessed by children. There were eight children with minimum resources, but they made ends meet and saw it all as a blessing. It would be later in my life that I realized how many material things I didn't have, yet I rejoice over the abundance of love and attention I received as a child. I hear people refer to growing up poor because they didn't have the possessions that others had: nice clothes, a beautiful home in a middle-class neighborhood, private schools, the best public schools, and private lessons.

I had what I needed. I lived in small homes that accommodated my family, and I didn't have the new clothes that my fellow classmates or playmates had. Mama was an excellent seamstress, and the clothes she made were much nicer than clothes from the stores. I was able to keep myself occupied playing games with my peers without the latest toys to keep me busy. What did I have? I had parents who knew that what I needed went beyond the dollars. I had a strong foundation of faith that would outweigh anything that money could buy. This foundation of faith was built on love providing much room to grow physically, emotionally, and toward Christ! Yes, my parents taught me that having faith in God, believing that all things are possible through Christ, would give me the strength, endurance, and understanding that would take me through life safely. I didn't understand it at the time, but as I continued to build on this foundation, I gained an understanding and would later learn that my parents were right!

Yes, a child does lives what he or she learns! When he learns to value what's important in life, he also learns to love his fellow man, to give more and take less, to treat others with kindness and respect, to honor his mother and father, to use words that are encouraging, and to not demean or belittle others. He learns to reach out and love selflessly, unconditionally, and with his or her whole heart. He learns to respect himself so that he knows when he's respected and he knows how to extend that respect toward others. He learns that God is in control and it is only God who will always be with him and in any situation. He learns that through God, his parents are the makers of strong roots that would sprout many branches that would guide him through life. I know that's what I learned. My parents were gifts from God, and those strong roots have defined who I am.

Mama

Each time I looked at Mama, I looked in admiration. She consistently greeted everyone with a smile. There was a seriousness to her expressions; her smile was pleasant yet inquisitive. She could communicate without speaking. Her smile had different meanings. She would smile in a pleasing way, yet she would smile and it would immediately suggest that she was about to question either my behavior or a comment I made at some point. She would smile in a way to let you know that she was aware of a lie that was told or that a lie was about to be told. That particular smile was a warning to get it together before it got to that point. Then there was her forgiving smile, which was reassuring and warm. It was her way of letting me know that everything would be all right and there was nothing to fear. These smiles came often and were generally followed by a warm hug.

Her eyes spoke peace and gave one a glimpse of her loving heart. She loved people, truly was inviting, and made every possible effort to accommodate those in need. From needing something to eat, something to wear, or just a friend to talk to, she was there for them. She had a huge heart and was a God-fearing woman who found it necessary to include the Lord in her interactions and to make it known that Christ was present in her life and in her home. She made me accountable to read verses from the Bible and to study His word. As I look back on my childhood, I now know that although I didn't read as much as was expected, I heard it through Mama's daily teaching. I was very young, maybe three years old when I learned Psalm 23 in its entirety. I memorized the words, but didn't know exactly what those words meant. I realized over time that the 23rd Psalm would be a constant thought in my mind as an adult and it would be my blessed assurance! Mama read her bible daily and walked around the house singing numerous gospel hymns and taught them to me and my siblings.

Mama walked with assurance. She knew who she was and had

no problems helping others to understand that. She lived what she taught us. She put God first and made it her business to make sure we knew who she was and who we were. I think I got it at an early age! Mama was proud and it was obvious in how she walked. She held her head up high and never allowed her head to hang down. She reminded me that holding your head down indicated that there was something to hide. "Hold your head up high and be proud of who you are," she would say. She had a very fast pace in her walk. Her thick black shoulder length hair would sway in the wind as she walked while at the same time, her dress swayed back and forth when walking and she didn't waste any time getting where she had to go. There was a rhythm to her walk. Today it would be defined as a swag. She always wore dresses, never pants in her life, as she was a lady, poised and proper. She didn't believe in wearing pants and she didn't believe her girls should wear them. I was a high school senior before I wore my one and only pair at that time.

Mama was soft spoken, but could raise her voice when she felt it was necessary. She was loving and taught me early in my life that children were one of God's most precious gifts. I was so convinced that children were that special, I made up my mind at an early age that I would not have children. It seemed like a job that I was not capable of handling. I didn't think that I could take on this task with the compassion that Mama had. She never taught that children should be spanked. She always said that children are to be chastised. She made it clear that parents are responsible for their children's spiritual growth. She would say that when we (her children) have children, we must take them to church. She explained that God will hold us accountable if we do not take our children to church. I always felt that I would be punished by God if I did not follow through with this expectation. This was another determining factor that helped me decide that I would never have children. When I was young, I was going to church because my parents told me that I had to. Like most children, I was thinking that when I grow up, I wouldn't go and if I didn't go and didn't have children, it would be okay. As a child I thought as a child and later learned that those childish ways would no longer exit.

My Mama was very intuitive. She knew her children and it seemed that she knew our thoughts before we voiced them. She was a woman of wisdom and where she gave advice, she did it in a manner that left me room to make a decision, allowing me autonomy while knowing that her advice would influence my decision. She allowed me to exercise critical thinking, or as she referred to "using your own mind." She allowed me to be an individual, to get to know who I am! She was keen on education. I would find out later in my life that Mama was an outstanding student in school. She had skipped a grade because of her intelligence and ability to excel beyond grade level requirements. She demonstrated her love for learning through her children. She took interest in our school work and often surprised me with her knowledge on topics I had not expected her to know. Mama had not finished high school, but was clearly knowledgeable beyond high school level.

Humility was something Mama knew much about. She was very humble and never boasted about what she knew. She gave herself no credit for her efforts, accomplishments or work she had done. She credited it all to God and taught us not to think selfishly. She reached out to help others and never expected anything in return. She gave and was not concerned about receiving. She loved unconditionally and made her children feel equally loved. She put her family first, after God and kept God in the forefront. She took nothing for granted and nothing was owed to her. She lived within her means and would not allow herself to be placed in predicaments that compromised the well-being of her family. She never compared herself to others, nor did she want or possess things because others had them. She was not one to keep up with the Joneses. She was confident in who she was and was not interested in how people felt about her. She believed that as long as she was living for the Lord, what others thought didn't matter. If she was talked about, she wasn't interested in who said what. She did not deem that as her problems. She knew that God would take care of it all and she wouldn't have to carry that burden alone. I became aggravated at times trying to figure out why she wasn't.

She loved the Lord. Mama could have been a preacher. As a matter of fact, I often felt as if she was. She provided a lesson in much of my behavior. She would sing songs that suggest how we should behave. She often sang a song when she wanted to remind my brother that he needed to change his ways. She would sing a song called "You Better Make a Change," and when my oldest brother was around after she had verbally expressed her dislike for his behavior, she would begin singing, "you better make a change, oh my Lord won't you hear God's call, you better make a change." We all knew it was for my older brother and I would work hard trying to behave so that there wasn't a song directed towards me. She often reminded us of how we should behave and I didn't realize until I was an adult that much of what she said to us was from the bible. She brought the bible to life in her daily living and I had much to gain living with her and having her as my mom. A child lives what he or she learns and my Mama stuffed each day I lived with her with much wisdom, love, kindness, humility, respect, and the ability for me to know who I am.

Mama was beautiful. Her high cheek bones accented her big bright eyes, her brown skinned complexion, her tall statue and the way she carried herself. She was a poised, elegant, classy lady. Although she wasn't working, she wore lipstick daily as well as perfume (or as she called it "smell good"). Her shoulder length hair often pulled back in a "French roll" highlighting her facial structure. She was as beautiful inside as she was on the outside. Mama presented herself well in her dress attire. She was always appropriately dressed for any and all occasions she attended. She was pleasant, nurturing and comforting. She liked having fun and made a way for us as a family to engage in family activity. It was obvious why she was attracted to Daddy. He expressed his attraction to her often as observed in how he looked at her.

In addition to her intellect, Mama was very creative. She could make anything and it was truly a blessing because her sewing talent made it possible for us to have new clothing regardless of the limited household budget. I took great pride in the things Mama made. I recall her making me a red plaid coat and it was lovely. She even made slips for me to wear underneath my dress for church on Sunday. I enjoyed the smell of new fabric and watching her save the scraps for her quilting. Mama didn't use patterns. She envisioned how the garment would look and made it based on just that. Her philosophy was "a good seamstress did not need a pattern to sew." She sewed for the family and our house was the drop off point for the neighbors when they needed clothing mended and when there was an outfit needed for special occasions. Mama was there to make it happen and they often left satisfied with her work and her company. As for us, walking around the house with missing buttons, broken zippers or ripped garments did not exist. Mama took pride in keeping our clothes in tack. Mama gave a clear message that she enjoyed her position as a wife and mother.

She was a stay-at-home mom. As long as I can remember, Mama was home all the time while Daddy worked. I have never known her to work, and I never asked her directly why she didn't work. It just wasn't relevant during our conversations. I was just happy that she was home when I left for school and home when I returned. Being home with her all day prior to starting school was really a pivotal time in my life. She approached everything with much significance while making me feel important and loved. She was my security and I trusted her and believed what she told me. Although she was home, she would inquire about the school day. She was available to leave home when needed and make herself available at the schools when needed. She was my first teacher and I was a little advanced in first grade because of her.

Mama never drove a vehicle, Daddy drove her and the family

to any place we needed to go. It didn't bother Mama that she didn't drive and was dependent on Daddy to drive her around. Daddy seemed to be honored to have that role, as he didn't appear to be bothered by it. The 1950s were known as the years of conformity. Things were beginning to change for women in the United States as a whole. However, that conformity was not applicable to the African American women. They did not have the "material Abundance" (khanacademy.org) made available to other women. Growing up, I never heard Mama or Daddy complain about the economy, what they didn't have, nor did they speak on racial issues. The consistent lesson in our home was to do my best and blame no one for anything that I lacked or felt that I should have. It was up to me to build on the foundation they laid for me through their teachings. Where things changed in our society during these times, life was consistent in our household. No excuses, no envy, no blame and no pity. My Mama was an amazing God-fearing woman who walked by faith and not by sight.

Daddy

Daddy was as handsome as Mama was beautiful. He loved wearing his hats and they complimented his good looks. He would dress to the "nine" when going to church and the pictures he took with mama were evident that he dressed up to pose with her. He wore suits to church and when he was working, he was in uniform. I used to love watching him shave using his old spice cologne. I still love the smell of Old Spice! I always thought that he looked like Santa Claus when he lathered his face before shaving. It never bothered him that I wanted to watch. I think he got a kick out of the amazement I showed as I watched him shave. It got to the point where he would let me know when he was going to shave, and he allowed me to stir and mix the lather before applying it to his face. He was suave and also walked proudly.

Each time I looked at Daddy, I saw strength and independence. He was a proud man who didn't want handouts, nor did he accept them. Aware of his limited finances and education, Daddy was a hard worker and did what he could to provide for his family. He always worked, and not once did I hear him complain about having to work as hard as he did and the fact that he did it alone. As a man in the 1950s and '60s, he rose above the oppression and discrimination to make ends meet for his family. He stressed the importance of working hard and getting a good education. Daddy did not complete high school, but he knew the value of getting an education. He wanted more for his children than what he was able to obtain. I saw him as my hero.

He was strong, and I never heard an argument between him and Mama. Not to say they never disagreed, as disagreement is inevitable in a marriage, but I never heard them argue. Daddy was wise and voiced his opinion. He provided us with words of wisdom so that we were able to make the right choices.

He was a provider. We didn't live in the best houses, but we didn't live in the worst. We had a roof over our heads, and although it might not have afforded us the amenities that our friends' and neighbors' homes had, it was my safe haven. Daddy was in charge, and there was a comfort in knowing that he was there. When Daddy was not buying food, he was out hunting. I recall him leaving with his rifle and returning with dinner.

He gave instructions regarding how to behave and was keen on being respected; he had no tolerance for disrespect. This was clearly exercised in our house. Daddy was Daddy, but he was also *sir*, as was any male adult—"yes, sir; no, sir" was my response when answering him. Mama was addressed as *ma'am*, as were other adult females.

When we ate, manners were mandatory; it was always, for example, "Could you pass the biscuits, please?" and followed by a thank-you. Daddy took pride in saying grace before each meal. At the time, I perceived it as routine. As an adult, I see it as a way for

Daddy to sit down and see the benefits of what God had provided through him. He was a caretaker and a loving father.

Daddy was the breadwinner of our home. As a little girl, I believed what I observed in my household. Watching him provide for his family taught me that it was the role of the husband and father to work and ensure that his family had what they needed. *Need* is the operative word. He could only provide for the needs of his family. He worked hard to make ends meet, and he found time to spend with us after he returned home from work. The attention he gave was more valuable than anything he could have purchased in stores.

He praised me and highlighted any accomplishment I made. It could have been something as simple as drawing the lines on the ground to play hopscotch. Daddy went beyond his limitations, financially and educationally, to make ends meet. His greatest contribution was his love. That superseded anything and everything that money could buy. There were times when he stretched his dollars and gave us some things that we wanted as well.

Daddy was a protector. He treated his daughters with the upmost respect and care. He had his dos and don'ts, and we were expected to follow his rules. Each morning after getting dressed for school or outside play, Daddy would sit me on his knee and tie my shoes. As he did, he would tell me his expectations for me at school or play. He would say, "When you go outside, do not leave the yard, and stay out of those blackberry patches." He would make sure my socks were in place to protect my legs from being scratched by the boughs. I looked forward to having those moments with Daddy. He made me feel safe, and as I believed in him, he made me believe in myself. He had rules for home, for visiting others, and for church.

Daddy drove us everywhere we went. Mama and Daddy were always together. He made sure Mama had what she needed in the house while he was at work. He provided that security for the family.

A Way That's Mighty Sweet

Daddy had a way of assuring me that everything would be OK. He even made medicine taste good. As a child, I was never sick, other than having the measles. We took our vitamins, and we had to take castor oil, which I dreaded, but I would not refuse to take it. Taking a spoonful of castor oil was one of the worst things I ever had to do as a young girl, but Daddy managed to make that a pleasant memory. He would give me an orange, soften it, and put a hole in it. Then he would instruct me to squeeze the orange and suck the juice from the orange immediately after taking that spoonful of castor oil. It worked, and I started to look forward to taking that castor oil. The orange gave it a sweet taste, and I was allowed to eat the orange afterward.

Daddy was also an artist and a musician. He never had music lessons, but what a pleasure it was to hear him play his harmonica. Daddy would sit on the steps of the house, in the living room, or in the kitchen and play his harmonica. I don't remember the titles of the tunes he played, but I remember the feeling I had when I heard him play. It was a joyous and happy time. His music planted in my heart what may have seemed to be missing in my environment. I felt the love and warmth that his music provided, and he would look at me while playing. When he took a break briefly to take his lips off the harmonica, he would smile pleasingly at me and then continue playing. I looked forward to hearing him play. To this day, whenever I hear a song with a harmonica playing, I see my daddy playing his harmonica, smiling, and patting his feet.

Then, there was his artwork. He completed numerous ink-sketched pictures. He would dip his feather-pointed pen into the ink and sketch his pictures. I often think about one of them—a picture of a house with a porch and many windows on a well-landscaped lawn. I often wondered if this was a house that he hoped to provide for his family. It looked like a blueprint for an architect. He saved many of his pictures and kept them in a little locked trunk, as these were valuable pieces of artwork. Daddy was a talented man.

Linda Aurelia B. Blackmon

    As a child, I didn't think anyone was anywhere as wise as my daddy. He was one of the most intelligent people I knew. He was a man of integrity, of high regard for the Lord, and one who took pride in all that he did. He taught me the importance of education, to strive for excellence, and to remember that only I could block my success. I learned at an early age that God was (and is) first in my life and that only I could determine the quality of my education. No one was to define that for me.

    I loved learning, and although I spent most of my preschool days with Mama, Daddy was always interested in what I learned. He placed strong emphasis on learning, and I knew at an early age—before I started school—that school was important. The more I learned, the more I wanted to attend school. Daddy provided the social lessons needed to balance my learning experience. He taught self-respect and reminded us that how we respected ourselves would determine how we respected others. There was no room for disrespect.

    Growing up in the sixties required more than tough skin; it required an in-depth understanding of who we were. Segregation kept races divided, and in doing so, education opportunities were limited. History tells us that the life span of an African America was seven years less that Caucasian (digitalhistory.uh.edu). My parents decided that segregation and the limitations society placed on the African American population would not be a barrier for their children. My home was a place where positive conversations took place, and my parents ruled out the unkind conversations that we might have heard when we were away from home and our parents. They defined who we were, based on the Bible and on their morals and beliefs. Thank God for them!

Daddy, the Disciplinarian

Like Mama, Daddy was a talker. There were so many lessons to learn from one act of unacceptable behavior. There were basic instructions on how to act while at home and how to act once we left the house. His expectations were not different. I learned that my behavior at home determined how I should behave once I left the house. Respecting each other at home was the lesson taught early in life. If or when it was not demonstrated elsewhere, the lesson continued once we returned home.

For years, I'd heard stories from others about their getting "whippings"; they were beaten and yelled at. At times, it seemed that problem-solving was about hitting or implementing some type of corporal punishment. Daddy didn't talk about hitting or physically punishing us. He and Mama talked about any unacceptable behavior and guided us on how to correct it. I think I love to talk because of all the talking that took place as I was growing up.

Hitting was not the answer to unacceptable behavior, but there was one time when I thought I would get a whipping. Mama and Daddy had to go somewhere, and they took me to a sitter. I was told to stay in her yard and to do what I was told. Disrespect would not be tolerated.

After they left, I decided to go to the nearby blackberry patch and pick some berries. I was young at the time and wasn't thinking about the dos and don'ts while my parents were away. I returned before my parents came to pick me up. They talked to the babysitter and said nothing to me on the way home. When we were inside the house, however, they let me know that the sitter had informed them that I had wandered off into the blackberry patch. Well, on that day, the lecture I received was far worse than any whipping I could have received. I cried because my feelings were hurt. I realized that I had disobeyed my parents. I thought that it was OK because I had followed some older kids into the patch.

Daddy gave me a one-to-one lesson on how I must think for myself. He explained that I could have said no and stayed in the babysitter's yard, as I was told. He said that I had to think for myself, or I could end up in trouble or harmed. I wasn't more than seven years old at the time, but I was old enough to understand the meaning of thinking independently, avoiding the influence of others, and—most importantly—being responsible for my actions. It taught me to make decisions based on what was right and not to allow others' opinions, likes, or dislikes to interfere with who I was.

Making the right decision was most important. It may have taken me years to understand what a blessing my parents were to me, but on the many roads I've traveled, life has taught me to appreciate them. They were and still are my heroes.

- 2 -

My First Teachers

> My son, hear the instruction of thy father; and forsake
> not the law of thy mother. For they shall be an ornament
> of grace unto thy head, and chain about thy neck.
> —Proverbs 1:8–9

I ENJOYED MY CHILDHOOD BUT NOT BECAUSE OF THINGS I HAD or wanted. I enjoyed the gifts of love my parents presented to me in so many ways. Learning from them was and is the most important thing I've ever done. They were both teachers. Daddy always talked about respect, dignity, and knowing who I am. Mama talked about being a lady and being careful when selecting friends. She always said, "You're as good as the company you keep."

They both made sure I practiced good manners and was on my best behavior at all times. Humility and respecting others were a must. They often assured me that God knew and saw all that I did. They would say, "He hears what you're thinking." I often wondered how that could be. What I knew about God was what my parents told me and what I heard in Sunday school. Reading Bible verses was a must; Mama encouraged me to memorize verses at an early age. The first Bible verse I learned was Psalm 23—the Lord is my shepherd, I shall not want. In those days, we had only one Bible to use in church and in our home, and it was the King James Version.

Church was mandatory, and that was that. Daddy drove us to church each Sunday, and I enjoyed that ride. It seemed like hours when I was young, but in reality, it was about a half-hour drive. On the way there, the ground rules were carefully reiterated. Mama and Daddy would take turns reminding me of what was expected. We would be entering God's house, and only godly behavior would be tolerated. To this day, I can hear Daddy saying, "Don't talk in church. Only the devil talks in church because he doesn't want to hear what the preacher is saying."

Mama was quick to say, "Be quiet and listen." We heard the conversation without distractions, other than the treats we had on the way to the church. Daddy had snacks in the car, and he would give us different types of cookies to eat on the way. I particularly like the cookies with the holes in the middle. I eat those cookies one at a time by placing the cookie on my pinky finger. I would eat around the edges of the cookie and would end up wearing a cookie ring. After admiring how evenly I'd bitten around the hole of the cookie, I would pop it into my mouth and then start a new one.

Once we were in church, I was able to demonstrate how well I was listening. Entering the church gave me a sense of security, a sense of peace, and there was a smell of what seemed to be powder and perfume. I enjoyed reading the advertisements on the hand fans that were passed out to keep cool. The adults were always given the fans first. I dared not ask for one, as respecting my elders was always a priority. It was times like those when I was to be seen and not heard. I wasn't really interested in fanning; I just liked reading the fans and chewing the half stick of chewing gum that Mama gave me. I kept quiet and listened to the pastor preach.

On the way home, Mama and Daddy would discuss the sermon and quiz me on what was said. In my own way, I was able to repeat some of the sermon, and that was enough to please them.

Mama had what she called *prayer meetings*. She would invite her friends over to the house, and they would read scripture and discuss what they'd read, followed by amens, head nods, and other comments that expressed their agreement with the text. Then, they would share experiences relating to what they'd read. They gave testimonies and praised God as they continued to read.

Mama would call my siblings and me into the room to present a song—she would tell us which song to sing. I have always loved to sing. Mama spent a lot of time teaching me how to sing church songs. One of the first songs she taught me was "Jesus Loves Me." Once I memorized that song, she taught me to sing "He's Got the Whole World in His Hands." Other songs I learned were "I Thank You, Jesus," and one of her favorites, "Sweeping through the City." Singing was so much fun. This was their routine at the prayer meetings, and I looked forward to this moment and enjoyed it. Mama and her friends would clap and smile, showing approval as we sang. Afterward, we would take seats and listen. Mama served refreshments after the study, and then her friends would leave. This happened weekly, and we sang each week.

Mama and Daddy practiced what they preached. Their kindness was unlimited, and they truly treated everyone with respect. They didn't just tell me what I needed to do; they showed me, and I wanted nothing more than to be like them. I had to get out of my own way so that I could be more like them.

Things I Remember

Mama and Daddy taught us by example. Their examples were more than going to church; they were about how we treated each other. We saw this in how they treated us and how they treated each other. I never heard them say an unkind word to each other, nor did they express anger toward each other in my presence. Daddy was the head of our household. He left home for work every day while Mama took care of the children. This was a perfect situation for me, having my mama home every day. She was attentive, loving, and caring. I remember being home alone with her when my siblings were in school. I was about five years old. At that time, kindergarten wasn't an option, so I would start school in the first grade. I wanted so badly to go to school because Mama taught me to love learning. During the day with her, she would teach me the basics. I knew all of the alphabet. I could read. I learned nursery rhymes. I knew how to add and subtract (mostly single digits). These lessons at home intrigued me and increased my curiosity. I wanted to learn more! I wanted to go to school. I decided to tell Mama that I was ready for school. I followed through with my plan and rushed to share my enthusiasm.

When I told her, she looked at me and said, "You can't go to school. You're too young. You must be six years old to start school."

"But I will be six soon", I said, "please let me go."

"They won't let you start early," she said.

Hearing this crushed me! I needed to start school so that I could learn more and so that I could leave with my older siblings. I immediately started crying, which was something I didn't do. I knew that crying would not get me what I wanted, but in this particular case, I wasn't crying to change her mind; I was crying because I was hurt. I didn't ask why because I knew not to question my mama—that would be disrespectful—so all I could do was cry.

Mama took me by my hand, walked me over to the sofa, wiped my tears, and began to explain to me why I couldn't attend school.

She said "Aurelia, there were rules for kids attending school and age is one of them. All kids attending school starts at the same age and you are not old enough. You will have to wait to start next year, and I will continue to help you learn while you're home with me."

I was already five and would be six shortly after school started. Mama explained to me that I had to be six at the start of the school year. I was convinced that I couldn't go, and as I struggled to hold back tears, Mama asked me a question.

She said, "Would you like to go to the school and talk to the principal?" Although I wasn't sure what that meant, I immediately replied with a yes! Enrolled or not, I would go inside the school building, and somehow, that was good enough for me.

We got dressed, and Mama checked in with me again to be certain that I wanted to do this. She reminded me that it was a long walk, and I might get tired. We lived in a house in woods surrounded by dogwood trees, and that made the walk more exciting. I loved where I lived; looking up at those trees was something to behold. I enjoyed skipping and catching butterflies on my finger, and I looked forward to doing this during the walk to school.

It was quite a walk, just to get to the main road that led to the school. I quickly said I still wanted to go, and I assured her that I would not get tired. So Mama and I were off to school to meet with the principal. I don't think she made an appointment; we just went.

Walking into that building was exciting; to this day, I remember how good I felt holding Mama's hand as I walked toward the principal's office. He was sitting behind his desk.

Mama introduced herself and me and then said, "We're here because Linda wants to start school this fall."

He looked at me and appeared serious. At the time, I thought he looked mean. He directed his conversation to me. "What's your name, and how old are you?"

I hesitantly told him "my name is Linda Brown and I am five years old, but I will be six in September."

He then explained to me about the rules, which sounded like the same thing Mama had told me prior to leaving the house.

"Well, Linda," he explained. "the deadline for the required age has passed, and you are too young to start." You will have to wait and start first grade next year."

That was so difficult to take in; tears began to roll down my face, and I quickly tried to wipe them away. I didn't want to cry in his office; I knew that I had to wait.

He handed me a tissue and said, "You really want to come to school?"

I nodded and replied, "yes sir."

"Why?" he asked.

I didn't want to talk anymore, but I managed to say, "I want to learn to read and write." As I spoke, I cried even more. It was hard for me to speak because I struggled pronouncing certain words. I was ashamed that I might say the wrong thing; I had hoped that I wouldn't have to say anything.

He was kind to me, and I stopped crying. He leaned back in his chair, pulled out some papers from his desk, and handed them to my mother.

He said, "Here Mrs. Brown, any child who wants to learn this badly needs to come to school. Please fill out these papers so we can enroll her"

He turned to me and said, "You are starting school this fall!"

I don't remember, but I do believe I said thank you. Mama smiled at me and nodded her head with much approval. I was only five but felt so grown and so big! I was going to school and couldn't wait to tell my siblings. Little did I know that it would be the first time I negotiated with anyone outside my home. I was elated, and the walk home was better than it had been on our way to the school.

Starting to school was exciting for me, and I couldn't wait. I wasn't concerned with what I needed to attend because I never had to be concerned about that. Mama and Daddy always took care of what I needed. I wasn't one to ask for anything, but I always was appreciative of anything they gave me.

I would no longer have those days alone with Mama. The one-to-one attention she gave me that helped me with learning the basics was coming to an end. I remember how proud Daddy was when he got the news. He came to me a few days before school started and handed me a brand-new book satchel. It was a pretty red plaid, outlined in black. It buckled on the front and had a pocket large enough for lunch and a handle to carry it like a suitcase. I was ecstatic! This was what the kids were carrying, but I never thought I would have one. I didn't expect it and wouldn't have dared to ask because he always gave me what I needed, but Daddy knew exactly what I wanted, and he provided it. I'll never forget his smile as he handed the satchel to me. That was one of my proudest moments.

Enrolling in school was a wish come true. I felt important and as old as my siblings because they no longer said goodbye to me as they went off to school each morning.

I was learning new things. I continued to have problems with speech and felt bad at times about asking or answering questions in class. The school provided me with a speech therapist, and that was a blessing. She was the sweetest, kindest person I had every met. I got to meet with her alone, and soon I was pronouncing words correctly and happily volunteering to ask and answer questions.

All was going well in first grade—until my beautiful book satchel was ruined. I had asked my first-grade teacher permission to use the bathroom. Many kids had asked before me, so by the time I asked her, she was convinced that kids were asking to get out of class. I really needed to go, but she didn't believe me. She directed me to go back to my seat and told me to stay there. I did as I was told.

Soon, I began to wiggle, cross my legs, and do whatever I could to keep from relieving myself in my chair. As I squirmed and wiggled, I became distracting to my classmates, and the teacher directed me to be still.

"Mrs. Washington," I asked, "Can I please go to the bathroom? I really needed to go. She again said "no."

I sat there, and after a while, I slowly urinated on myself. The stream of urine flowed down the chair onto my satchel, and a puddle formed on the floor. When a classmate noticed that the floor was wet around my chair, she thought I had spilled something from my bag. The teacher saw where I had urinated and pulled my chair over by the window. She lifted my dress so I could dry off but still would not allow me to go to the bathroom.

At the end of the day when I went home, my parents were not pleased when I told them what had happened. I was more upset about my book satchel than I was about the humiliation I had experienced. Mama cleaned my satchel, and it was good as new. I was able to take it to school a couple of days afterward. I don't know what Mama and Daddy said to the principal, but the next day the teacher apologized to me, and it never happened again. My classmates never teased me for what happened. I think they knew that it was the teacher's fault.

I enjoyed school for the duration of time that I attended that particular school. We relocated to a different district after I completed second grade. I started a new school in third grade. The summer before fourth grade, I hit another milestone in my life. We were on a tight budget, and although I wanted a bike, I wasn't going to ask for one. It wouldn't make sense anyway because I didn't know how to ride one. I rode tricycles that belonged to friends, but I had not learned to ride a bike and had not thought of learning until one of my friends invited me to ride her bike. I couldn't tell her that I didn't know how to ride. I would be a fourth-grader soon, and I was embarrassed to admit that I didn't know how.

"Linda, it's your turn to ride, take it", she said. So I kindly accepted her invitation to ride the bike. To demonstrate that I knew what I was doing, I decided that I would ride down a hill. I didn't think about the danger in it, I decided that I would go for it and dared not anticipated about the possibilities of getting hurt. The excitement was larger than any fears! I took the bike and rolled down that hill like a champ! I stayed up and stayed on the bike without braking, and I gently touched the brakes as I approached the bottom. What an experience! There was one problem; Daddy was standing at the top of the hill when I returned.

He had a habit of appearing just when I thought the coast was clear. I remembered the time when he told my sisters and me not to walk to school. He thought that the school was too far away for his girls to walk. He planned to talk to the school about sending a bus to our home. The minute we thought he had gone to work, we sneaked out of the house and walked to school. Before we reached the end of the property that led to the main road, Daddy jumped out of the bushes and rushed us home. He did get us a school bus, and we didn't have to walk to school anymore—and we also learned a lesson. He could be anywhere and always had a way of working things out.

As I approached the top of the hill where I had taken off to show my bike-riding skills, I saw Daddy looking down at me with his arms folded. My friends stood on either side of him, and I wasn't sure what to expect. They were all cheering and clapping as I slowly but surely approached the top of that hill. I had gotten Daddy's permission to go outside to play with them, and I figured that he might have come outside just to check up on me. But for him to witness me taking off on a bike and taking the risk of riding down a hill brought much concern, as I wasn't sure how he would react. I made every effort to respond cheerfully to my applauding friends and was so glad they couldn't feel my heart racing as I approached them.

I huffed and puffed my way up the hill. Riding down had been easy, but walking back up was taking a toll on me. My friends were cheering in disbelief at the way I'd gone down that hill. The next person to ride asked me to hurry up so that she could take her turn, but I was taking my time hoping that Daddy was not mad at me. I didn't want to disappoint him, but I couldn't continue to procrastinate. I made it to the top and thanked my friend for letting me ride her bike.

Daddy looked at me and said, "It's time to go back to the house."

I said goodbye to my friends and held on to Daddy's hand as

we walked back to the house. Before approaching the yard, Daddy stopped and said to me, "I saw how you rode that bike. Had you ridden it before?"

"No," I said, "that was my first time."

"I can't believe that was your first time," he said. "You did an excellent job riding down a hill for the first time." He looked at me and said, "You need your own bike. I'm going to get you one."

Wow! My own bike! I was so happy and looked forward to getting that bike. I didn't ask when I could get it because it didn't matter. I knew that when Daddy was able to deliver that bike, he would. This became my new proudest moment.

Third grade had been great; I loved my teacher, Mrs. McIntosh. She was so kind and spoke with such respect to all of her students. It was because of her that I didn't want that school year to end. During my third-grade year, a major event happened. I wasn't into politics and knew very little about it, other than who the president was. One day in particular, however, it seemed that everything stopped. Mrs. McIntosh apologized to the class for her tears and announced that the president of the United States, John F. Kennedy, was dead. She explained why she was crying, and after the announcement, we continued with our work.

When I got home, Mama was also crying. When asked what was wrong, she too informed me that the president of the United States was dead; someone had killed him. She was watching it on news. I wondered why she was crying when she really didn't know him. It was then that she explained that that president stood for equality and wanted people treated fairly. It was what she and Daddy had always taught me—to treat everyone with respect. Mama would say, "Behave yourself, be sweet, and don't be ugly." Other than the death of the president, my third-grade year was very special to me.

My fourth-grade teacher was nothing like my third-grade teacher. Mrs. Paige was stern, even abrupt at times, and she seemed to expect to catch everyone doing something wrong. I was careful not to say or do anything that would cause her to call me out. The last thing I wanted was for her to contact my parents and report any unacceptable behavior.

Mama and Daddy took school very seriously and had always stressed the importance of education. I loved going to school and I loved learning, but I couldn't help but think that Mrs. Paige was looking for something to report. I paid attention to her instructions, did my work, and was always eager to submit my completed schoolwork. I was able to focus on my schoolwork and did what I had to do to get my work done. I knew Mama and Daddy would be proud.

A Turn for the Worse

While in school, there was a lot of talk about a new Broadway-type production coming on TV—Rodgers and Hammerstein's *Cinderella*; all the kids were talking about it. We were all eager to watch how the wicked stepsisters and stepmother would treat Cinderella, isolating her from the family, as well as the magic of watching a pumpkin from her garden turn into a carriage to take her to the ball. We had watched all the commercials about this new whimsical production and couldn't wait to see it. It was scheduled to air on February 22, 1965. This was the beginning of the second semester of my fourth-grade year. *Cinderella* was a main event, and we were overwhelmed with excitement as we looked forward to watching this broadcast.

School was the same as usual on February 22, other than the excitement about watching *Cinderella*. The teacher had to hush the class more often than usual to stop talking, but amazingly, she did not discipline or punish anyone for talking. I remained quiet, fearing get caught and have a bad report go home to my parents. It was more difficult than usual for me to focus on my work, but as long as I was quiet, I didn't have anything to worry about. It seemed as if the day was longer on the twenty-second, but finally the dismissal bell rang, and we could go home. My best friend, Daisy, and I rushed home as fast as we could so that we could complete our homework and do whatever we needed to do before it was time for *Cinderella*. I knew that Daddy would most likely be home early enough to watch it with us.

Things went as planned after I go home. Mama had dinner ready when I returned from school and kept a plate warm for Daddy—he would be home a little later. I had a new baby brother who was only two weeks old at this time, and he was quietly resting.

Later that evening, I found my place on the floor to watch *Cinderella*. The broadcast started, but fifteen or twenty minutes into it, we heard sirens and saw lights flashing outside in front of the house, practically in the yard. Suddenly, our interest in *Cinderella* was gone. Once the ambulance sirens stopped, I could hear people talking. I wanted to see what was outside. I went outside with my mother and a sibling, but as I ran out into the yard, a neighbor grabbed me and directed me back into the house. There were only adults out there. I did get a glimpse of what they were looking at. There was a white sheet over what appeared to be a body.

I looked out the window from the house, and I saw neighbors crying, along with my sibling. The crowd blocked my view of what was happening, and the ambulance took off.

Mama was crying after that ambulance left. She called my siblings and me close to her and gave us the bad news—news I didn't want to hear. She told us that Daddy had died. Daddy often rode to work with a coworker. He would walk down a path from his drop-off point, less than five minutes away, to get home. That night, as he was approaching our yard, he had a heart attack and fell dead. A neighbor had called for help.

This changed my life as I knew it. The days following Daddy's death were vague. I vaguely remember the funeral service, but I do remember viewing his body and wishing that he would wake up. I remembered the burial and the feeling I had as I walked away from his burial place.

Mama did her best, as she grieved, to console me and explain death and why it happened, biblically. It was obvious that she was hurting, but she remained strong for us. It had only been two weeks since she had given birth to her eighth child, and she was doing all that she could to hold her family together without her husband. We were surrounded by family and other relatives, and soon afterward, we picked up life from where it was before Daddy died.

There were still many uncertainties, but I could not approach Mama with questions. There was an emptiness, a void that I felt only Daddy could fill. He had taught me so much, and each day, I'd looked forward to hearing new things that he would tell me.

I could no longer look forward to him coming home after work.

- 3 -

Moving on without Daddy

> The Lord also will be a refuge for the
> oppressed, a refuge in times of trouble.
> —Psalm 9:9

AN INSTANT SHIFT FROM TWO PARENTS TO A SINGLE-parent home was a major adjustment for me. So much rushed through my mind. As a nine-year-old, I wondered about so many things. I wondered why my daddy had to die. I didn't understand why some people lived and others died. I hoped that my mama wouldn't be taken away next; if that happened, who would I have? I thought about the things Daddy did with me and pondered, from time to time, who would do them now. Daddy was my security. He made me feel safe when I was afraid.

I thought about a time when we were having dinner. As Daddy was saying the prayer before we ate, blessing the food, I thought I saw someone peeping in the dining room window. Once he completed that prayer, I screamed out in fear that I'd seen someone. My siblings didn't believe me. I'm not sure if my mother believed me, but Daddy, without a word, excused himself from the table, got his hunting rifle, went outside, and fired the gun in the air.

When he returned, he said to me, "No one is going to bother you." We continued with dinner, and nothing else was said about what I'd seen. I felt safe that night and slept well because of him.

The next morning, Daddy took me by the hand and told me to come with him outside. I was so glad to go out because the ground was covered with newly fallen snow. I looked up at the trees and noticed that the beautiful dogwood trees were covered with snow. They were so pretty during the spring and summer, when the pink-and-white blossoms made it look as if the sky was made of flowers, and they smelled so sweet. The property was surrounded with all kinds of trees—fruit trees were in the back of the house, with scents that accented the scent of the dogwood trees. The front yard was full of flowers. Mama's planters, made from old tires, overflowed with flowers. She loved planting flowers each year and watching the ones from the previous year sprout new blooms.

Now, the entire yard and trees were blanketed with snow. As we went outside, I noticed little paw prints in the snow, headed in different directions. I was searching for untouched areas, hoping that Mama would treat us to some of her homemade "snow cream"—her ice cream made from snow was always exciting and certainly worth waiting for.

As I stood there gazing at the scenery, Daddy tugged at my hand as a sign to come with him. We walked around the house to the windows of the dining room, where I thought I'd seen someone peeping while we were eating. As we approached the window, Daddy pointed to footprints on the ground and said, "Look at that. I ran that person off who was peeping in the window. They won't come back!" I was so relieved, and later in life, when I looked back on that day, I knew he was assuring me that I really did see someone and that he believed me. I was relieved to see those footprints, and I felt what I had always known that day—that Daddy would always protect me.

I thought about the days when he would sit me on his knee and tie my shoes and make sure that I was dressed warm enough to go outside in the cold. I thought about how much I loved sitting down with him and listening to him play the harmonica. He played it with such enthusiasm and joy. To this day, I think of him each time I hear a harmonica. I also thought about how he would draw and allow me to watch him as he sketched with ink and made perfect lines.

I thought about the long drive in the country on Sundays to church. I loved looking out of the windows, watching the animals as we drove by and looking at the landscape of the country homes—seeing the barns of different sizes and how they were used as we drove by the fields of corn, tobacco, and other vegetables grown by local farmers. The flowers along the roadside and the blossoms on the trees were always beautiful.

Sitting in the back seat with my siblings, I always tried to listen to what my parents were saying. They spoke in a quiet tone, almost a whisper. I recall getting caught by Mama on one occasion. She turned around to me and said "Aurelia"—only Daddy called me Linda—"don't be an eavesdropper." I immediately slid back into the seat and never did that again.

Who would drive us now? Mama never drove a car; Daddy did all the driving.

I thought about the times I would anxiously watch for him to come home after hunting and about the times when he praised me when I'd made him proud. I could no longer make him proud because he was no longer with me. I thought about the expectations he had of me after I made him proud—there was always room for improvement. He emphasized becoming better at what I did, not because I could then earn more money but because it would make me a better person.

Daddy was a humanitarian. I thought about the bicycle he had promised to buy me. I had hoped that I would get it in the summer of that year. Whenever he told me that would do something, he always followed through. As a nine-year-old child, I couldn't help but think about that bicycle. Now, he couldn't get it for me, but I knew that had he lived, I would have gotten that bike.

Then I thought about Christmas. It was early in the year when Daddy died, but Christmas was always a big celebration in our household. It was exciting, from the moment we would clean the house until the time we decorated and watched the lights glisten on the tree. Then, as Christmas Day approached, I waited eagerly to see what Santa would bring. Mama and Daddy made this a special time for us. The meaning of Christmas, the birth of Jesus Christ, was clearly taught to us. It wasn't about us or what we wanted. I don't recall ever being asked what I wanted for Christmas. It was always a mystery and a surprise on Christmas Day.

We helped Mama with the extra cleaning prior to decorating the house. We decorated the windows and made them look as if it had snowed. The tree was last to be decorated. Mama would string popcorn for the tree, and she would put out nuts and candies that added a festive smell to the house. Daddy always cut the tree down and brought home a real tree for us to decorate. The fresh-cut tree made the house smell nice, and I knew that once the tree was decorated, Christmas was surely on its way.

Nothing went under the tree until Christmas morning. I loved waking up to find presents underneath the tree. Daddy didn't wrap gifts; he made individualized boxes for me and my siblings. My name was written on my box, and it was filled with all kinds of toys. He also put fruit and candy in the boxes. Apples and oranges added to the Christmas aroma to which I grew accustomed as child. I wondered if that would continue. Would Mama be able to do this without Daddy? Who would help her?

I had other thoughts, such as what would happen when I got sick? Daddy always gave me medicine when I had a cough, fever, or just needed vitamins; he took care of it. I remembered how he'd helped me to take castor oil by offering me orange juice. I felt that only he could hold that teaspoon of castor oil to my mouth, tell me to swallow it quickly, and wash it down with fresh orange juice. Daddy knew how to fix things; he was my safe place. Now he was gone, and Mama would have to care for me and my siblings alone.

As time went by, Mama organized the house and finalized the loss of her husband and my daddy. I learned later that Daddy had a heart condition and had been getting medical treatment for his heart. I never heard him complain about being tired, although he must have been tired. He was a hard worker, and his daily routines were consistent—he left at the same time and returned at the same time each day. There was no indication that he was sick. He always had time to play and give me the attention that I was now learning to do without. Mama explained that God calls us home. She explained death to me, saying that it was a part of life and that we were not to grieve as much as celebrate God's calling to bring Daddy home.

It didn't make sense to me at the time because I wasn't trying to see how my daddy's dying could be a good thing or that I should understand it. Over time, I learned that my interpretation of Mama's teaching was not what she meant. It was about moving on and knowing what I could not control, while understanding that God was in control. Mama went as far as to tell me that, someday, she too would be called to God, and she would want me to go on with my life and remember the things she taught. She assured me that Daddy would want the same thing, and I still had to honor and obey him. Mama was very calm as she told me these things, and I felt a sense of peace, hearing that from her. I still had her, and I believed that I would be OK. I was thankful that I wasn't alone. Nevertheless, I still missed my daddy and concluded that I would focus on what he had taught me.

Finishing school that year was stressful. I had taken off a few days from school for the funeral and to adjust to my new life without Daddy. Upon my return, I felt as if everyone was staring at me. Nothing was mentioned about my losing my daddy, just stares. Mrs. Paige had nothing to say to me about what I was going through, but she was quick to tell me I had schoolwork to make up. She loudly called my name in front of the class, telling me that I had a project due, and I must turn it in the following day, or I would get a failing grade. The assignment had been given to the class while I was attending my daddy's funeral. I kindly asked her

A Way That's Mighty Sweet

if I could have an extra day because I wasn't able to do it because of the funeral. With a stern stare, she snapped, "No."

I thought, *It doesn't matter that my daddy died.*

Although I asked for an extra day to complete that assignment, I did not expect her to give me any extra time. She didn't seem to be that kind of teacher; she never appeared happy. In my short years of school experience, she was my least-favorite teacher. Mrs. Paige was scary, always speaking to the class as if we were being scolded. She was a tall lady and stout, and as she walked very slowly around the room, she would drag her feet. She was quite intimidating. I felt as if I might have done something and was in trouble when she approached me.

She walked toward my desk that day, waving a sheet of paper. She slammed the paper on my desk and said, "Here are your instructions—no excuses."

The assignment was to make a United States map. After I outlined it in pencil, I would have to make a mixture of table salt and glue. Next, I would pour the mixture into my outline, being careful not to go beyond the lines. Once it dried, I would have to paint or color it and label each state. This was a messy assignment, and I never liked getting my hands dirty. My immediate thought was, *I'm not doing it. I'll just throw it out and take the failing grade.*

Then I thought about what Mama had said to me—that Daddy would want me to go on with my life. I knew that he would not have wanted me to miss an assignment for any reason. This was a quick lesson for me to end my pity party, be responsible, and complete the work. This would mark the beginning of my knowing what I could and could not change. Daddy once told me that I was responsible for my decisions. I couldn't bring my daddy back, but I could carry on with the lessons he taught me and be the best person I could be. Daddy would always live on in my heart.

As time went by, I slowly accepted that things had changed and would be different forever. I was settling into a new lifestyle and Mama showed such strength and control as the new head of our household. She continued to do what she did when Daddy was alive—she cooked, cleaned, and made sure that I attended school every day. She kept Daddy's teaching alive and consistently reminded me of the importance of studying and making good grades. Daddy had planted the seed of going to college. Mama kept it nourished and stayed on top of my schooling. Rules didn't change, as I'd thought that they might. I still had to be inside at a certain time and could only play with kids that met her approval. Mama kept routines as normal as she possibly could, and there was no misunderstanding as to what I could or could not do. Mama was clear, and she made sure that God was the center of our household. I got biblical lectures more often after Daddy died.

Transportation was a concern for us. Daddy did all the driving when he was with us, and now that he was gone, we would have to take a bus, a taxi, or walk. Mama did a lot of walking, and I walked with her to get to places within walking distance. I struggled with the definition of "walking distance" from time to time. Mama's walking distance was confusing to me, as I believed, on numerous occasions, that we could have used a car ride. But she was fine with walking, and after a while, I was fine with it as well. There was much to be said about walking—good conversation and hearing stories about how she grew up and that she had to walk twenty miles to school each day. She would say, "We're not walking far." I thought differently, but there were times when we reached our destination sooner than I had expected.

Christmas was different now that Daddy was gone. The fresh-cut Christmas trees were no more. Who was going to chop down a tree and bring it home? Mama couldn't, and neither could my siblings or I. So each Christmas, we had what I called a "fake" tree. It was one of those trees that came in a box, and we put it together. Christmas was still Christmas and remained my favorite time of year. I thought about all the things Daddy did at Christmas—the toys under the tree, boxed by him and carefully placed for us to enjoy on Christmas Day. I thought about the time when we left milk and cookies out for Santa, and one of my siblings caught Daddy eating the cookies and drinking the milk.

I wondered if Mama would be able to give us the same type of Christmas that we'd had when Daddy was here. I knew what I could do to make it easy on her.

"Mama," I told her, "I want to help you with Christmas."

"How can you help?" Mama asked me.

"Santa doesn't have to come this year," I said.

She looked at me strangely. "Why?"

"I know there isn't a Santa Claus because he isn't real."

"Tell me why you think there's no Santa Claus," Mama said.

Mama had a cedar chest where she kept important things. It was a beautiful piece of furniture, made from cedar wood, and always smelled freshly made. It opened from the top and was used for storage. It was so shiny, and I always wanted to see what was in it, but I never thought about opening it. Mama had made it clear, over the years, that I was not to go into the cedar chest without her permission.

When I was four years old, Mama was doing my sibling's hair. She needed something from the chest and asked me to go look in the chest and bring it to her. I happily went into the chest to retrieve what Mama had asked. When I opened the chest, I saw all kinds of things, including Barbie dolls, coloring books, paper dolls, spinning tops, and other toys. I had to search for what she wanted, and once I found it, I closed the lid on the chest and took it to her. I never said anything to anyone about what I'd seen in that chest.

Months would pass before Christmas. As always, the gifts were not placed under the tree until Christmas Day. On this particular Christmas, all of the toys looked familiar to me. I saw the dolls, the spinning tops, the games, and coloring books that I'd seen when I opened the chest. I was convinced that these were the same toys and that Santa could not have delivered them early because he delivered toys on Christmas Eve. Again, I said nothing.

I did not tell Mama or Daddy what I knew. I believed it would have displeased them to know that I was on to the big secret of Santa Claus.

Now, Mama couldn't believe what she heard. I never had told her that I wondered why they would say there was a Santa when there wasn't. She looked at me in awe and had a smile on her face. I was glad it was a smile and not a frown, so I decided to keep talking.

"I'm telling you now because Daddy isn't here to help you with the toys. I'm OK if you can't buy me anything." I believed that telling her would free her of worrying about having enough money to purchase toys without Daddy. I waited for a lecture and maybe some scripture about what I thought was inappropriate behavior.

Mama smiled even more and said to me, "Since you know now, I'm going to bring you with me to buy toys!"

That was an answer I never expected. She was OK with me telling her what I knew and even more so because I never shared my findings with my siblings.

I went with Mama to get the toys that year. I was amazed at all of the toys I saw in the store. Mama allowed me to pick out some things but not to select anything for myself—she wanted me to be surprised when I saw what she had purchased for me. She never told me not to tell anyone what she bought, but I knew that it was important to keep that to myself.

That first Christmas without my daddy was enjoyable—it wasn't the same, by any means, but we were able to enjoy it. We decorated as usual, and there was much joy as we remembered the reason for the season. It was all about Jesus Christ. I was happy with the things Mama gave me.

It was the first Christmas of many after the death of my daddy. With my mama by my side, taking care of me, and by the grace of God, the path to my future could only head in a positive direction. I was so thankful that I still had my mama. As much emptiness as I felt in Daddy's absence, I didn't feel alone. Mama was able to fill any void I had during that time. It had to have been difficult for her, but she never complained, nor did she let down her guard when it came to us children. In years to come, she would make it clear that she wasn't alone because she had God.

Fifth and sixth grades remained for me in grammar school as I adjusted to my new norm. Those two years were exciting for me. I had a fifth-grade teacher I really liked. Mrs. Kelly made learning fun and exciting. She was a petite lady, always smiling, and she made the kids feel important. Her approach to teaching was very engaging. She asked for opinions and allowed her students to participate in meaningful discussions. She knew some of the kids in the class on a personal level, but she treated everyone the same. I knew her outside of the classroom and because of that, I made sure that I met the expectations of her class. She knew Mama personally, and I didn't want to give her any reason to call Mama with a negative report. I made sure that all my assignments were turned in on time and my class participation was at its best. I was a quiet child and never talked to others during class.

Sixth grade was just as exciting. Mrs. Farris was a strict teacher, but, in my opinion, she was always fair. There was a firm rule of no chewing gum or eating candy in class. Corporal punishment was allowed in school in those days, which consisted of getting one firm blow of a wooden paddle on the hand if the teacher believed your behavior warranted it.

During my elementary days after my daddy died, I walked to school each morning with my friend Daisy. Some days, we shared candy on the way—apple candies, or as we called them, "apple twists," which were actually Jolly Ranchers. Those candies always discolored our tongues, and my tongue was either red or green by the time I got to school. I didn't know that Mrs. Farris would check our tongues at the beginning of class.

She had us line up in rows about fifteen minutes after school started, which gave us time to eat candy and get caught. I remember thinking that I was going to be in trouble if my tongue was still discolored, although I had not eaten the candy during class. She called for the students sitting in the first row to come up first. One by one, she said, "Let me see your tongue."

Some students had eaten candy prior to being called up and bravely took their punishment without explanation, as they were guilty as charged. Then a student came up, and before showing her tongue, she pled innocent and kindly told Mrs. Farris that she had eaten the candy on the way to school and did not deserve to be punished. Mrs. Farris, however, told her to hold out her hand, and she hit the child's hand with that paddle.

After seeing how my classmate had failed to convince Mrs. Farris that she had not eaten the candy during class, my pulse raced, and I was overcome by fear. I did not want to face her, although I too was innocent.

Suddenly, Mrs. Farris yelled, "Next row line up." Now it was my turn to stand and wait for a punishment I had not earned. I watched students return to their desks, shaking their hands as a means to cool down the pain.

"Linda, come forward."

I slowly walked up to her desk and kindly said, "Mrs. Farris, I had a green apple twist on my way to school."

She instructed me to open my mouth and stick out my tongue. She looked at me and said, "You may return to your seat."

I took a deep breath and scurried to my seat, wondering how she knew I was telling the truth. She didn't play favorites in any case. Shortly after she finished punishing students for eating candy in her class, she went around the classroom with her hands opened and asked students to deposit their candies into her hand. She made it clear that she would not return it; as she went back to her desk, she dropped all of the candy into the garbage pail. She then explained that she would not accept lies and said, "I can tell if candy was just eaten or if it was eaten on the way to school. The color is darker when it's fresh." She advised the class to have their candy before entering her class.

As for me, I decided not to eat any candy prior to getting to her class. I knew that Mama would not have approved of me eating candy so early in the morning.

Mrs. Ferris's class was my favorite year in elementary school after Daddy's death. I focused on learning and enjoyed the assignments in class and the homework she assigned. I've always loved reading, and with the memories of Daddy and Mama's ongoing encouragement, I could only succeed. Toward the end of that school year, Mrs. Farris made an announcement to the class. She had chosen the three students with the highest average in the class, and she would reward these students with a pizza and a trip to see Holiday on Ice!

I sat in my chair, thinking that I would never be chosen for such an event, but as she called out the names, the last name she called was mine. I was elated but feared that I would not be able to go because we didn't have a car anymore. How would I get there? Who would take me? Would Mama allow me to go?

Mrs. Farris asked the other two students and me to stay a few minutes after class. At that time, she gave us information and asked that we take it home to our parents. She would provide more details once she received approval from our parents.

I rushed home and gave Mama the information. As she read the materials my teacher provided, she smiled and told me that she approved of my going. Mrs. Farris would pick me up at my house and drive me and my classmates to the coliseum. Mama was extremely proud because attending this trip was solely based on grade average and the teacher's selection. I could hardly wait because the other girl chosen was a good friend of mine and the boy was kind and very well-mannered. I was thankful that Mrs. Farris had recognized me, and I was extremely grateful that Mama had approved. I couldn't help but think how proud Daddy would have been.

It appeared that the weekend would never come. After what seemed like a long and drawn-out week, it was Friday evening, and I made plans to attend this big event the next day. It was advertised on television—figure skaters glided across the floor, dancing, lifting each other, and doing all kinds of tricks. I couldn't believe that I would actually be there!

The next day, I was up and eagerly waiting for Mrs. Farris to pick me up. I was ready to go. Mrs. Farris pulled up in front of the house, but she wasn't driving. Another sixth-grade teacher from the school, Mr. Grant, had agreed to accompany her on the trip. She stepped out of the car and met Mama at the door. I waited until they finished their conversation before heading to the car. Mrs. Farris told Mama that we would return later in the afternoon or early evening. She planned to take us for pizza after the show. She assured Mama that I would be OK and that she would look after me. She told Mama that I was a good listener and was obedient, which was another reason why she chose me.

Mama waved goodbye to me, and with a smile, she said, "Behave."

I hopped into the car and took the window seat because I didn't want to sit near the boy, although I never verbally expressed that. I asked my friend Lilly if it was OK with her if I sat on the end, and she agreed that I could.

Once I was in the car, Mrs. Farris announced, "We're on our way." In those days, wearing seatbelts was optional, so we were not encouraged to wear one. Thank God for His mercy that we made it there and back without incident.

The drive from Burlington to Greensboro was about twenty-five minutes. Upon our arrival, Mrs. Farris gave us her expectations prior to going inside and finished with, "Behave the way you do in class, and you will be fine." With a reassuring smile, she asked us to stick together. She had our tickets and would present them at the door for us.

I was amazed by the size of that coliseum. I couldn't believe that it would be filled with people. This was my first outing of this size. Other than school, I had seen a lot of people at church and at community church events. The city park had sponsored community activities, such as Easter egg hunts, that a large amount of people attended. But this was different. These figure skaters were celebrities. I had just watched them on TV commercials, and now I would get a chance to see them live.

Mrs. Farris gave the tickets to the person at the booth, and she guided us to our seats. I was really excited because we actually had front-row seats. We had a very close view of the skaters! I couldn't wait to give Mama a full report of my observations because I knew she would be excited as well.

As the show was about to begin, Mrs. Farris kept looking back anxiously, saying, "He needs to hurry and get back here." That was the first that I'd noticed that Mr. Grant was not in his seat. The music started for the introductions, and the lights were dimmed, indicating that the show was about to start.

Suddenly, Mr. Grant appeared, breathing heavily, as if he had been running to his seat. Before he sat down, he handed each of us our own cotton candy! I had never had cotton candy and couldn't wait to taste it. We all thanked him for buying it. I waited until Lilly took a piece of her cotton candy because I wasn't sure how to eat it. I thought about biting into it as if I was eating an ice cream cone. After watching Lilly, though, I pulled a piece off the top and popped it into my mouth. I was so pleased with how it dissolved in my mouth, and the sweet taste was better than I had imagined. Mrs. Farris smiled at me; I think she gathered that it was my first time eating cotton candy.

The show was phenomenal and exceeded my imagination. The dancers glided along the ice with such ease and grace. They moved to the music and spun around, at times so fast that I could hardly see their faces. The male skater would lift his female partner onto his shoulders, assist her with flipping over, and land her on her bottom as she slid on the floor between his legs. It went on for what seemed like a long time, and then there was intermission. During this time, they prepared the ice, and that, in itself, became a show. We watched how they removed the old ice and refreshed the floor with new ice; the machine packed it down so that the skaters would have a new floor to finish their routines.

It was an event that I would never forget. I have always believed that Mrs. Farris created this event to help me cope with the loss of my daddy. At times, she would ask me how I was doing, and she would ask about Mama. I arrived to class late a few times, and she never penalized me for it. She knew that I was struggling with the loss of my father, and her kindness was a blessing for me.

The skaters returned to finish their routines. During their finial routines, they each did a solo skating act. The crowd cheered, and at the end of the show, people threw roses out on the floor as a sign of their appreciation.

As we got up to leave, Mrs. Farris and Mr. Grant asked if we had enjoyed the show. We all started talking at once as we shouted out our favorite parts of the show. As much as I loved the skating, I really enjoyed watching the stripping of the old ice from the floor and putting down new ice. The person who did this process explained that the old ice had scrapes and loose ice from the skating. The old ice could interfere with their performances and possibly cause injuries, so new ice was needed to complete the show. I enjoyed watching them add the new ice and smooth it down with a huge machine that appeared to be smoking. I learned that the ice was so cold that it generated what looked like smoke.

Mrs. Farris and Mr. Grant said that we would stop on the way home to get pizza. I not only wasn't familiar with any pizza places at that time, but I wasn't even aware that they existed. Mr. Grant parked the car and went in to get the pizza for all of us. We each had our own individual pizza, and it seemed like a lot. He distributed the pizza and went back inside to get sodas. They allowed us to eat the pizza on our way home and didn't appear to be concerned about us dropping food in the car. I made up my mind that I would be careful. This trip reminded me of the times my daddy took me on long trips as we snacked on treats that he provided. This was truly a celebration for me and was an occasion I have never forgotten.

The ride home was great. We ate most of the way, and as we got closer to home, it was bittersweet for me. As much as I didn't want to see the day end, I was excited about telling Mama about my experience. On the way home Mrs. Farris gave us feedback regarding our behavior.

"Listen you all," she said, "I am very proud of your behavior in the coliseum.

I'm just proud to have you as students. Continue to pay attention and make

Good grades in school." We instantly began to smile as she talked.

"Also," she added, "stay away from negative people and you will do fine."

At that time, none of us hung around anyone in our class. We did our work and stayed out of trouble.

Mrs. Farris told us that because we were such good students that we should be friends with each other. I already considered Lilly as my friend, but now I knew it was OK to talk to her during recess or during the little time we had before class started.

Mrs. Farris opened my eyes to new things that day. She introduced me to pizza, cotton candy, a major public event, and a new experience shared with my peers. She let me know that teachers do care about their students, not only in the classroom but beyond the classroom as well. I was the first one to be dropped off. It was early evening, and I was tired from excitement. Mrs. Farris gave Mama a positive report and waved goodbye. I told Mama about my day and how much I had enjoyed watching the show. I told her about the pizza and the cotton candy. It was obvious that Mama was happy that I had enjoyed myself.

It was one of the best school-related moments I'd had since Daddy died. Going to school became more exciting. I loved school and looked forward to going, but now I had a teacher I really liked because I knew that she truly cared.

For the rest of the school year, we prepared for middle school. I was completing sixth grade and heading for seventh grade. I didn't know what to expect, and because I didn't know, I took it all in stride and looked forward to moving up another grade. During that time, I would be introduced to desegregation. By the end of my sixth-grade year, a decision was made to end segregation in my school system.

- 4 -

Another Transition

> Follow peace with all men, and holiness, without
> which no man shall see the Lord.
> —Hebrews 12:14 (KJV)

I BEGAN MY SEVENTH-GRADE YEAR IN A RACIALLY MIXED school. Although race, discrimination, and prejudice were not discussed in my household, I had attended an all-black school from grades one through six. Very little was discussed in school about desegregation, and there was no advice or discussions regarding the differences I might face in an integrated school. Mama and Daddy didn't talk about black and white issues. It was never discussed, but they had measures in place to limit my exposure to the racism and prejudices of this world and of our community.

I don't recall experiencing any fear or anxiety about going to a "white school." My parents never spoke harsh words toward any race or anybody. They only spoke about the Bible, how to treat people, and how to live as God intended for us to live. They placed emphasis on my behavior and made me accountable for all of my actions. I learned that I was not to blame anyone else for the choices I made, and I wasn't allowed to hate anyone or to use the word *hate*.

Teaching me right from wrong included being respectful to everyone and especially to my elders. Color or race was not a factor, but how I treated them was. The same behavior was expected everywhere. It didn't matter if I was in church, in school, a department store, or even on the playground or visiting neighbors. I had to be respectful and watch how I carried myself. We couldn't say "bad words," have verbal fights of name-calling, or demonstrate disrespect.

By the same token, I was taught not to tolerate disrespect. If I was being disrespected, I would tell the person who was disrespecting me that I didn't like being disrespected. If it was an adult, I was to convey that disrespect to my parents and leave it with them. Physical aggression or fighting was not tolerated. There would be consequences if that happened, and if I was ever in a situation where it might happen, I was to walk away. Daddy did give me one exception—he said that the only time he would tolerate my putting hands on someone was if someone actually spat in my face. He was not encouraging hitting anyone, but he could see how that could cause a physical reaction. If it should come to that, he would lean a little to understand a physical reaction.

I spent all my early education years in a school where all educators and students looked like me. I had not been in any situations where I experienced discrimination firsthand. I never used public bathrooms growing up (other than in school), and I never drank from public water fountains. As a rule, before we went anywhere, we were told to use the bathroom. We clearly understood that we would not use the public bathroom once we were out. It was different when going to visit a relative; at that time, it was OK if I didn't use the bathroom before leaving the house. I drank from the fountain only when I was in school and that wasn't often.

Mama kept portable, collapsible cups in her purse. If we got thirsty, she would expand the cups, get water, and give it to me. Growing up, I was never exposed to public signs on doors that were blatantly discriminatory or other means indicating that we were not equal, although they were there. I realized as I got older that Mama's planning kept me from being exposed to those signs, and because of that, I never saw them. I saw more of them on TV during my adult years than I saw as a child.

Now, I was on my way to a new way of learning, and I didn't quite know what to expect. Daddy was gone, and although Mama discussed my moving to another school, she did not discuss race issues. She simply reminded me of who I was and what was expected of me. That boiled down to my being respectful to everyone, staying away from trouble, and choosing my friends carefully so that I was surrounded by those who had the same morals and principles as I. She always said, "You are as good as the company you keep."

In my mind, it was just another grade, and I was prepared academically to go. I looked forward to going to middle school, and the uncertainty was not discouraging. I had gone through changes I never thought I would have to face when Daddy died. I felt that I was ready for whatever would happen, and I believed that if I could go through Daddy's death, I could go through anything. The worse had happened, and I was ready to move on.

The summer before seventh grade would introduce me to more problems. As a tradition, we always visited relatives' farms and helped out whenever we could. One day, while I was at the farm, helping with tobacco, I was attacked by bees. They stung me in numerous places, particularly my arms and legs. The pain was excruciating, and it took a while before the bees left me alone. The bee stings became sores, and I feared that I might not be able to start school on time. It wasn't until I was stung that I felt anxious and afraid; I felt that if the sores did not heal in time, I would have to miss days at the beginning of the school year.

The pain was unbearable; it was difficult to walk, and there was much swelling. Mama treated the sores, kept them clean, and wrapped them, per instructions from the doctor. By midsummer, there wasn't significant improvement, and Mama informed me that I might not be able to attend the first week of school or maybe longer because the sores weren't healing fast enough. I became quite tearful and begged Mama to let me go to school.

"I have to wait and see how things are," she said.

I felt like I had prior to starting first grade. I was anxious to see what this new school was like, but like first grade, I felt sad because I didn't think that I would be able to attend.

As time went by, my sores showed some signs of improvement. Mama estimated that I might be able to go to school, but I wouldn't be able to wear anything on my legs. This wasn't just seventh grade; it would be the first time I'd get to wear stockings, or *nylons*, as we called them. Mama continued to clean and dress my sores. It had gotten to the point where I could leave the dressing off. Mama said leaving the dressing off would help the sores to dry, and they needed to dry so that I could wear stockings. She warned me that there would be scabs, and they might not look too good. I didn't care! I just wanted to attend school and wear stockings.

As the first day of school approached, however, Mama told me that I could not wear nylons because the sores were not dry enough, and the stockings would stick. I was devastated. I had to wait to see if I would be there on the first day.

A new school year always meant getting new clothes. Mama did her shopping for me, and she had included nylon stockings with my school clothes. I was excited to know that I could actually wear nylons. I never liked wearing socks but never complained because I learned to be thankful for what I had and not to wish for anything more. At times, I may have wished but never verbalized it.

Mama didn't just hand the nylons over to me; she decided to give me a lesson in how to put the stockings on without tearing them. When I began wearing stockings, we didn't have pantyhose; we had individual stockings, with garters to hold them up. I had to put the garter on first so that I could attach the nylons to the garter. Mama carefully demonstrated how to put them on, starting from the toes up to the upper thigh. Then, I would clip the stockings from the front and back of each leg. I caught on rather quickly, and Mama was so proud of how I was able to do it the first time after watching her.

I believe I caught on so fast because I had wanted to wear stockings for a long time. I didn't think there was a chance of my wearing anything on my legs. I was thankful that my sores were healing, although the scabs might show. I never told Mama, but I didn't want the scabs to show—that would be too embarrassing. Nonetheless, I was ready for school; my sores were healing, I had the nylons I wanted, and, hopefully, my sores would heal. I was on my way to the seventh grade.

Soon, I would have a resolution for my condition. Fishnet stockings and window-pane stockings had just come out. I hoped that Mama would let me wear a pair of those. I presented her with the idea of my wearing either the fishnet or the window-pane stockings. Mama looked at them both and told me the window-pane stocking might be better suited because of my sores; the fishnets would stick to the sores more easily. The fishnet stockings had smaller, boxed-shaped openings, so I decided on the window panes, and they were perfect. The window-pane stockings were made with a yarn-type thread and consisted of little squares, shaped like small boxes. These boxes would provide enough separation from each other, leaving a wide enough opening to prevent my sores from sticking, while looking very fashionable. Mama purchased me a couple of pairs, and she was pleased with how they looked on my legs. I was excited again to return to school.

Attending Middle School

Anticipating middle school was exciting but a little scary because I didn't know what to expect. My best friend, Daisy, would attend school with me, and that made it easier. We had been best friends since the third grade. We walked to school during our elementary school years and spent much time after school, playing and visiting each other. We lived in a tight-knit community, where it really took a village to raise children. The parents in our community knew each other, and respect was given to all adults. Daisy's mother and Mama were close friends, and we were more like family than friends. Daisy shared my excitement for attending middle school, and we were excited because it was a bigger school with more teachers, and we were also excited that we would have to change classes. We were switching from a one-teacher classroom, teaching all subjects, to at least six teachers teaching six different subjects—or so we thought.

Entering the seventh grade would end my walking-to-school days. Daisy and I were excited to ride the school bus. We wondered who would be our bus driver. Bus drivers during those times were high school students who were trained to drive school buses as a paid job, and they attended the high school associated with the middle school. Once school boys were old enough to have a driver's license, they could drive the school bus.

On the first day of school, we lined up at our bus stop and waited anxiously for the bus to come so that we could meet our new teachers and new classmates. Daisy and I hoped that we would be in the same classes or at least the same homeroom.

The bus was filled from the front to the back. There was much chatter about things that happened during the summer and students wishing that there would be no homework. Daisy and I talked between ourselves, hoping that we would like the school and the teachers. Although we were attending an integrated school, that topic never came up in our conversation. We were only hoping for a good day in school. I was concerned about my sores showing, but Daisy assured me that the sores were not noticeable, and I believed her. Daisy and I were always truthful with each other. We had a friendship built on honesty, trust, and respect for each other. We could say anything to each other, and neither of us was ever offended. We appreciated each other's honesty, and that never changed, even throughout our adult lives.

We arrived at school and were welcomed by teachers standing at our bus stop. Along with greetings, they instructed us on how to leave the bus and enter the school. They glanced at our schedules and directed us to our homerooms, informing us that the teacher would provide more information. Daisy and I were not in any classes together, but we had the same lunch wave, and we decided that we would meet up for lunch, if we were allowed.

The school was so much bigger than either of the elementary schools I had attended. My first school only had seven rooms, a principal's office, and a milk room. The milk room did not accommodate people but had an icebox that kept the milk cold for kids who wanted to buy milk. The second school, from grades three to six, had about twelve classrooms, a principal's office, a cafeteria, and a gym. Now, this middle school had much more. There was a gym, an auditorium, a cafeteria, a library, a music room, math labs, typing labs, principal's office, assistant principal's office, clerical offices, guidance counselors' offices, and numerous classrooms. There were two levels to the building, and there was a football field outside and an open area that was used for gym classes.

I thought the teachers were great. They were very helpful and attentive to the needs of the students. There were teachers in the school that all students could identify with, although there were a smaller number of African American teachers.

I was excited again to return to school, and I adjusted well in middle school. This was where I first realized that I really liked singing. I'd sung for Mama and her prayer-meeting friends since I was little, but now, I discovered that I loved singing in larger groups. I signed up for chorus as an elective course. In doing so, I joined the school choir and enjoyed every minute of it. The choir instructor was very pleased with my voice and told me that I should take lessons "on the side" and really train my voice. I thought nothing of what he said, and I never told Mama. I knew if I told her, she would have made a way for me to get those lessons. Because we were living on a tight budget, I didn't want to add more to her responsibilities. She was giving me what I needed, and she was doing it alone. I was content with being in the choir.

Mama was concerned that my grades might be affected by moving to middle school. She never said it, but she was constantly telling me to study, listen, and stay away from those kids who caused trouble. I knew that moving from a small, segregated school to a much-larger, integrated school could surely impact my learning. Mama had reasons to be concerned. Things were different, but for some reason, I felt more relaxed and in place. My grades improved, and I did better than I had done in elementary school. My love for reading increased, and although I never liked math, I was managing and making the grade. I worked hard to finish my lessons, and I made friends. Daisy and I had mutual friends and chose them wisely. We were true to our teaching in regard to being as good as the company we kept. Like the two of us, our friends focused on school and making good grades.

Race and ethnicity did not seem to be an issue, and if it was, our school experience was not negatively impacted. There was one occasion, however, when Daisy and I believed that there might be a race problem.

This was during the time of political campaigning for president of the United States. A former governor was running, and his political platform was segregation. His campaign talked about how he wanted to end desegregation. I knew very little about politics at the time, but it was clear that this particular candidate was against unity, and he was advocating for a divided society.

We were on our way to school. It was the second year that we rode the school bus. We were in the eighth grade, and by this time, the middle school had been rebuilt at a location where we would have a longer bus route to school. We were excited about riding the school bus a second year, as by now, we had gotten used to it.

While on the bus, we always kept our conversations between the two of us and were careful to stay out of others' conversations.

On this day, there was much mumbling among the African American students. We could hear bits and pieces of conversations regarding blacks and whites. I began to feel uneasy, nervous, and extremely anxious because of the remarks students were making in this regard. Daisy and I stopped talking and quietly waited for anything that might occur.

As the bus approached the next stop, we could see students holding signs. We couldn't see what was on the signs from a distance. The bus stopped, and white students entered the bus with signs that supported the presidential candidate, although they said nothing. Some of the black students became angry instantly and began to provoke the students carrying the signs. They began name-calling, and this caused several students to go back and forth with racial epithets from both sides, and some students threatened others. It was intense and appeared that fighting would take place.

The bus driver, who was a high school student, pulled the bus over and asked the students to take their seats. He said that he would radio the school, requesting assistance, if they didn't stop. He added that students could get expelled from school if he had to wait for help. His speech was effective; the students sat in their seats, and the students holding the signs tucked them under the seats. There were no further altercations, and at the end of the day, school officials entered the bus before it left and gave all students clear expectations regarding required behavior to ride the bus.

The signs the students had with them that morning were confiscated, and the parents were contacted to pick up their signs. It was an awakening moment for me and for Daisy. Although school had gone well for that day, it was a relief to return home without incident. We hoped that the next day would be better. I had my first glimpse of racism, and I saw it firsthand. It was a moment that I didn't want to relive.

Mama always wanted to hear how school went for me. I didn't want to do anything that would cause her worry, so I stayed on top of my schoolwork and homework. I knew she wouldn't tolerate anything other than my best. So I strived to do my best and prioritized my studies.

I couldn't wait to tell Mama about the situation on the bus. After she heard the entire story, as well as the follow-up lecture we received before coming home, she barely reacted. She asked if anyone had approached me during this encounter. When I told her no, she told me that I did the right thing by staying out of it. She reminded me that I couldn't control how others thought, and when people did or said things that were hurtful, it had nothing to do with me. It was all about them because they weren't happy with themselves. Sometimes, saying hurtful things to others made them feel better. She reminded me to avoid saying hurtful things to others, although they might say them to me. When and if it happened, I was instructed to walk away and avoid getting into trouble. Remembering the words of my father, I hoped that no one would spit on me.

My adjustment to middle schcol was a positive experience. I had no incidents of any kind and focused on my classes. Although I was not seeking to make friends, interacting with other students was easy. I was content with my best friend, Daisy, and together, we befriended others. I was excited because I was getting closer to attending high school and was looking forward to graduating and going to college. I was so thankful to have Mama but often wondered how things would have been if Daddy was still here. So much had changed, and my life as I knew it was no more.

I had become a young lady. Girls my age were talking about boys they liked and would snicker and giggle when a boy they liked crossed their paths in the classroom or while changing classes. I made up my mind in middle school that I didn't have time for boys, nor did I express any interest in them. At times, I would see girls my age (not yet sixteen) hiding under staircases, kissing boys. I thought it was so gross; I would rather read a good book or complete a homework assignment than waste my time thinking about boys. I was determined that I would not get married, and having kids was certainly out of the picture. Boys were the last thing on my mind. I liked that nursery rhyme that said boys were made of snakes and snails and puppy dog tails!

I remember having a conversation with Daddy about marriage. I can't recall what prompted the conversation, as I was very young at the time, but we often had one-to-one conversations. Daddy told me about the kind of man I should marry. He emphasized the importance of marrying someone who loved the Lord and who put his family first. He explained that a man is to take care of his family and be responsible. He defined *responsible* as someone who worked, went to church, and took care of his home. A responsible man would take care of his wife and children and make sure bills were paid and that there always was food on the table. There were many dos and don'ts about marriage. He told me that dating and marrying someone from a home that was still intact—meaning a two-parent household—where he could learn responsibility from his parents was ideal, but that wasn't always the way it was.

He told me that there were good men in military, yet there were some who returned home from service without having learned responsibility.

I was convinced by my own thinking that I would not get married. I had babysat on many occasions, and as much as I enjoyed babysitting, I had no regrets when saying goodbye to the little ones when their parents returned.

I found it disturbing to see my peers getting all giggly and excited when they saw a boy they liked. It was difficult to imagine being married to any of those boys in middle school. I looked forward to getting my education and having a career, where I would not have any of those concerns. I was ready to move on, and boys were not included in my plans!

- 5 -

Changing the Things That I Can

I can do all things through Christ which strengtheneth me.
—Philippians 4:13 (KJV)

ENTERING TENTH GRADE WAS NOT WHAT I HAD HOPED IT would be. We had moved to another house prior to my tenth-grade year, and with that move came a new school district, a new house, a new community. I was spending what I thought was the most important year of high school in a new school. While I still was attending middle school, the new high school was completed, and my friends and I spent our ninth-grade year talking about how we couldn't wait for the first day of school in another brand-new school.

Then we moved, and I was so disappointed to be away from my friends. Daisy and I talked on the phone almost daily. We were no longer within walking distance from each other, and that limited our in-person conversations with each other. I missed visiting her at her home, hanging out in her room, and having our girl talks.

Mama knew how much I'd wanted to be in high school with my old classmates. She was apologetic, saying, "Don't worry, baby. You will be back in school with your friends. This isn't permanent." Mama didn't owe me an apology. She was doing the best she could alone, making a home for us. I was so thankful to have her as a mom and dared not ponder what it would be like if I didn't have her. She reminded me to do well in school, regardless of where I attended, because it was up to me to do my best and nobody else. I told her that I would, but I would learn that was easier said than done.

I realized that I would have to do things differently, and I became quite comfortable in communicating with Daisy the best I could at the time. We talked over the summer and compared notes about our upcoming first day of high school. We shared which courses we had and only wondered what classes would be like. Although we were about three or four miles away from each other, we didn't walk to visit each other. We visited occasionally when Daisy's mom would bring her over. We both decided that we would make the best of our school years, even if it meant that we would graduate from different schools. Nevertheless, we would graduate from high school at the same time. I had reason to believe that we would graduate together from the same school. Mama had told me not to worry, and once she said that, I believed that she would find a way to get me back in the school district where I once was.

When I began my tenth-grade year, I was not excited. I was still feeling down because I wasn't where I wanted to be, but I decided that I would do my best and try not to let Mama know that I was disappointed to be in that school. It was a good school; it was just very old, and I didn't like the way it looked. I could not point out any other reason why I didn't like it, other than it was old.

I liked all of my teachers, and I made friends there as well, but no one could compare to my best friend, Daisy; we remained close. I dived into my classes with an open mind and focused on doing the best I could. Mama didn't need anything to worry about. She had prioritized her children and ensured that we got what we needed. I always appreciated that she did not remarry. She never talked about it, but I don't think I would have been able to live with someone else becoming the man of the house, although I would have tried. We were fine as we were, and Mama seemed content. That was good enough for me.

Linda Aurelia B. Blackmon

I experienced my very first progress report in this school. I was taking a Spanish class, and Mr. Alegar was very kind and thorough in his teaching. He went over everything clearly, but I often indicated that I understood the content of the course when I did not. I had a very passive attitude and wasn't interested. I found the class boring, but I had to take a foreign language, and it was either Spanish or French. I had taken Spanish in middle school and did OK, but I didn't like it then. I wouldn't take French because one of my sisters had taken French, and I wanted to learn a language that she didn't know. Hindsight says I should have taken French so that she could have helped me with it, but that was the attitude of a fifteen-year-old who made poor choices. It was indeed a lesson learned and one I have never forgotten. As an adult, I mentioned this to my sister, and we had a great laugh.

My other courses went well, probably because I liked them. At midterm, progress reports were sent home when students were not doing well in their subjects. I had never received a progress report at any time during my school days, so I didn't expect to receive one this year. When I did, I was devastated! Mr. Alegar asked me to see him after school. I had no idea what he wanted. I figured it couldn't be serious because I turned in my homework, and I didn't talk during class. My heart started racing, and I dreaded seeing him.

The last five minutes that I had to wait for his class to end felt like an hour. Finally, the bell rang to end the school day. I had selected this class as the last one during the day so that I could go home afterward. I was proud to have made that decision—until that day. I felt that I might need time to calm my nerves before going home, but it was too late.

After everyone had left the class, I walked up to his desk. He looked at me and said, "I have something for you." I said nothing; I just waited for him to continue. He gave me a sealed envelope and said, "This is a progress note. You are to give it to your mother. I have to ask you—what is going on? You seem to be on task,

A Way That's Mighty Sweet

yet your grades are not what they should be. I've talked to your other teachers, and we all agree that this is not your work. I have to inform your mother. These grades count toward your overall average that you will need to graduate. You have to do better. Your mother will go over the report with you. You must do better, and I know that you can."

I took the progress note and responded, "I will." Then I went outside to line up for my bus ride home.

Riding home that day was the worst bus ride every. It was worse than the one where students were carrying racist signs. I cared very much what my mama thought of me and cared less of what others thought. I couldn't see what was in that envelope, but he told me it was a progress note, and I knew that wasn't good. I had not heard of anyone bringing home a progress note because they'd done something good. I noticed so many things on the way home to which I previously had paid little attention. As the bus drove away from the school, I noticed how beautiful the landscaping was and how the old but well-kept school was on a well-groomed yard that looked like a green sea. There were so many ways to enter and leave the school, as there were doors everywhere, and I watched kids running to their buses, trying not to be left behind. I noticed how different my route was to get home, as compared to the last school I'd attended. As I noticed the rapidly moving surroundings, I remembered that I missed it all and wanted to be back there. This ride was much longer, but on that particular day, it seemed shorter. I kept thinking that I hoped Mama would not be too angry. Then I thought, *What if I'm failing tenth grade? Will I have to stay back and postpone my graduation? What if I can't graduate with Daisy?* I felt that my dreams would be gone, and I couldn't bear the thought of failing.

After many stops and turns, the bus approached my street. I didn't like living on the dirt road. It was so different from what I was used to, but it was in a small private community. I remained thankful to be there because I had my mama. The bus stopped, and I got off and slowly walked to the house. As always, Mama was waiting with open arms and smiling. As she hugged me, she asked, "How was school today?" She always asked that, so I was ready for it, but I was not ready to give her a response, and I dared not lie to her.

I put my books down and pulled out the envelope. "Here. Mr. Alegar told me to give this to you." I tried to walk away as she sat down to open it, but she motioned for me to sit down. She opened the envelope, and her expression immediately changed. That's when she asked if I knew what was in the envelope.

I quickly responded, "No, he said you would go over it with me."

Mama looked at me and shook her head. I felt like crying, but I knew that my best reaction was to be quiet and let her ask the questions.

Mama handed me the envelope and told me to read it. I slowly smoothed out the page—procrastinating—and then read it. I was hurt and ashamed. The note stated that I had a D average in that class. I had never received a D in any class or schoolwork. He specified in the progress note where the areas of improvement were needed—test scores, pop quizzes, class participation, and correct homework. He wrote in the comments that I would need to bring the average up if I was planning to have the required GPA to graduate. Although it was passing to most, it wasn't passing for me. I was striving for an A and no less than a B average.

I could see the disappointment in Mama's eyes. I had heard other kids say that when they brought bad grades home, they got punished, and their punishment was getting their behinds whipped. Well, I wasn't worried about that fate because Mama didn't believe in hitting. She always said, "Children should be chastised, not whipped." Her chastising meant ongoing lectures combined with scripture. At that moment, however, I was hoping for the whipping punishment because once it was done, it was over. Lectures were ongoing because there was follow-up and reminders of my responsibilities and the outcomes of my decisions. I said nothing. I waited for her.

"Why do you have a D average?" she began. "Are you doing your schoolwork?"

I didn't know at the time that it was really a trick question. I told her, "I am doing my work."

"If you were doing your work, your teacher would not have needed to send the progress report home! Don't try to fool me. I wasn't born yesterday." That was a confirmation that I had better acknowledge my lack of attention toward my work, own it, and decide how I was going to get it right.

I told her, "I really am paying attention in class at times. I don't talk but just think about being at my other school."

"That has nothing to do with it," she said. "A *D* is unacceptable and only you can fix it. You I don't have a choice but to do your work as its assigned and prepare yourself to graduate. I don't want you to try to just pass. You must try to get an A. If you try to get an A and end up with a B, at least you did your best. What happens if you try to pass? A D is passing, and you know that's not acceptable, so try to get an A. I don't want to see any Cs."

I looked at her and said, "OK, Mama, I will work harder and do my best."

She wrote on the comment section of the report, telling my teacher that she had seen the report and that she would work with me at home to assist with bringing up the grade. She told me to read it and asked if I knew what she meant. I said no. She explained to me that she would be checking daily to see my assignments.

I knew I could do better and realized that my pity party was over, and I had to demonstrate strong efforts and gain attainable knowledge in that class.

I was so relieved and gladly returned the progress note to Mr. Alegar the next day. He opened it and smiled as he said, "I see that you are going to work toward getting that grade up. I know you can do it."

I couldn't help but think that if he was so sure I could do it, why did he send the note home? I took on a new attitude and did better at focusing on my work. I studied, and when I didn't understand assignments or class discussions, I raised my hand for clarity and at times met with him during my study hall to gain a better understanding of my assignment. I was determined to work as hard as I could to obtain an A, although I still did not like the course. If I could avoid another lecture from Mama, it was worth it.

Shortly after that, I was called to the office of the guidance counselor. After what I had gone through with my grade, I felt anxiety stirring in the bottom of my stomach. My nerves were racing as I left my classroom and went to her office. As I entered, she smiled at me and motioned for me to have a seat. I had not sought any assistance from the guidance counselor, and I wasn't interested in any at that time.

She began, "Linda, there is a new program this summer at one of the colleges. It's an educational camp. Students are selected based on their grades."

I couldn't help but wonder if she knew about that D in Spanish that I could possibly receive. She went on to tell me that teachers had recommended me and strongly believed that I should have one of the spots there. It was hard to take more of this conversation without asking her if she knew about the progress report, so I asked her.

She said yes and further explained that Mr. Alegar had spoken to her, and he believed that, after communicating with my mother, I should be fine.

I couldn't believe it!

She then said,

"This program is also about potential, and all your teachers feel that you would do well there. Would you be interested?"

I quickly said, "yes!"

The excitement, however, quickly shifted to gloom and wonder.

I thought about the progress note and was very concerned about what Mama would think. *How can I approach her with a request to go to summer camp?* Surely she had not forgotten about that progress report. *Oh my,* I thought, *what am I going to do?* I wanted to attend that camp badly! It would be my first time staying on a college campus—and for six weeks! I thought that because it was an all-expenses-paid program, Mama would lean more toward allowing me to attend. I quickly dropped that thought, however, because I knew that paid or not, Mama would make it happen if she thought it would provide some benefit for me. She would not base her decision on monetary reasons, especially if I was not meeting her expectations for doing my schoolwork. Well, I could only wait and face the outcome, regardless of her decision.

As I was heading back to my Spanish class, I thought about that summer camp. I thought about all of the things that were in my favor during this tenth-grade year. I had a job in the school, tutoring students in typing, for which I got paid. I was taking a drama class and had landed a part in the play presented by our class. That was fun, and Mama was pleased that I was doing something that I really liked. My other courses were going well, and she recognized that I was working hard in my Spanish class. She had commented earlier that she hoped that my efforts would be worthwhile and that my grade for that class would improve. I hoped so as well. I wanted to graduate, and I really was trying.

After I entered the Spanish classroom and sat down, Mr. Alegar asked everyone to quiet down and prepare to learn. He called out my name, and I was startled, thinking, *What now?*

When I didn't answer, he said, "Linda, please see me after class."

I politely replied, "Yes, sir."

I had entered that classroom with much enthusiasm and a readiness to learn and to absorb all that I could and to focus on the lessons. I looked around and noticed that a few of my classmates were smiling, as if they were pleased that I had to see the teacher after class. Several students had to stay after school due to their behavior, and they seemed delighted that I might have gotten into trouble, and it was now my turn to stay afterward. Their expressions didn't really bother me. I had learned not to let others bother me, and it was paying off. I gave them no reaction and tried as hard as I could to focus on the lesson.

I felt drained from the pressure I was feeling and anticipated having to take another bad report home to Mama. Finally, the class was over. I had not participated as I had in the past, so I was expecting a lecture on lack of participation. At this point, I didn't care. I figured I would face the music, even if I didn't like what was playing—and I was convinced that I would not.

After all of the students had left the classroom, he asked me to come up to his desk. As I was approaching his desk, he opened his desk drawer and removed an envelope. He looked at me and said, "Give this to your mother."

I just stood there in shock but somehow asked him, "What is it?"

"It's another progress report. The term will be over soon, and I want your mother to see how you are doing."

I started to cry, but I can't recall what exactly happened. I was numb and could barely think. I felt faint and couldn't say anything; it was probably best that I didn't. As I reached out my hand to take the envelope, he told me to read the report. He had not sealed it because, this time, he wanted me to see it before I delivered it home.

I was thankful for that and slowly pulled the report from the envelope. I opened it and couldn't believe what I saw. I had earned a B! I was overwhelmed with excitement and relief. Before opening that envelope, I had seen nothing but dark clouds and attending summer school, forfeiting the summer camp program, or—worse—waiting an extra semester to graduate.

He must have noticed my relief, and he congratulated me. "You've worked very hard," he said. "I knew all along that you could do it." He then sealed the envelope and noted on the outside that he had allowed me to read the note. He signed his name after his comment, and I was so thankful for that.

The bus was waiting for me when I got outside. Mr. Alegar had informed the teachers on bus duty to have the bus wait for me. I quickly hopped on the bus and saw that a friend had saved me a space on her seat.

"Are you in trouble?" she asked.

"I am not," I told her. "Mr. Alegar wanted to tell me that I had improved my Spanish grade to a B." I was sure to speak loudly enough for those kids to hear who had smiled when they heard that I had to stay after class. Those smirks instantly disappeared, and that was the end of that.

The bus ride home that day didn't happen fast enough. I couldn't wait to get home to give Mama this news. When we finally got to my bus stop, I got up before the bus actually stopped, yelled bye to my friend, and ran home to give Mama that progress report.

I rushed in the front door and could smell Mama's turnip greens and cornbread cooking. She always had dinner started by the time I got home from school. She heard me running into the house and asked why I was running.

I showed her the progress report. I had held it all the way home because I didn't want to have to go through my book bag to find it before giving it to her.

As she took the report, she looked at me and smiled. She saw Mr. Alegar's comment on the envelope and she said to me, "There must be good news in the report. Is that why you're so happy?"

I smiled as I was trying to catch my breath and said, "Just open it."

Mama opened the report and read it out loud, and I could hear the excitement in her voice. After she read it, she gave me the biggest hug, and she gave warmest, most loving hugs you could ever receive. She said to me,

"See? I knew that once you put your mind to it, you would do just fine. Were you trying for a B or an A?"

I proudly responded, "I was trying for an A. The B is my average now, and I'm still working on an A for my final grade."

Again, she smiled and said, "A B is very good. Keep trying for that A because you're better than average. That is why you don't make Cs. Cs are average."

I was happy to be back in the mix of students who were graduating. Mama was happy as well.

That evening at dinner, after Mama blessed the food and it was served on our plates, she announced that she had some news. I had no idea and couldn't imagine what that news was. After she had said grace, I had emotionally left the table—I was sitting there, but I was thinking that several years after Daddy's death, it still felt different at mealtimes. I wondered for a minute, before Mama got my attention again, if Daddy would have been proud of me as well. That moment was short-lived, as I heard Mama continuously asking me if I was listening. I assured her that I heard her, and she began to tell her good news.

"Do you remember those people who were here last week?"

I said yes. I remembered that a man and a lady had come over to meet with Mama. I had learned early to stay out of grown folks' conversations, so when they came over, I left the room and gave them some privacy. It wasn't my place to ask what they wanted because I knew that if it was something Mama wanted us to know, she would share it.

"Well," Mama continued, "that was Mr. Compton and his secretary, Miss Tiffany. Last week when they visited, they talked to me about new apartments that are being built. I applied for one but didn't want to tell you until I knew if my application was approved. When they were here, they asked many questions about how I would pay for the apartment and the size of my family. After answering their questions and completing the application, they told me that they would give me a call if we were selected as tenants for this new development. Well, today they called to tell me that we will be moving into an apartment. All of the units are not complete as of yet, but some of them are completed, and the one we're moving into is ready for us to move in. We will be moving in the first of the month!"

I couldn't believe what I was hearing.

Before I could respond, she said, "Wait, there's more! Our new apartment is in your old school district. You will be graduating high school with Daisy and other friends you attended middle school with!"

This was better than good news; this was great news!

Mama said, "Remember, I told you it wasn't permanent and not to worry. I knew you would be back at your old school."

"How did you know?" I asked her

"God always make a way if it's his will," she said.

"God knows what's best. You have to have faith and pray. God will always make a way."

That day was one of the best days ever! I was overwhelmed with excitement and visualized walking around the new school that would be a year old when I got there. I immediately called Daisy and told her the good news. She was as excited as I was. She yelled to her mother, but her mother knew already—Mama had kept her in the loop. Daisy and I couldn't figure out how they were so successful in keeping this news from us. We instantly concluded that it didn't matter; what mattered was that we would be classmates again. We looked forward to being able to relate when we talked about certain events or matters that took place during the school day.

Mama said she would call the school and start the transfer process so that we would be able to attend sooner than later. Although Daisy and I would be attending the same school, we would not ride that same school bus because we were on different bus routes. I was moving across town, and we would be farther from each other but close enough to visit by car. I could hardly wait to leave and was happy to finish the school year with my old friends. As I was lying in my bed, fighting sleep that night, I could hear Mama singing, "I know the Lord will make a way, somehow." Her prayers had been answered.

Things didn't go as smoothly as I had hoped. At the beginning of the following month, we moved into our new apartment. It was great! The community was still in the process of developing, and it was interesting to watch new housing units being built around us. The lawns were beautifully landscaped, and there were shopping centers and a grocery store within walking distance. The bedrooms and bath were upstairs in the apartment, and the living room, dining area, and kitchen were downstairs. I was excited about having the bedrooms upstairs, as it provided some privacy. I was extremely thankful for a washer and dryer hookup, as we'd had to go to the laundromat to wash clothes, and I never liked that. Mama loved having the clothesline already hooked up in the backyard. She always loved hanging the laundry outside to dry, as she believed the fresh air was good for the clothes. I, on the other hand, wished that clotheslines didn't exist!

We were the first tenants in the unit, but families steadily moved into the other units.

Prior to moving, Mama had been successful with the school-transfer process. With the paperwork completed, I would soon be with my former classmates—but not as soon as I had hoped. I would have to finish the school year at my current school.

Mama said the principal and the counselors had agreed that it was best that I not transfer in the middle of the final grading period. Mama also said that because we were no longer living in the school district of my current school, they would not send a bus to pick me up. I would have to walk to school or see if I could get a ride.

I knew that getting a ride was out of the question. No one in my family had a car, and there wasn't anyone nearby who could transport me daily. I made up my mind that walking wouldn't be a problem; I was up for the challenge. So, I would not start school with my friends until the beginning of my junior year. I was disappointed but thankful that Mama followed through, and I didn't have to wonder or hope that I would graduate with my former classmates. I now knew that it was going to happen, and that was worth the walk. I assured Mama I would be OK with walking to school. School was almost over for the year, and soon, this would all be behind me.

Walking to school, however, was not as easy as I thought it would be. It was a long walk, and because I had to leave earlier than most kids who walked to school, it seemed as if I was the only one awake at that time. It was very quiet, and there were no other students walking in my community; it felt a little scary at times—walking through the neighborhood to get onto the main road that would take me through the downtown area before getting on the street where the school was located. Cars would swoosh by, appearing to be in a hurry to get to work, while others would look at me suspiciously and slow down.

I would walk faster and faster. The cars would move along, and I would continue my walk, hoping to get to school soon. As I approached the end of the street, there was a huge building that I was afraid of walking past. It was a coffin company, and the thought of looking at the coffin on display in the window—with the curtains drawn back to display the entire coffin—really rattled my nerves. My imagination got the best of me on a daily basis.

I decided that I would run past this building each morning. Walking home was not as scary because people were around, and I had to walk on the opposite side of the street to adhere to pedestrian laws and I didn't have to see the coffins inside that building. It was such a relief whenever I saw familiar places that indicated that the school was nearby. By the time I arrived, I was tired but well awake and ready for my lessons.

After several days of walking, I complained to Mama about

the walk. It was too long and I was scared at times. Mama said she would see what she could do. She didn't tell me what she was going to do about it, and it wasn't my place to ask her. I knew that in due time, she would get back to me with any plans she might have in place, and she did just that.

Mama spoke to the school officials and told them about the long walk. With only a little time remaining in the school year, she asked if there was a way they could provide transportation for me. The school did have buses that came to our community, but they were for students with special needs. These buses picked up the students regardless of their districts and took them to their assigned schools. These buses were shorter than regular school buses, and the capacity was less than half the number of students assigned to the larger buses.

Mama informed me that I would be riding one of these buses. I was thankful and didn't mind riding with these kids. I was happy that I didn't have to walk. This arrangement reminded me of the time when Daddy approached the school system during my first year of school and negotiated a bus to pick up his daughters because he felt that the walk was too long for us. They had complied, although we were in walking distance. I felt special to have parents who really looked out for my best interest.

I knew that kids would most likely tease me because some of them would make jokes about the kids riding on the "short school bus" and call them names. I felt that I would be called names for riding this bus, but to my surprise, I was not. Riding this school bus was a blessing. The students were so kind, and there weren't any arguments or disrespectful conversations on that bus during the little time I was assigned to ride it. I wasn't tired when I got to school, and I didn't have to leave home as early as I had when I was walking.

I was able to register for my courses at the other school and prepare for my summer program. I had much to be thankful for.

My Summer Camp Experience

School was finally over for the year. I did it! My GPA was above a B average, and Mama was so proud. My grades arrived prior to my leaving for camp, and Mama summarized my tenth-grade year of school. She reminded me of how I hadn't wanted to be there, but I had made the best of it. She reiterated how proud she was that I brought that grade up in my Spanish class. She also praised me because that was the only class where I had problems. She told me that she was proud of me, and she knew that I could do it. She said to me, "Remember who you are. You can do anything if you put your mind to it. God is always with you, and he will always make a way." Mama had always said to me that I was her child, but I was God's child and God always came first. Her telling me that I must remember who I am was her way of reminding me that I was God's child first. It would take years for me to truly understand what she meant.

The time had come for me to go to summer camp. It was a four-week camp (instead of the six weeks I was originally told). My paperwork arrived in the mail. There was a list of things I needed to bring with me. Mama started checking off things that she would need to buy. It would be my first time away from home where there were no relatives. I was anxious but eager to go. Mama checked off sheets, towels, pillows, and other bed linens. She felt that I should bring new ones with me. I needed toiletries and hygiene products, and I wanted some new clothes. I had saved a little money from the work program during the school year and was able to contribute to the expense of purchasing new things. Mama arranged for her brother to drive me to the college. It was about a half-hour drive from my house. I would begin the week after school ended.

It was a very busy time, preparing for the camp. Mama went over all the dos and don'ts and her expectations for me while I was away from home. She covered everything from choosing friends carefully to remembering that I was as good as the company I kept. I heard that so often, practically every time I left the house. I would have to associate with friends who had the same morals and beliefs as I.

Mama also reminded me to talk to the adults if there were problems and not to take matters into my own hands. She was always concerned that I would have difficulty controlling my anger if I was provoked. I had never had trouble at school or challenged anyone in an aggressive manner for any reason. However, she had witnessed me expressing anger toward my siblings when I was provoked or appeared provoked. Mama reminded me to pray daily and to remember that God was with me.

I was becoming a little hesitant and more nervous about going after I heard all the dos and don'ts. I would have no family around, and it was family that provided me with that sense of security.

- 6 -

New Challenges

God is our refuge and strength, a very present help in trouble.
—Psalm 46:1 (KJV)

THE DAY FOR MY DEPARTURE FINALLY CAME, AND MY uncle was there to pick me up and take me to the college campus. He brought along my two cousins, his two sons, and after the car was packed and all goodbyes were exchanged, we were off. Although I was in the car, looking back at Mama, I could still feel her warm, loving hug. That was enough to sustain me and keep me focused on what I needed to do.

The drive to the college seemed never-ending. My uncle was a slow driver, and as we were in transit to the college, my anxiety grew due to his driving. Nevertheless, he had taken time from his schedule to drive me. Mama was appreciative, as was I. There were signs indicating that we were near the school, and I couldn't wait to get there. I fell asleep as we were approaching the school. The drive reminded me of the car rides I had when Daddy was still with us, as it was long enough to get a little snooze, but I missed the conversations that took place during those drives.

I thought about how my parents would talk between themselves in the front as we kids sat in the back, supposedly minding our business, only I always tried to listen to what they were saying. Mama would tell me to sit back and stop eavesdropping.

Suddenly, the car came to an abrupt stop. Uncle Anthony was

frustrated when a car cut in his path as he was turning into the driveway of the school. "Look at those knuckleheads," he said as he stopped to enter the driveway.

As we drove up to the school, we asked for directions to the dorm where I would be staying for the summer. When we reached the dorm parking lot, we saw cars parked, with families removing suitcases from the cars and heading into other dorms. I felt happy to be there but was already missing Mama, my family, and my friends.

Uncle Anthony parked the car and said, "This is it. Come on, boys. Grab her luggage, and let's get her settled in so that we can head back home."

William and Lance took my luggage and headed with me to my dorm, as Uncle Anthony checked the car to ensure that nothing was left behind—he had made it clear before parking that he had no intention of leaving anything. We were almost in the dorm by the time Uncle Anthony locked the car and headed up. We stopped for him, but he motioned for us to go ahead and said he would catch up.

As I entered the dorm, I gave the lady at the desk the letter with the instructions I needed to receive a key and to get settled into my room. I told her that the boys were my cousins, and they were bringing my luggage up and would leave after dropping the luggage off.

She smiled, said OK, and pointed us in the direction of my room. She was very pleasant and well dressed, and she told me that I was going to enjoy the camp. We headed up, and I unlocked the room. My cousins dropped the luggage on the floor and sat on the bed, claiming to be very tired after bringing the luggage up. Uncle Anthony had not made it to the room, so I looked around to see where everything went. William and Lance decided that they would wait until Uncle Anthony got there, and they remained seated to let me know that their jobs were done.

As we waited for Uncle Anthony, the door to the room was

abruptly pushed open, and an angry old woman entered. She immediately yelled at me, telling me that I had already broken a rule.

"Boys are not allowed in your room!" she shouted. "They have to leave now! What is the matter with you, letting boys up here? You two, out now!" She pointed to the door.

I tried to tell her that they were my cousins, and they would be leaving. "They only carried my luggage to my room, and my uncle is on his way up to take them back."

Boy, was she a mean-looking woman! She stood there with one hand on her hip as she continued to point to the door. Her eyebrows were raised. She was wearing a dress that fell to the middle of her legs. Her hair was bushy and up on her head, and she had a stern, rough voice! She didn't sound lady like at all—nothing like the lady who had given me the key to the room and who had no problem with my cousins coming up.

She yelled to my cousins, "Get out!" That's when Uncle Anthony came into the room. He immediately asked what was going on, and I quickly told him what had happened.

He assured that lady that they were my cousins, helping to bring up luggage, and they were leaving with him.

She explained that she was in charge of the dorm and would be staying there as well. That was news that I didn't want to hear. After she left the room, Uncle Anthony told me that it would be OK, and he and the boys had to head back. They said their goodbyes and were gone.

I watched them from my room window as they pulled away. I sat on the bed and thought about being alone. I was not going to have a roommate, and I had never been alone. As I looked at my schedule, I noticed that I had to be at the cafeteria soon to get my schedule for the week. This was an educational writing camp. I would participate in creative writing assignments as well as recreational activities. I put some things away to organize my room and then headed over to the cafeteria.

When I arrived, there were about four girls in the doorway, greeting students as we entered. They introduced themselves as the "welcome wagon," and I sensed sarcasm but worked on not showing my frustration. The lady back at the dorm had tested my patience, and I was trying hard to avoid reacting and showing that I was angry. I went into the building, took a seat, and waited for the orientation to begin.

It was a long process because there was a question-and-answer period, and people asked a lot of questions, some of which were unnecessary and a waste of time—at least I thought so. I was very tired and wanted to go to bed. I read over my schedule and discovered there was a lot taking place during the four weeks of this program. I would have writing courses and several activities all week. I signed up for swimming and couldn't wait for the activities to take place.

They would show us a movie each week. There were games planned in the Student Union, writing contests, and talent shows, and we had a meal schedule where we would meet daily to eat. It all seemed so interesting and exciting, but I was tired and wanted to go to bed. I'd told Mama that I would call the next day, and I planned to write to her weekly. I took a shower and went to bed and was prepared for the next day.

Classes there were very interesting. It was like being in school, and I looked forward to writing. We created our own stories, and the teachers gave us scenarios and situations for us to use as foundations to create stories. These would be submitted for the contests. I never liked competing, and I wasn't concerned about winning anything. I figured if I got something out of the lesson, I had already won. That's how my parents taught me as a child—competition was not of interest unless I was competing against myself.

Mama had signed a permission slip for me to take swimming lessons prior to my coming here, and my classes were going well.

I enjoyed writing and was always eager to read the comments the teacher included when grading my papers.

I learned a lot that summer. I became the ping-pong champion. I played ping-pong often; I had never played before, as my school did not offer ping-pong. I learned about creative writing, and I wrote poetry and short stories. One of the instructors advised me to have some of my writings published. At the time, I thought nothing of it.

I did well with swimming lessons until one day, as the swim instructor was teaching me how to float, I somehow ended up at the bottom of the pool. When I returned to the top of the pool, I immediately told her that I was quitting. She tried to convince me to stay with it because I only had a week left.

"You weren't drowning," she said, "and you managed to swim to the top of the pool without help."

At that point, I was thinking that she didn't try to get me out. I assured her that I was quitting.

"I have your certificate ready. Your mother will be disappointed if you quit."

I wasn't worried about Mama getting upset because I quit swimming lessons. She told me that it was up to me to take the lessons, so I was certain that it was my choice of whether to stay with it. I didn't trust the instructor anymore, and I followed through with quitting.

My only complaint about the camp was seeing a scary movie the first week I was there. I didn't want to tell Mama that I was scared because I didn't want her to worry or have any doubts regarding allowing me to go. The movie they showed the first week was *Psycho*, in which a lady is murdered in her shower. It would take me years to get over that scene and to take showers with no one in the house. I never told Mama about that, and I never watched that movie again until many years later.

I was able to participate in a talent show and sang with two other girls. That was a lot of fun, as I met kids from different areas of the state. Overall, it was a good camp. I got a chance to see what college life was about, and I enjoyed every minute of it.

In a few days, it would be over and I would return home to prepare for my junior year of high school. I was looking forward to that.

I missed my family and wanted desperately to return home. I missed Mama's cooking, her hugs, and the looks she gave me when I needed to be redirected. Mama was kind and loving. She gave enough for her and Daddy, and she tried hard to fill the void that developed when Daddy died. I needed to see her, to feel her, and to have that sense of security that only home could give.

I was ready to go home, but returning home was bittersweet. I would miss the independence I had at the camp. There was very little redirecting and needing permission for certain things. There was that dorm counselor who watched us like a hawk, but I made sure I stayed within the rules and gave her no reason to call me to her office or suspend my privileges, as some students were.

My uncle picked me up and drove me home to Mama. She was so happy to see me, and when she hugged me, I was so relieved. I felt safe and secure again. I didn't have to wonder what she was doing or if she was OK. We hurried into the house, and as I unpacked, I filled her in on my time at camp. When I told her that I quit swimming lessons and the reason for it, she told me that it was OK because it was important that I felt safe, and only I could make that decision. She wasn't concerned about my not getting the certificate.

I showed her the award I'd received for my writing, and she was very pleased. She told me that it would help me with school and that I should continue to do well. She told me that she was glad that I was home. She went into her room and gave me an envelope. It was my new schedule for school! I was really excited. Although I knew I would be going to high school with Daisy, now it really seemed real. It was in writing!

The letter also included summer programs where I could work

and earn a little money before school started. Mama said it was OK to apply for the summer work, as it was only two weeks, and that would give me a little pocket change. I was excited about earning a little money to buy some things I might need for school. Mama always got what I needed, but any time I could contribute and save her a little money, I wanted to do it. She never asked for any money that I earned and strongly encouraged me to buy some things I wanted for school. She always advised me to save as well.

Now things were really shaping up. My enthusiasm was overwhelming, and I couldn't wait to tell Daisy that I was home from the camp. She and I had written each other letters while I was away and stayed in touch. I called Daisy, and we exchanged happenings during the time I was away. She was happy that I would be returning to school with her, and she updated me on old friends and warned me about teachers about whom I should be concerned. We planned to do some shopping together before school started.

I was able to get a job with a work program called Neighborhood Youth Corps. I was a summer camp counselor for the two weeks before school. The camp provided activities for small kids, ages five through ten. The camp was in my community at a nearby park. The children participated in camp games and creative activities. There were about seven kids assigned to my campsite, and there was another counselor with me. A bus dropped them off each morning and picked them up in the afternoon. It was an easy job, and it was within walking distance of my house. This was my last assignment before school started, and I was relieved when it was over.

Daisy and I decided to shop for school supplies. It was apparent that my junior year would not be that much different from sophomore year. After buying a few notebooks, pens, and pencils, our supply shopping was done. We didn't need as many supplies because we had a study hall. Instead of six courses we only had to shop for five. Having a study hall lessened our course load and by doing so, we needed less supplies. We took the city bus downtown and were careful to get home on time.

By the end of the summer, we were ready to return to school. I didn't need as much for school because Mama had bought me a few garments when I went to camp. Those were still practically new, and I could wear them to school. This would be the year that we started preparing for college.

Back in School

School was back in session, and I was back on the school bus and back with my old friends. The classes were designed similar to classes at the other high school, but this high school was a new school, only one year old, and beautifully designed. I was thrilled to be back.

As life goes, however, good things don't last forever! I was greeted by many of my old friends, but, surprisingly, some weren't as friendly or happy to see me. They had their own agenda. I chose to ignore them and move on with getting acclimated to my new surroundings. I knew that my last two years of school would be at this high school, and I wanted to make the best of it. There was so much to do, and although I was looking forward to studying, I was also thinking about other things that would take place during those last two years.

There were the junior and senior proms, planning for graduation, and all the perks that came with being a senior. Other social events would take place, and there were always girls talking about cute boys, although I still had no interest in boys. My thoughts were occupied with the ideas of the future senior perks, and I couldn't wait for that! In the meantime, I was adjusting to my new school, settling into my classes, and getting to know the teachers and students.

One of my favorite courses was Health Occupations. I was

thinking about becoming a nurse after graduating from high school so I signed up for the Health Occupations course. The teacher was wonderful—very caring and compassionate toward people in general. She made learning fun, and she managed to give students individualized attention when needed. I learned basic nursing skills in this class—how to take vital signs and make up different types of hospital beds.

Mrs. Mavis enjoyed teaching this class and prepared us to complete in a statewide bed-making contest. It was a big event, and I was thrilled to be included in this endeavor. I had Mrs. Mavis for my junior and senior years of high school. During my junior year, Mrs. Mavis asked me to ask my mother if Mrs. Mavis could visit with her. I became concerned because I didn't want to ask Mama if it meant getting another progress note. The last thing I wanted was to tell Mama that another teacher wanted to talk to her about me.

But it was different this time. Mrs. Mavis told me that she just wanted to meet the woman who had raised such lovely daughters. Mrs. Mavis had taught three of my sisters who were grades ahead of me. With this knowledge, I quickly said that I would let my mother know what she had asked. Mama said it was OK for this teacher to visit her and talk. Mrs. Mavis did visit our home, and she and Mama had a nice "girl talk" kind of chat. Mama was pleased to receive the positive feedback from Mrs. Mavis about me and my sisters.

Senior High Highlights

After two weeks of that junior year, I was convinced that I did not want to be in a study hall; it was a waste of my time. There was too much talking and playing around from the other students, and I wanted out. My counselor told me that because we were well into the semester, I could not change study hall to another subject, but I could take a driver's education course. In order to take that course, I would have to meet with the principal.

As much as I didn't want to meet with the principal, I decided that I would indeed speak with him about dropping study hall and taking Driver's Ed. I didn't want to talk to him for fear that he would find a reason to speak with Mama. He knew Mama, and that made me nervous, but I followed through and met with him. When I entered his conference room, I saw an enormous oval-shaped table with about ten chairs.

All the chairs were occupied by students making cases to change classes or to talk themselves out of being disciplined. It was difficult to hear what each person said to him as they approached the seat next to him to plead their cases. When I entered the room, he seemed surprised to see me. He quickly directed me to take the seat next to the person at the end. I did as I was told and waited, patiently and quietly, as each student took his or her turn to meet with him.

My turn finally came, and after he asked what my concern was, he immediately associated me with my sister, who had attended high school under his leadership. She had worked for him while in school, and he remarked to me how smart she was as a student in his school. I proudly agreed with him, and then, as he requested, I explained why I was there.

At first, he said the class had started, and I would need to catch up. I assured him that I could and I would. I really wanted to start driving. He agreed that I could take Driver's Ed and gave me a form to give to my counselor. I would start my Driver's Ed course the next day.

All of this was great! The only thing I had not done was get Mama's permission to take Driver's Ed. I was only fifteen but turning sixteen in a month or so. I emotionally prepared myself to let Mama know and hoped that she wouldn't tell me that I had to wait. I was nervous and was scolding myself for making this decision without her approval. *Oh, boy, what was I thinking?*

On the same day that I was granted permission to get out of study hall, I told Mama as soon as I got home. I dared not delay telling her, as that would surely have made matters worse. I explained to her that I couldn't get any studying done in study hall because of all the noise, and I wanted to do something useful with my time. I told her that I would understand if I couldn't stay in Driver's Ed because I had not gotten her permission, but I'd had to act on it because time had already expired to drop study hall and take on another course.

Mama did not hesitate to tell me it was OK. It was as if she was pleased that I had signed up for the course. She said, "You should think about driving and getting your license."

With her approval and understanding, I was more eager and excited about changing the class. I was ready to go.

While fellow classmates were dreaming of going to the prom for the first time that year, I had no interest and decided that I was not going; I didn't anyone to ask me. That year, we also had a Sweetheart Ball. It was a smaller version of the prom and was presented by a committee, which I was on. I served as the historian for that committee, and my responsibilities consisted of keeping records of the planning process for this ball. It would be the first time the school had presented such an event.

I had declared over and over that I would not attend that ball. I didn't want to go through the hassle of buying a gown and other accessories that were needed. The faculty told me, however, that because I was a member of the committee, I would have to attend; I had no choice. This was upsetting because I really did not want to go, and I didn't want Mama to have to be concerned about buying a gown. I was working part-time in the school's work program, but I didn't want to spend my money on that. I had to go home again with news that Mama didn't need to hear.

When I told Mama that I had to go, her first question was, "How are you getting to the ball?"

I hadn't thought about that. "I don't know," I told her.

"You will not be riding with any of the kids at that school because I'm concerned about safety."

I didn't want to ride with anyone and had no plans to ask for a ride. On the other hand, we didn't own a car, and I had to be there. "Because I can't get a ride, I will have to quit the committee."

"I don't want you to quit because you are too far into the committee and have responsibilities. I will see what I can do."

This was concerning to me because I had no idea what she meant or what she was going to do to get me there. She had ruled out getting a taxi, so I just had to wait and see. I starting thinking about a dress and borrowed one from my sister.

I also thought about letting the committee know that I might not be able to attend because of a lack of transportation. As much as I didn't want to say that to them, I did tell them that I could not attend the Sweetheart Ball. I also let them know that my mother did not want me riding with other students, so I couldn't get a ride with anyone.

The teacher who supervised the committee advised me to stay with the committee. Because we still had some time, he would also see what he could do to help.

I told Mama about my conversation, and she said that she was working on it as well. A few days later, the assistant principal, Mr. Morgan, called me to his office.

"I've heard about your transportation problem," he said. "Because I've been assigned to monitor the event, I would be willing to drive you to school."

I was mortified to hear that the assistant principal would drive me to the Sweetheart Ball. Mr. Morgan was a very nice old gentleman. As nice as he was, he still was the assistant principal. He told me that he would come to my house to talk with my mother and assure her of my safety. As much as I wanted to lie and say that the matter had been resolved, I told him that I would let Mama know that he wanted to meet with her.

"I'll work around her schedule," he said.

If there was ever a time when I wanted to tell a premeditated lie, that was the time. I dared not follow through with that plan, though, because Mama often said that she despised lying. She would have recited the Ten Commandments to me, and I didn't feel like being preached to. So I went with the truth and communicated everything Mr. Morgan had said.

Mama was OK with that plan. She said she would ask him questions regarding transporting me to the ball and determine after that if I would attend the Sweetheart Ball.

At this point, I was just numb! I had nothing to say but OK. I hoped that I wouldn't have to ride to school with an old guy who everyone knew was the assistant principal. It was too much to bear. I had stomach cramps just thinking about it, even though I knew that Mama had my best interest at heart. I also knew that she was going to pray about it before she made a decision. She always talked about praying and doing what was right by the Lord. I heard her, but the Lord knew that I was not following her example regarding prayer.

Mama and Mr. Morgan met at our house. I was allowed to be a part of the conversation, although I had nothing to say. I didn't want to be there. I was bored and, for the first time that I could remember, I would have rather been washing dishes or just cleaning anything than sitting there, hearing how Mr. Morgan would drive me to school and keep an eye on me during the event. I felt like Mama was talking to my babysitter, one who was happily compliant in giving her a blow-by-blow report!

I was devastated and no longer wanted to be on the committee or attend that ball, but I knew that I had no choice. Mama got details from Mr. Morgan regarding when he would pick me up and when he would bring me home. While he was there, she informed me that I must be on my best behavior and went over all the dos and don'ts. Mr. Morgan assured her that he knew there would be no problems because I had demonstrated nothing but exemplary behavior. Mama smiled, thanked him, and saw him to the door.

The Sweetheart Ball

The night of the ball finally came, and I still was hesitant to attend. I was dressed up in my sister's gown, but I didn't primp as long as I usually did because I didn't care. Mama said I looked pretty. I thought, *At least she's happy about it.*

Mr. Morgan came to pick me up, as scheduled. He told Mama that he would have me home as discussed and reminded her that he would be chaperoning the event. He would be there to keep everyone safe.

Mama thanked him again and said to me what she always said: "Be sweet." That meant, *Stay out of trouble, be kind, remember who you are (God's child), and respect your elders.* I could be nothing but sweet that evening because I didn't want to go. I responded, "I will," and walked toward Mr. Morgan's car.

Mr. Morgan opened the back door and said,

"I'm your chauffeur this evening. You have your own chauffeur."

"Thank you Mr. Morgan", I said as I entered the car.

It was as if he knew that I was not happy about him driving me and wanted to make me feel better. I thanked him, and as we took off, I wished that the ride would soon be over.

This seemed like a very long ride, but I was OK with it, as I was hoping that by the time I got to school, everyone would be inside and would not see me entering the building with the assistant principal. Every time we stopped at a light, I hoped it would get stuck and delay us.

Mr. Marshall had always been the protective type of man. If he saw kids having problems that did not warrant disciplinary actions, he would step in and give brief lectures regarding behavior.

If he saw a boy disrespecting a girl, his lectures were a little more than brief, and sometimes it may have led to disciplinary actions. He was all about respect, and he modeled what he expected. He was very kind and cared about the students. As we rode along, getting closer to the school, I could see the last turn that would take us into the school parking lot. I had my fingers crossed and looked around, hoping not to be seen.

As we drove into the lot, Mr. Morgan did not go to a parking space. He drove around near the entrance but stopped the car near the sidewalk, where no one was walking, and said to me, "I'm letting you out here so you can walk in alone. I don't think you want to be seen walking into the gym with the school's assistant principal. When the event is over, I will meet you in this same place after most kids have gone."

I was so thankful. I would have to stay a little longer because I was on the committee, and I would need to make some notes regarding the event before leaving.

The night was perfect! I worked throughout the entire event but enjoyed it. I didn't want to dance with any of the boys, and having to work on the committee was the perfect excuse to be busy and avoid having to make up reasons why I didn't dance. I just wasn't interested. I was glad that I attended and couldn't wait to get home and thank Mama for letting me go. It was a good experience, and because of it, I was totally convinced that I didn't want to attend the prom my junior or senior year of high school.

Getting My Driver's License?

I finished my Driver's Ed course and was now ready to apply for my learner's permit. At the time, there was no car in our household, but I had arranged with a cousin to allow me to practice using her car. I passed the test in class and felt that I was ready to take the written test at the Department of Motor Vehicles. At the end of the course, I was given the book used by the DMV to study in preparation of getting my permit.

I didn't study as I should have because I felt that since I'd passed the class test, I was ready. Mama had to accompany me to the DMV because she would have to sign for me to get my permit. After I took the test, I was confident that I had passed. I told Mama I was all set and was just waiting for the results. Mama seemed pleased as we waited.

The attendant for the exams came out and gave me my results—and told me to return in a few weeks and retake the test. I had not passed the test. Had I not been in a public place, I would have cried on the spot. I was hurt, embarrassed, and ashamed!

Mama looked at me and said, "Study the book, and we can come back." She never scolded me but encouraged me and told me to keep trying. I gathered that because it wasn't school, it was OK.

I studied the handbook from the DMV, and I was ready the next time. I realized that what I thought was confidence before was nothing less than a cocky attitude. I remembered that Daddy would always say that being prideful could get in our way of doing what's right. He would say, "Pride can kill you." Years after his death, I began to understand what he meant.

Mama quizzed me prior to my returning. I believe that she read the book and familiarized herself with the laws and rules of driving. There were times when I would give the wrong answer, and Mama would say, "You don't know that." She would say the answer as it was written in the book without any prompts.

Now, it was time to put my preparation to the test and to take it a second time.

I went into the room guarded, almost emotionless, fearing that I might forget what I knew. I took the exam and turned it in, hoping that I would pass the exam but also prepared to take it again if I had to.

Mama and I waited patiently, and soon my name was called to come to the desk. I was asked a few questions and then was congratulated for passing the exam. I was issued my learner's permit and could now drive with a licensed driver in the car. My cousins were available to assist me and allowed me to drive as they rode along. I would be eligible to have a driver's license at sixteen, and I was determined to have it by my senior year. I drove with my permit while in the eleventh grade, and by summer, I was ready to try for my driver's license.

My cousins had given me their seal of approval and had labeled me a good driver and ready to try for my license. I was underage so Mama would still need to sign for me to have a driver's license. This time, she had some ground rules and went over them with me before I went to take the test. She told me to study the book and to know all the answers. Although she didn't say anything when I had to take the permit test a second time, she told me that she would not go with me a second time to get my license.

She made it clear, because I needed her to sign for it, that I was not old enough to do it on my own. Therefore, she would only make one more trip to the DMV.

"If you don't pass the driver's test this second time", she said, "you will have to wait until you're eighteen years old to get it on your own."

"I'm going to pass it this time Mama", I said, "I studied and I'm ready."

That thought brought all kinds of discomfort to me. I thought, *That's two more years!* I would be in college by then and would not be able to get my license. I knew that I had to get it, so I studied the book several times before going to take the road test.

The day I went to take the road test, it was very scary. Mama was with me, and although she was sending me pleasing smiles of support, all I heard was, "You're going to wait until you're eighteen to get your license if you fail the test." I knew what I had to do to get that license. I sat there, wrapped up in all kinds of nerves and mixed emotions, while Mama looked so calm and at peace. She didn't seem to be worried at all, but why would she? Her rules were clear, and in any case, it was a win/win for her. She was OK with walking and taking taxis or calling her brother if she needed to go somewhere. She never had any interest in driving.

I needed to have my license; it was a benefit for high school seniors to have their licenses. Seniors were allowed a senior pass, which authorized them to leave campus during lunch and eat where they pleased. Daisy and I had dreams of leaving campus and having lunch at Hardee's. Daisy had plans to get her mother's car, and I was looking forward to my sister Edna buying a car so I could drive it.

I had reasons to be concerned, but knew I had to focus on passing that test. The examiner came out, called my name, and said, "Let's go." My cousin came with us so that I could use her car for the road test. I had driven her car many times and was comfortable driving it. The examiner was a big man, emotionless, and very stiff-necked. He wasn't friendly at all, and I was nervous getting into the car with him. He directed me where to go, when to turn, when to stop, and when to signal, and he used terminology that indicated which driving technique to use. "Make a three-point turn; parallel park."

I felt as if I was doing fine for a minute. Then he told me to make a left turn. I made the turn, but he had a look on his face that concerned me. I kept driving until he directed me back to the DMV parking lot and told me to park. He then took his clipboard with drawings on it and began to tell me about that left turn I'd made. He said that I'd made it too short; had a car been there, I might have hit it.

I could feel tears welling up in my eyes as I visualized Mama's face—and me standing in line, two years later. My ability to have that senior perk vanished right there in that moment.

Then the examiner looked at me and smiled a little. "You did very well. The left turn was minor, and you can fix that. I just wanted you to know. Congratulations. You have a driver's license."

I couldn't get into that building fast enough to tell Mama that

I'd done it! She was excited and told me that she knew I would get it because I knew the answers. I even told her about the left turn. As we continued to talk and hug, my name was called again, and I went up to take my first driver's license picture. At age sixteen, I had my driver's license, and I couldn't wait for those senior perks.

My junior year had been great. I was very selective when I chose friends, so they were few but loyal and believed what I believed. Our morals were similar, and we put our studies first. We weren't interested in hanging out after school or impressing our peers to be like everyone else. We were individuals who followed the teachings of our parents and practiced doing the right things. That behavior came with opposition from other peers. For no apparent reason, I was taunted for being "different." Mean girls have always existed, but at the time, I didn't realize that's what they were. I learned that girls thought I was stuck-up and too sophisticated. I was taught to be careful of the company I kept because those peers also represented who I was. I stayed true to that when I selected friends. I never disrespected anyone. I later learned that people have their own impressions and/or opinions, and usually, it was all about who they were. This was something I had not experienced in the other high school or anywhere.

Things were really changing. My senior year would mark the end of another chapter of my life. I often felt cheated because Daddy didn't see me grow up; I wondered what he would think about me driving. As much as I missed him, I was so thankful to have Mama. She was available to listen to me, to hear what happened at school, and she gave me advice on dating and how to conduct myself as a lady. She was keen on my behaving like a lady and exhibiting proper behavior.

After looking at several schools, I decided to attend junior college, receive an associate's degree in nursing, and continue to a four-year college afterward. Mama was OK with this plan and endorsed it 100 percent. In the meantime, I was enjoying my senior privileges.

I was using Edna's car while she worked and using my senior pass to go off campus for lunch. I also had a part-time job and had my own bank account. Mama was always interested in what I was doing in school. She made sure I had what I needed, and she too was preparing for me to go to college. She was also looking beyond college and made an attempt to start a hope chest for me.

She came into the kitchen one day as I was sitting there, working on a puzzle. Mama always had five-hundred-piece puzzles for us to work on in our spare time. I enjoyed doing them, even more so when she sat down and worked on them with us. On one particular day, Mama had some trinkets in her hand and gave them to me. She told me that she was starting a hope chest for me. I persuaded her to discontinue doing that because I had no intention of getting married. Where some girls dreamed of getting married and becoming mothers, that was the farthest thing from my mind. I liked children, especially my baby brother and my nieces and nephews. I was content being a baby sitter for family and friends when needed. Mama liked seeing me with them and often gave me advice while babysitting. After the conversation about the hope chest, she concluded that I would not have children and jokingly said, "I won't live to see you with children." It was not in my plans because I just wanted to finish high school, go to college, and start my career.

My senior year of high school would present me with challenges I'd never experienced. On one occasion, I was approached by a group of girls. It was the first time I was ever threatened or challenged to fight. We were riding the school bus together, and they called me names and threatened to beat me up. I didn't acknowledge them in any way; I continued to act as if I was reading a book. I didn't know all of these girls personally, just one of them, and I didn't want any trouble. I just wanted to be left alone. I wished I had driven that day. I'd done nothing to initiate this encounter.

One of the girls happened to be the daughter of one of my

mother's friends. I was surprised to see her there and could not imagine why she was a part of the group. We always got along and had never had any problems. I just sat there, hoping that I would get to my stop sooner rather than later. When it was time for me to get off, I got off without incident. I said nothing to them, and they eventually stopped their taunting. I was shaken and couldn't wait to tell Mama what had happened.

I nearly ran into the house to tell Mama about my experience. I thought that she would hug me and say, *Don't worry baby; it's going to be all right*. Well, to my surprise, it didn't go that way. I was prepared for the pity party I thought I would receive, and it didn't happen. I told Mama about the incident and made it as dramatic as I possibly could.

She was quiet as I reported the details. I made sure to tell her that she even knew one of those girls.

"Mama", I said, "I just had problems with some of the girls on the bus! For no reason, they threatened to beat me up. I said nothing to them and ignored them because I didn't want to get into any trouble."

"What did they do", she asked.

"They were calling me names and challenging me to fight them. One of those girls was Jackie. She was the main one and it didn't matter that we were friends."

She quietly let me finish without interrupting and watched me the entire time I was speaking.

Then she said, "Sit down, Who do you think you are? Do you really think that people won't bother you because you did nothing wrong? Look what they did to Jesus Christ! You're not better than he is, so why is this bothering you?"

I didn't know what to say in that moment. I quietly searched for the right words to use, and all I could say was, "Oh." I knew that Jesus was crucified and died on the cross. I wasn't reading the Bible in those days, although I watched Mama read that Bible daily. She often recited what she read as a means to keep God's Word in our household.

She continued, "Remember when I told you that people will say and do mean things? They don't need a reason. Jesus did nothing and they crucified Him! You hold your head up and keep on ignoring them. You didn't do anything wrong."

I was devastated but dared not tell her that I wasn't clear with the Crucifixion at that time. I had been in church all my life, and now I realized that I had not paid attention as I should have, in church or at home. Holding my head down represented, and I had nothing to be ashamed of. I did just that, but the next day when I went to school, I saw one of the girls and decided to ask her if she wanted to finish what she had started the day before, now that it was just the two of us. She walked away from me, and I continued to my next class. I was relieved that she had gone her way and I mine. It would have been trouble for me, had it gone differently and if Mama had been notified that I was in the principal's office.

My school year was coming to an end. I was asked to go to the senior prom, but I decided not to go. All my applications were in, and I was looking forward to preparing for college. I would be leaving home, and I was excited about that. Although I would miss Mama, I was ready for the experience. I had planned to major in nursing, but the nursing school I visited was not appealing to me, so I decided to attend a junior college and major in pre-nursing. I figured that I would decide during my time at that school if I was still interested in nursing. The school guidance counselor was helpful with answering questions about the school. I was satisfied that it was accredited, and it was small. I liked the idea of going to a small school as opposed to a very large campus. I checked the mailbox constantly to see if I had received my acceptance letter.

Prior to graduating from high school, I received my letter. I was accepted to a very small junior college. At the time of my high school graduation, I was seventeen and would not be eighteen until a month after the college admission date. A form was included in my letter of acceptance, telling me that because I was underage, my mother would have to sign a permission form, authorizing me to attend college and to live on the college campus. I'd been excited about going to college and had bragged about leaving home and being on my own, but Mama was quick to remind me that if she chose not to sign the permission form, I would have to wait until the following semester to enroll. She reminded me because I consistently danced around the house, singing that I was leaving for college.

I quickly humbled myself and apologized for being so cocky and misguided regarding leaving home. I was about to start college as I did in the first grade—underage and needing authorization from a parent. I was thankful that Mama was allowing me to leave, knowing that I was underage. I knew that she trusted me and wanted me to excel in all that I chose to do. She was my rock, and I could only wonder what I would do if I lost her. I was glad that she was there to see me finish high school and prepare for college.

- 7 -

Leaving Home

Fear thou not; for I am with thee: be not dismayed; for I am thy God: I will strengthen thee; yea, I will help thee; yea, I will uphold thee with the right hand of my righteousness.
—Isaiah 41:10 (KJV)

WHAT A FEELING IT WAS TO WALK UP ON THAT STAGE, receive my high school diploma, and toss that tassel on my graduation cap to the other side, denoting that I'd done it—I had graduated from high school! It was a great moment, and I was so pleased to see Mama smiling. As always, her smile and joy were expressed with a big hug, and I enjoyed every hug she gave me. The screams and cheers of my classmates, family, and friends were overwhelming.

It had been an interesting time. Our graduation date was changed, and we didn't graduate as soon as planned. I was on pins and needles, hoping that it would not change again. It finally happened, and I then got ready to prepare for college, which I had long waited for. I thought about Daddy; I felt his presence through Mama. I knew in my heart that he would have been proud as well.

Now it was time for me to focus on packing and (again) checking off the things I needed to take with me. Through my excitement, I pondered on leaving home and being away from Mama. As much as I wanted to leave, I wanted to stay. She was very supportive and shared my excitement, encouraging me and reminding me that I would be fine. I wasn't going far, only about an hour away, and that was a consolation for me because I could come home whenever I wanted or needed to.

The summer was filled with preparations, calling friends, and comparing notes about where we were all going. We exchanged addresses, promising each other that we would stay in touch. Mama signed the permission slip, and during the summer, I was issued information regarding my dormitory, my roommate, and student expectations regarding policies and rules of the school. It was the basic dos and don'ts of the school.

The pictures were inviting, and my excitement grew after reviewing the information. I was ready during midsummer, and at that point, it was a waiting game. I was waiting for Mama to approach me with a speech of dos and don'ts. I think, at the time, not only did I expect it, but I looked forward to it. I managed to talk myself into being a nervous wreck, thinking of what Mama might say. I knew she would tell me to act like a lady, watch out for the boys, and remember what I was taught. She might tell me to be in my room at a certain hour and stay away from certain kids; remember that "birds of a feather flock together," meaning to choose friends with the same morals and values. She might tell me to find a church and make sure I attended regularly and to keep God in my heart. When I was in high school, she told me to be nice to the boys that I didn't like because if I was mean to them, they might talk to boys I truly liked, and they would not want to have anything to do with me. I thought, *That's a really good tip*. I never had a reason to think that way in high school, but it might be helpful in college.

My thoughts got the best of me. I had worked up enough anxiety that I felt as if I had actually had a talk with Mama. I also knew that it was too soon to get that lecture. She would most likely wait until it was time for me to leave before lecturing me. Although I had packed for school, Mama kept adding little things to my luggage—toiletries, an extra comb, towels, soap, and shampoo. As time went by, she also added things to the trunk she had bought for me so I wouldn't need too many suitcases. My sister Edna packed an alarm clock; she knew how much I loved to sleep and said I would need it to wake me up. Mama wouldn't be there to wake me up, and I couldn't afford to miss any classes.

Looking at the majority of my things in that trunk, the vision I had of leaving and going to college was now a reality, but the bliss I had envisioned was not there. I was growing up, and it was a feeling I'd never had before. It was bittersweet, and I wondered if I should go, as planned, or wait until the following semester. After much debating with myself, weighing the pros and cons, I knew I had to go. I also knew that Mama would not approve of my waiting when things were already in motion. I was about to enter my freshman year of college.

My bags were packed, all my paperwork was in, and another sister volunteered to drive me to school. Prior to my enrolling, Edna had driven me up to look at the campus, but she was not available to drive me up for the school year. My sister Renee and her husband, Albert, would be at the house early in the morning to take me to school so I could participate in orientation. My registration would begin a day after my arrival.

Mama approached me the day before leaving. She said, "Come here, gal." She always said *gal* instead of *girl*. "I want to talk to you before you leave."

I thought, *This is it. I'm going to get a lecture after all.* I was prepared because I had gone over things in my head that I thought she might say. She and I sat down on the couch, and I asked her to wait. I ran upstairs to get a picture of me with a poem on the back that I had dedicated to her. When I gave it to her, she read the poem, smiled, and gave me a hug. I loved seeing her smile; she didn't have to say anything. The love and appreciation radiated through her eyes, and it was evident that her heart was glad. When she hugged me, it wasn't just her arms embracing me; her love for God and her spirit embraced my heart and enveloped me in a feeling of warmth. It was like a blanket on a very cold day. I waited for her to start the lecture.

Mama, however, didn't lecture. She looked at me and said, "I'm not going to tell you what you should and should not do. You already know those things because we raised you. You were already told what to do and what not to do. Nothing has changed, so I'm telling you that you know what to do and what not to do. It is now up to you to make the right decisions, and I know that you will."

I was stunned and didn't know what to say at first. I felt myself getting a little nervous. Yes, I knew right from wrong. I was taught throughout my life, from the day I was able to understand English, but I wanted to hear it! Then I thought, *She trusts me to make the right decisions.* Although that was my plan—to do what's right—what if I forgot something? What if I needed to hear it again? I was not in a good place that day. I just told her, "I will remember what I was taught, and I will make the right decisions."

I then asked, "Can I can call you if I need to?"

She quickly said, "You can always call me. Everything is going to be all right. God is with you."

That was a little scary because I didn't have her faith, and I wondered if God would be with me.

Saying Goodbye

Finally, the day came for me to leave. Renee and Albert arrived and helped load the car for my one-way trip to the school. I said goodbye to Mama and my family and was on my way to school. I watched the neighborhood become distant as we drove away. I could still see Mama in the yard, waving as we turned the corner. I was so glad that she didn't look sad; she looked pleased, as if she was saying, *Well done.* I was not the first child in my family to go to college, but Mama took nothing for granted. She made my departure special, as if I was the first to leave. I waved to her until we were completely out of sight of our apartment.

Soon, my anxiety in leaving would fade. I faced forward and anxiously waited to arrive at the school. I had very little to say on my way there and kept checking the time, hoping that my arrival would be sooner rather than later. I was tired from the excitement and fell asleep.

We finally arrived—I was awakened from my sleep when I heard, "We're here." Renee was shaking me, telling me to wake up. Albert began unloading the car. I took my papers from my purse and headed toward the dorm entrance. I stopped at the office. A lady introduced herself as Mrs. Jones as I handed her my papers. She quickly reviewed them and told me,

"Your room is ready. Your roommate has not arrived, but since you're the first one here, you have first choice of the bed, desk and dresser.

She returned my papers to me and pointed us in the direction of my room.

"Someone will be up later to go over some things with you."

As we walked up the stairs, I thought, *This is an old building*. The outside reminded me of an old refurbished house, almost like a castle, but it still needed work. When we entered the building, the door squeaked and the floors creaked. There was a large gathering room on the first floor, referred to as the parlor, where students could watch TV and socialize. There were a few students in there, and they waved to me as I passed by. The students seemed friendly enough. I just had to get past the ancient look of this building. I wondered, *Why did they name the dorm Asphalt Hall?*

As we went upstairs to the second floor, the steps creaked even more. We kept walking until we found my room on the right of the hallway, as Mrs. Jones had directed. When I entered the room, I wanted to faint. There were two beds, two dressers, and one closet that my roommate and I would have to share. I decided to take the bed closest to the door and the dresser in the corner. I didn't want to stay.

Renee and Albert set my trunk on the floor. Albert immediately left and said he would wait in the car. Renee stayed with me for a few minutes as I started to unpack and put things away. She helped me take out a few things and then said, "We have to get back. We want to avoid as much traffic as possible." She hugged me and left.

I went to my window and watched them drive away. I wondered, *How could they leave me here?* I'd been here less than an hour and was already missing home. I knew I had to stay, but I didn't want to at that time. I continued to unpack and put away my things. I managed to get everything where I wanted it, and I was careful to take only half of the closet space. Some things I would have hung in the closet were folded and put in my dresser.

As I lay on the bed and cried to myself, I decided that I would stay in the room. I didn't feel like socializing or meeting anyone. I was having a private pity party that Mama would have shut down, had she been there. It wasn't acceptable to feel sorry for myself. Although I wasn't sure of all her reasoning, I thought about her saying to me that if Jesus could go through what he went through, who was I to have any disappointment? I put on my "big girl pants" and decided to go to freshen up in case so it wouldn't appear that I'd been crying.

As I was getting up to go to the bathroom, someone knocked on my door. It was one of the students Mrs. Jones had assigned to show me around the campus and go over the plans for the next few days. Her name was Bonnie. She was very cheerful, upbeat, and pleasant to talk to. Being around her made me feel better for a while. She showed me the laundry room, the dorm kitchen, and the bathroom, and she explained the rules for each area. I was glad to have someone to talk to but was horrified when I saw that bathroom. The showers were all in one big open space and reminded me of a jail. About eight shower heads were lined up on the wall, where everyone would shower at the same time. I did not like the idea of showering with other girls. I made up my mind that I would get in there early, before everyone showered, or late, after everyone had showered.

Bonnie explained that the parlor was also used for dating.

"Girls are allowed to entertain their dates in the parlor and with other students", she said.

"Okay", I said, "It's a large room."

That wasn't a concern for me; I didn't plan on dating, but if I dated, I wouldn't mind sitting in there with other dates. I had nothing to hide and didn't need privacy when dating.

Bonnie showed me the boys' dorm, located at the top of the hill. We didn't go inside, as girls couldn't go into the boys' dorm without permission, and the boys could not enter the girls' dorm. In both cases, they would have to meet in the parlor, where they were visible to everyone. We went to the Student Union, where there were game rooms and a TV; Bonnie said that many school functions and activities took place there. We walked up the road to the administration building, where we would register the following day. I was given a tour of the classroom building and the school library. We also went to the dining hall, where we would have dinner that evening and where all meals were served.

After walking with Bonnie and becoming familiar with the school, I felt much better. She was a sophomore and had nothing but positive things to say about the school. Despite the old, disgusting-looking showers, I was beginning to adjust and felt that I just might like the school. After the tour, we spent time in the Student Union and then left for the dining hall to eat.

The food was tasty and appeared to have been cooked and prepared there. The ladies serving on the line were pleasant and very welcoming. They explained what everything was and gave heaping portions—too much for me. I didn't have much of an appetite and asked for the minimum. As we sat at the table, we started to engage in conversations with other students—freshmen and sophomores. They were very helpful, and after I asked many questions and listened to others, I felt as if I belonged there.

I was still a little upset because I felt as if I'd been dumped off. I knew I had to be there, but I'd wanted more time with my family, as this felt so permanent. I managed to focus on my peers and make the best of getting to know them and acquiring information for the following day. Dinner was over, and it was time for me to head back to my dorm. I was tired and decided I would spend time alone in my room and go to bed early.

I said good night to my new acquaintances. As I entered the building and walked toward Mrs. Jones's office door, she stopped me. "Linda, I have a message for you," she said as she handed me a folded note. I opened it, and it was a message from Mama, telling me to call her before I went to bed. I was so happy she had called, but I'd never given her the number; I wondered how she got it. The one thing Bonnie forgot to show me was that there was only one pay phone in the dorm. Mrs. Jones pointed to the phone and told me to just dial the operator, and I would be connected to my house.

I called home collect. Mama answered the phone.

"Hey, baby, how are you doing? Did you unpack yet?" she said. I was delighted to hear her voice. I had decided that I wouldn't call her collect much because I didn't want to add charges to her phone bill. We had talked prior to my leaving, and she told me that it would be difficult to for me to call a lot for that reason, but she had called me.

I explained everything that had taken place. I told her about the tour and about the bathroom with the open showers. She told me not to worry about it—"Just take your shower, and go on about your business." I told her that I missed home already. Although I couldn't see her, I could tell she was smiling when she reminded me of how happy I'd been to leave home. She reminded me that other than God, family is all we have, and I could always come home on the weekends and school vacations. She assured me that time would fly by, and I would be graduating soon.

"How are you doing Mama?", I asked.

"I'm doing fine. I was just calling to see how you're doing and if you had settled in."

"I miss you, and I missed being at home, but I am going to be all right."

I didn't want her worrying about me. She was not to know that I'd been crying earlier. The phone call was short because we were careful not to add to her phone bill. I felt so much better that night after talking to her. Her calm and loving demeanor comforted me, and that night, the warmth I felt rocked me to sleep.

Adjusting

The next day, I decided to walk the campus, meet people, and register for my courses. I was able to see what type of programs were available. They had a gospel choir, so I thought I would join it, and I decided to join their Higher Education Achievement Program (HEAP) organization. I also had to sign up for a work study program that would help pay my tuition. After that, I had the first semester of my freshman year organized, and I was ready to go. I made it a practice to sign up for early-morning classes so that I could have the afternoons to study and do assignments. I was feeling good about the school in all aspects and looked forward to learning and graduating.

As time went by, I became well adjusted. I had been there for most of that semester without going home. I limited my phone calls and had called maybe once since the night I got there. I wrote to Mama and to some of my high school classmates. We stayed in touch and updated each other routinely on the schools we were attending and gave dates regarding when we would go home, hoping to catch each other during our home visits. I had gone home the least. Mama had called me and asked why I hadn't come home for the weekend. It was difficult for me to get home because we didn't have a car. On one occasion, a neighborhood friend who attended the school with me offered me a ride home. His brothers were picking him up, and there would be enough room for me. I kindly turned down the opportunity for a free ride home.

Mama called me shortly afterward and asked when I would be home. I used my same excuse—that I didn't have a ride. She then said that my neighbor told her that he had offered me a ride home, but I had said I wasn't coming home. He sold me out! He told Mama that I could have gone home with him and his brothers, but I said no. His mother and Mama were very close. Although they were neighbors, they were like cousins, so riding with them would not have been a problem, but I was enjoying being at school and wanted to get well adjusted to the school before going home.

Mama insisted that I come home the following weekend; I would get a ride with my neighbors. I was OK going home but highly frustrated with my neighbor for telling on me. I did not hold back in letting him know that I did not appreciate his doing so. He found it funny; he paid no attention to me and offered me a ride the following weekend, knowing that I was not going to decline.

I called Mama and told her that I was coming home. She was pleased, and so was I. I just needed a boost because I was getting too comfortable and overlooking the importance of home. I think she missed me and wanted to see me as much as I missed and wanted to see her. I was wrapped up in school and would have lost my grounding, had Mama not insisted that I make that trip home. I think she knew that, so I graciously went home.

- 8 -

Strong Roots

> Honour thy father and thy mother: that thy days may be long upon the land which the Lord thy God giveth thee.
> —Exodus 20:12 (KJV)

I GOT A RIDE HOME WITH KEVIN AND WAS THANKFUL THAT he and his brothers were so generous. They treated me like a sister, and, as usual, it was a pleasant ride home. As we turned the corner, I could see Mama standing at the edge of the yard with her arms open, waiting for me to get out of the car and walk into her warm and loving hug. I never understood how she was always in the yard, waiting, when she knew that I was coming home. When I asked her, she would say, "I just know." Mama always took the time to thank Kevin and his brothers for bringing me home, and she would tell them to thank their mother as well. The minute I stepped out of that car and into her arms, I was glad to be home.

As I went into the house, I started upstairs to my old room, but Mama told me to set my luggage down. She took me into the dining room, and I noticed that there were two coffee cups on the table—a regular-size cup for me and her "coffee hound," the larger cup for her. She loved coffee and drank it regularly. I could smell the coffee perking from the kitchen and hear the sound it made from the old percolating coffeepot. It smelled so good, but as I sat at the table, I wondered if I would really have coffee with her or if she was going to make me feel as if I was having coffee. As a young child, I always wanted to have coffee because she drank it. She would fill my cup with milk and add about a tablespoon of coffee, just enough to change the color of the milk. She would add a little sugar and allow me to drink that. I was satisfied that I was drinking coffee because it looked and tasted different from milk.

When I was a senior in high school, I had a teacher who wanted to give his students a relaxed way of writing. He got permission from the principal and parents to allow us to have coffee while we were learning to be creative writers. Mama permitted me to have a real cup of coffee at that time. It was instant coffee, but it was *coffee*, and it was a treat.

I asked no questions as she went into the kitchen and placed the cream and sugar on the table. I was preparing for milk with coffee. I had not drunk coffee without her permission, as much as I had wanted to. I waited for her to tell me when I was ready.

Mama went back into the kitchen and poured herself a cup first. She looked at me, paused for a moment, and began pouring me a cup of coffee—yes, a full cup of Maxwell House coffee, her favorite brand—and left room for me to add the cream. I marked this day as my official promotion from girl to grown. At least, that's how I saw it.

"Thank you", I said to her as she poured the coffee. To validate what I'd witnessed, I remarked, "You're letting me drink real coffee?"

"Yes, it's time to have coffee, if you want it", she said.

"You can add the cream and sugar to your liking."

I added the cream and two spoons of sugar, unlike the one spoon she always added. To this day, that was the best cup of coffee I've ever had. It was good, but it was not just the coffee; it was the conversation and the time we spent together while enjoying that coffee. Our conversation continued as we worked on a five-hundred-piece puzzle. Once we completed it, we glued it together and framed it, as we had done for several years. It was like old times, and I was overjoyed to relive those moments.

On this particular day, Mama decided to talk to me about Daddy. I never had a conversation with her about him until that day. Although she didn't say it, I think she was checking to see how I was feeling about Daddy. I had not mentioned him to her since the time of his passing. She talked about how he took care of the family and how he didn't want her to work. There was a time when she couldn't work due to medical reasons, but when she was able to work, it was decided that she would stay home and take care of us. She spoke of him with admiration. When I told her how I saw him, she seemed pleased.

She was never lonely when he went off to work because she had us at home with her. She had always seemed to enjoy her role as mother and wife. It was good to be back home, and I couldn't wait to enjoy her home-cooked meals. Her banana pudding was my favorite dessert, and because I loved it so much, she taught me how to make it. I never made it when I lived at home because being "domestic" was not my goal. It was fun to help her when she made it. We continued to talk about Daddy as we sipped on coffee, and I filled her in on some of the things I was doing at school.

Once I finished my coffee, I went upstairs to my old room to unpack the few items I'd brought with me. Mama came up with me; I thought that was a little strange, as she never followed me upstairs unless she was already going up. When I entered my old room, I noticed a little black poodle dog on my bed made from yarn. It was so cute, and as I walked over to the bed, Mama asked if I liked it. Of course, I liked it.

"A friend of mine makes them, so I had one made for you," she said.

"Thank you. I would like to take it back to my dorm."

"That's OK."

What a pleasant surprise! Mama normally did things to make me feel special, but this was so different. She had this made for me and wanted to see my reaction when I saw it. As I stood there hugging the dog, she went to her room and returned, asking me to hold out my hand. I put the poodle down and reached out my open hand, ready to receive whatever she had in her hand. She dropped a pair of earrings that she had purchased for me. They weren't gold, but they were more valuable to me than anything because she bought them for me. There was a shopping center near our house, and Mama walked there occasionally. I knew that she had to have walked there to get these earrings. She did all of this for me. Again, I thought, *It's great to be home.*

Mama made several phone calls to relatives, announcing that I was home for the weekend. We had dinner that evening and had discussions regarding my grades and how I liked being at school. I had an A average at that time, and if things continued as they had been, I would make the Dean's List. Mama assured me that I would. She was very excited about me joining the gospel choir.

"We have a church on campus," I told her, "and the choir occasionally travels to local churches in the community to sing."

She seemed pleased with that.

I was able to see some of my siblings that first day, and the evening was sealed with Mama's banana pudding. It would be difficult for me to return to school; I had forgotten about the comfort I had at home because of Mama.

As I continued to settle in that evening, Mama came to my room and nonchalantly told me that I would be singing at a church on Sunday. I was surprised, to say the least! When I asked which church and how, she said,

"Last Sunday, when I was in church, they announced that they would welcome people to sing for their church anniversary. I told them that you would sing if you were here for the weekend. When you told me you would be here, I called them, and they added you to the list."

As politely as I knew how, I said, "But Mama, I don't want to sing on Sunday."

"I have not *asked* if you wanted to sing. It's not about you; it's about the Lord. Therefore, you will sing on Sunday." As firm as she was, she was very calm, and she actually said it lovingly.

I just wasn't feeling the love in that moment because I truly did not want to go. I just said, "OK, Mama, I'll sing." I knew I was going to sing because she *said* I was going to sing, but saying OK gave me a false sense of choice, and that was good enough for me. She did allow me to choose the song I wanted to sing, with her approval. This was the beginning of my singing at churches of Mama's choice when I visited home on weekends and holidays. We continued to talk about my experience on campus.

Mama was concerned about my eating. I had lost some weight, and she was concerned that I was getting too small. I assured her that I was eating well, but I was more active than I had been when living at home. I promised her that I would try to eat more and stop losing weight. I caught her up on my social life. At that time, I was not interested in dating, but Mama gave her approval for me to date, if I chose to do so. She also gave me tips about dating; she would say no sex before marriage, and the best way to avoid that was to limit physical contact. She talked to me about kissing and said it could lead to other things. Then she talked about respect and how I should be treated. She would always say, "If you can't be the table, don't be the tablecloth. There's only one table, but the tablecloth can be changed over and over again." She was simply saying not to date anyone who was not serious about the relationship and who needed to have more than one girlfriend. It was good to get her advice and to hear her teaching. She had said this before, but somehow, it felt different at that time; it was advice I needed to hear again. I had developed an interest in dating and took heed to her advice. It seemed like preaching before, but now, it was encouraging and necessary.

I came home as much as I possibly could during the remainder of that year, although it wasn't as often as Mama would have liked. I looked forward to weekend and vacation visits home. The people and things I grew up with were at home, and I needed to stay rooted to where I'd come from. Mama would call to check on me from time to time. I tried not to call her too often because I didn't want to add to her phone bill. She had once asked me to slow down on the calls, but when I did, she called to tell me that I wasn't calling enough. We came to an understanding that she would call me and have better control of managing the phone calls.

As a freshman, I had become well adjusted to living away from home. While I had gained much independence, I craved being back in Burlington with my family; it was my safe haven. I had done well with my grades; I made the Dean's List both semesters, and that achievement was announced in my local newspaper. Mama always made a big deal of seeing my name in the paper, and she made sure all of her friends and some relatives were aware of it. She was proud and celebrated each announcement when I visited home.

Toward the end of my freshman year of college, I was offered an opportunity to become an exchange student. In doing so, I would attend another college out of state and return to North Carolina to graduate with my associate of science degree in pre-nursing. If I agreed to become an exchange student, I would go to work immediately after completing the AS degree. I informed Mama of this opportunity, and she encouraged me to take the opportunity to see if I liked it. I told her that I was not going because I didn't want to leave home. I really didn't want to be too far from her. The opportunity was in Maryland, and that was too far for me. I wasn't comfortable being an hour away. Although Mama gave me her advice, she let me decide if I was going, and I decided to stay in North Carolina, receive my associate of science degree, and enroll in a four-year school for my last two years and obtain a bachelor of science degree in nursing. She was OK with that plan and supported me wholeheartedly.

Linda Aurelia B. Blackmon

Becoming a Sophomore

When I reached my sophomore year, I was looking forward to attending a four-year school and looked at schools where I might attend. As I got closer to reaching the deadline for applying to schools, I was engaged in extracurricular projects. I was a member of the Student Government Association (SGA), an education enrichment program. I taught dance to youth in an after-school program, and I was enjoying my work study program. Working as a tutor was one of my work study responsibilities, and in doing so, I was able to have discussions with students about their course work. They often shared their concerns. I had several students each week, and it took a while before I realized that I was overwhelmed and overloaded with the extracurricular work I was doing. It was starting to take a toll on my weight.

Mama had commented about my weight during one of my weekend visits. I assured her that I was doing OK because I felt that I was. But now, I was very tired, and it finally registered in my mind that I needed to cut back on something without compromising my grades. Looking back, this is something I should have prayed about, but my prayer life was through my mama. I didn't want to quit anything I was doing, but I knew I had to talk to Mama about it first.

I learned at an early age that there was nothing that I couldn't tell my parents, and now this would hold true for Mama. She had reminded me numerous times after Daddy's passing that if there was ever a problem or if I did something, it was best that I tell her before anyone else did. Although I'd done nothing wrong, I thought I would tell her and ask for advice in this regard. Once I told her how overwhelmed I was and that I was struggling, she instructed me to speak with an adviser at the school. She said that they had my schedule and other activities in which I was involved, and they would advise me accordingly.

I followed through with her instructions and spoke with an

adviser. After reviewing my courses and extracurricular activities, she suggested that I drop the social club I'd joined. I couldn't drop work study because it was paying for my tuition. She also suggested that I speak with the instructor overseeing my tutoring assignments to see if she could lighten my load a bit. After talking to that instructor, she removed one of my tutorial sessions. I'd been overwhelmed, fearful of making the wrong decision, and needed some guidance, but I hadn't known how to approach it. I knew Mama would have a solution, and she did.

Mama was proud that I'd followed through and didn't allow fear to cause me to do anything that I might regret. I was thankful that my mama was available for me to talk to and to receive such guidance. She was looking out for my best interest, and this situation made it evident that I needed to come home more. She needed to see how I was doing, and I needed to be near her. I remembered the feeling I had when Daddy went outside to scare away what I thought might be a burglar. Again, I was being protected, and I was thankful that home was waiting for me on those weekends and whenever I needed a respite from school. Mama reminded me again that God was always with me and that I was not to forget who I was—a child of God—and to remember what I was taught.

This situation did not compromise my studies, and school continued as usual. I maintained my GPA, but I had gained interest in boys and dated while I was there, causing my outlook on life to sway a bit. I was having second thoughts about getting married someday, but the idea of children had not changed. I was quite comfortable with the decision to not have any. If I had children, I would want to be the mother to them that Mama was to me. I wasn't sure that could happen, but I was certain that I would not have as many.

My sophomore year would be the year I would meet my future husband. I had dated during my freshman and sophomore years. I thought a couple of relationships were serious, but I later realized that neither one was serious.

Talking to boys and having an interest in them caused me to think about my parents and all they had taught me. As I got older, I wanted more to have Daddy with me. I thought about the foundation he and Mama laid for me—honesty and putting God first and then family. It's not something they preached every day, but they talked about it when the situation warranted it, and they practiced it every day. Daddy practiced it until he died, and Mama was still carrying the torch, ensuring that I did not sway or slip away from the stronghold they had in place for my growth. I knew that the person I chose to marry had to be kind and responsible, and because I was taught for as long as I could remember, education was necessary. Daddy told me early in my life that a man has to be responsible, work hard, put God first, and take care of his family.

Daddy showed me how it was supposed to work. He was the breadwinner of our family; Mama took care of the home and the kids. She didn't work outside the home, but she made things a little easier for Daddy. She was a very skilled seamstress and made most of our clothes. She showed me, through her caring and loving nature, that a wife is a helpmate for the husband. I knew from watching her that it was important for a wife to be there for the husband so that he could take care of the family. She also showed me that throughout a woman's life, as a widow, a mother, and a single parent, she was introduced to strength she never knew she had. She showed me this when Daddy died.

I witnessed lessons she had not planned to teach, but she taught them well because of who she was and because she was placed in situations that she could not change. I was at a stage of my life when I was able to put the pieces of life together and build on the foundation that my loving parents, by the grace of God, had laid for me.

The thought of dating frightened me. I didn't want to lose

focus on my courses and risk a low GPA. From the brief dates I had, I learned that I was easily distracted when dating. Now I knew why it was important for me not to date in high school. I was allowed to but didn't have the time and wasn't trying to make time.

I was nervous and worried that I had begun to like boys. I called Mama and told her that I was interested in dating.

- 9 -

A Turning Point: Scattered Emotions

> This I say then, Walk in the spirit, and ye
> shall not fulfil the lust of the flesh.
> —Galatians 5:16 (KJV)

IT WAS THE END OF FEBRUARY 1975. I HAD GONE HOME FOR the weekend. I was feeling a little down and decided to go out with my sister Edna and my best friend, Daisy. Mama was OK with me going out because I was with my big sister. Daisy's mother gave her approval as well. We drove to Greensboro and attempted to go to the Cosmo Club. When we arrived, the club had reached their capacity, and they weren't allowing anyone to enter. Rather than go home, we decided to go to Cosmo II. It was a step down from the other one, as it was smaller and didn't have the most popular groups, but we were able to get in before they reached their capacity. It was a great evening. All we did was dance, dance, dance! I literally danced my blues away.

I had decided to take a break from dancing when this tall guy approached me. He was wearing loud burnt-orange bell-bottom pants, a colorful flowered shirt, brown platform shoes, and an Afro. My first thought when I saw him was, *Oh my goodness! He's not my type, but then again, it's only a dance.* As we danced, we talked and shared information about our interests, family, and career goals. He was from Connecticut and was in the army, stationed at Fort Bragg, North Carolina. He had attended school for a while but decided to join the army and pursued that career track. He worked for the dental company there and was a dental hygienist. He too was from a family of eight children, but he was the oldest. His name was James.

I couldn't believe that everything I didn't want in a boyfriend and had tried to avoid in the past actually had my undivided attention! I didn't like bell bottoms, platform shoes, loud colors, or Afros. But there I was, dancing, talking, and getting to know him. Despite of his attire, there was a connection, and I saw real potential for a relationship. He and his friend, an army buddy, were in Greensboro that night to see a concert. The Ohio Players were performing at the coliseum, but when James and his friend attempted to purchase tickets, they were sold out. Like us, they were looking for somewhere to go since they were already in Greensboro. They ended up at the Cosmos II, as we did. We both found that interesting, and I thought, *It must be fate!*

I listened to his stories about his family and found them interesting. I learned that night that he loved fishing. He had learned to fish as a young boy with his father, and now he boasted about being a great fisherman. Then he told me about his father's boat. I thought he was in for a rude awakening—I didn't fish, didn't clean them, and would have to learn to cook them if we made this a lifelong relationship. I decided that it wasn't relevant to tell him that at that point; we had just met and didn't know each other. Plus, I wasn't seeking a lifelong relationship. I was just in the dating stage, and that was enough.

I mentioned the school I was attending; I felt confident that he would never find it, so I had no reason to expect him to visit me there. He was very charismatic and energetic and seemed to care about what I thought and how I felt. He was complimentary and extremely talkative. We established a very comfortable rapport; talking to him was easy. It was almost as if I had known him prior to that night.

James and I danced until it was time to go home. It wasn't

until later that I learned that he had approached me earlier that evening for a dance, and I had told him no. He asked why I had turned him down a few times to dance before I finally said yes? I loved dancing, and I'm certain that it was because I needed a break. Whenever I felt tired from dancing, I would say no to anyone asking to dance so that I could rest. I never danced with anyone more than once when I went out because I didn't want to lead him on or give anyone the impression I was there with a date. But with James, it was different. That night as we were leaving, I gave him my phone number, and I gave him my real name. Since I had started dating, my friends and I had an understanding that we would never give our real names or phone numbers to anyone. We were out dancing and only dancing, not looking for relationships. We didn't expect or want to hear from the men again, so we made sure of that by giving fake names and made-up phone numbers.

This time, I broke the code. I didn't take his phone number, however, because I felt it was inappropriate to call boys. He would have to make the initial phone call and several more afterward before I would call him.

He walked me to the car, and Edna drove Daisy and me home.

It was late when we got home. Daisy was dropped off first and then me. When I went inside, the house was quiet; it appeared that Mama was asleep. I felt accomplished, thinking that I had entered the house without Mama knowing it and had possibly avoided a lecture regarding coming home too late. It was around one in the morning, and I had never stayed out that late while living at home or while I was in school. The school had a curfew of eleven o'clock every night, at which time the dorms would be locked. I was usually in before nine and socialized with my dorm mates once I returned.

Mama didn't expect that I would be out that late, but she wasn't worried because she knew that I was with Edna. I quietly and quickly prepared myself for bed. I couldn't wait to rest my tired feet. They were actually sore from all the dancing I'd done that evening. I soaked them for a while before turning in. When I went to bed, I reminisced about the evening. I thought that James most likely would not call me. Before I knew it, I was asleep.

It's Time to Dance before the Lord!

The next morning, I woke up to the aroma of bacon in the air—not just any bacon but the Canadian bacon Mama often cooked. It was early; I looked at the clock and couldn't believe what time it was. It was 5:30 in the morning! I laid there, wondering why Mama was cooking so early. She was always up early, but that day, it seemed earlier than usual. I thought that maybe she was helping someone cook for church, or maybe she was cooking a big breakfast and wanted a head start. I snuggled up to my bed covers and decided I'd eat later. My plan was to try to disregard the aroma of that bacon and finish my sleep. I thought that I needed more sleep after such an active night.

As soon as I fell asleep, I heard Mama calling me. It was close to six o'clock. Usually when I came home from school, she allowed me to sleep until at least eight o'clock. Before I could answer her, I heard her footsteps coming upstairs. The pounding of each step place strong emphasis on the seriousness of her coming to my room. I knew I was getting a lecture. Then I heard my name: "Aurelia, Aurelia!"

So much for an extended sleep. I turned over and started to get up as I answered her, hoping to be on my feet before she came into my room.

By the time I sat up, however, she was in the room. "Didn't you hear me calling you?"

I said "yes", as I rubbed and batted my eyes, hoping that would help me to wake up. "I'm coming."

She looked at me, shook her head, and directed me to come downstairs.

I went downstairs wearing my pajamas, careful not to waste any more time. I would get dressed afterward and take a nap.

When I went into the dining room, the table was set, and breakfast was ready. She had made biscuits, Canadian bacon, and eggs. She was brewing the coffee and told me to sit down.

I didn't want to eat that early because I was tired.

"Can I eat later?" I asked Mama

"No", she answered. As she poured the coffee, she asked, "Did you bring home clothes for church?"

I had not planned to go to church, and I was so tired from all of the dancing the night before that all I wanted to do was sleep. I mustered up the nerve to say

"Mama, I'm too tired to go to church. I didn't want to eat now. I planned to eat later."

That was a mistake; I'd set myself up for a lecture I didn't want and felt that I didn't deserve. It was too late because the lecture was coming, and I had myself to thank for it.

Mama looked at me and asked, "How was last night?"

"It was fine. We had a nice time." I tried to make it sound good by saying,

"We came straight home after driving Daisy home."

"I wasn't born yesterday," she told me. "You can't fool me."

She decided to tell me how things went.

"Don't think I didn't hear you come in this house at one o'clock in the morning. I was OK with it because you were with your sister. The problem is that I heard you trying to sneak in here. You know better than that! And I saw how you were walking into this dining room. What's wrong with your feet?"

"I did a lot of fast dancing and my feet are sore because of it", I said. Although the dancing was appropriate, Mama would not have approved of slow dancing because that required some physical contact. I decided not to complicate my situation any more than it was, so I did not tell her that I slow danced as well.

It didn't matter; my fate was sealed. While I was out dancing,

Mama had planned the following day, and there was nothing that I could do about it. She continued her lecture.

"You will not eat later; you will eat now. I made breakfast now, and you will eat now if you're planning to eat breakfast. It's your choice."

She was not yelling, but her speech was firm and assertive.

"We are scheduled to be at church around nine o'clock so that you can attend Sunday school and prepare to sing."

I couldn't believe it.

"I didn't know that I had to sing," I responded. "I don't want to go to church."

"You are going," she said. "You should have thought about that when you were dancing all night. You danced for the devil; now you can dance for the Lord today."

So, it was settled. I had to eat breakfast and prepare to go to church. I had brought an outfit home that I could wear to church, as I knew that there was always a chance that I would attend. Mama usually told me by Saturday if I was singing. This time, it was different; she told me the morning of. I hoped that I wouldn't fall asleep in church, as I didn't need another problem that I couldn't explain.

I finished breakfast and got dressed, and Mama and I were off to church. Although I didn't want to go, it was worth spending time with her. Once I attended church, sang, and appeared to be focused while in church, she was OK. I knew that she knew I was struggling because I was overly tired. As always, Mama made me feel good about the situation. She was clear that I was wrong to dance all night (or, as she said, dancing for the devil) and wanting to sleep in rather than serve the Lord. When church was over, she told me that I did a good job and to remember that no matter what I did, God comes first.

After we got home, I told Mama about meeting James. I told her where he was from and that I had danced with him for the majority of the night. I thought that maybe she would feel better knowing that I wasn't dancing with too many boys. She told me that I could invite him to the house so that she could meet him. By then, it was time for me to organize my things so that I could return to school that evening. Mama suggested that I take a nap so that I would be rested and ready to go when Kevin and his brothers picked me up, so I did.

It was a good visit. I was beginning to miss her humming hymns prior to my leaving. She wasn't OK with me coming in as late as I did, but it was more of an issue of me sneaking in, thinking that she wouldn't know. After talking to her, I knew that was deceitful. I made up my mind that I wouldn't do that again.

In the meantime, I figured that when I was planning to hang out, I would spend the night at Edna's. She had her own place, and it would be easier and less disturbing for Mama. Mama was OK with my spending the night with Edna, and I only stayed with Edna on one occasion after that night. I went to church every time Mama told me, and I graciously sang when needed.

After I returned to school, James and I stayed in touch by writing letters, and he called the dorm when he could. A week later, James surprised me with a visit. I was in my dormitory room when a classmate knocked on my door to tell me that someone was there to visit me. She didn't know who he was, even though she knew all the students on campus. It was late in the evening, past dinner. I went down to see who it was, thinking that it might be a relative making a surprise visit. I was really surprised to see James there with his army roommate. We spent time together that night; it was the first of several visits from James.

James and I saw more of each other, and it was time to introduce him to my family. He picked me up from school and drove me home. He quickly became familiar with everyone. He won my mother's heart the moment she met him. He offered to assist her with her flower garden. Mama took pride in her garden and often weeded her plants to keep them growing. The day James came to visit, he noticed some weeds growing in her flower bed, and he offered to weed her flowers. Mama was OK with that and was very pleased with his results.

Mama made her homemade scratch applesauce cake for that Saturday. She had always made it for us, so it wasn't anything new. She gave James a slice, and he loved it and raved nonstop about how good it was. He spent most of his time in the kitchen with Mama, assisting her with what she was doing, and he made Kool-Aid for her. Mama liked him and thought he was a "good boy." My sisters, on the other hand, were not as pleased. James had mischievous ways of getting to know them. He teased and aggravated them, often causing them to chase him because of something he playfully snatched out of their hands. He played innocent when Mama got involved.

James's and my relationship was growing into something I had not expected. I wasn't sure that it was something I wanted to happen at that time. We were seeing a lot of each other, and we were intimate when we saw each other. This relationship had grown against everything I was taught. At one point, it was frightening because I was supposed to wait until marriage before engaging sexually. I was worried about what Mama would think of me if she knew I was in such a relationship. I knew it was wrong, as I had heard it in church and at home.

Mama has lectured on numerous occasions about fornication and that it was a sin. I also thought about the time when Mama learned that someone we knew was pregnant—she was younger than I was. She told me at that time that she wasn't worried about me because she didn't think that I would do such a thing. I was already doing what she didn't think that I would do. I was lying to her! I wanted to tell her, but I didn't know how or if I should. I went on as if nothing was happening.

After several months, I was overwhelmed with our relationship. I thought we were moving too fast, and it was wearing me down emotionally. I didn't want to disappoint Mama, and I wasn't sure if it was what I wanted. Still, I wasn't being pushed; my actions were my own. I couldn't figure out how I'd become so involved after I had been so grounded and strong in my decision. I needed to think about this a little longer. I needed space and time to sort out my own behavior so that I could make a clear and conscious decision. In order to do this, I had to inform James that we needed to take time apart. We did just that in May of that year.

It was difficult to stay focused. I felt guilty because, deep down, I knew that I had strayed from my teaching. I didn't like the person I saw each time I looked in the mirror. I wasn't pleased with who I had become; I needed to make a change. Mama and Daddy had always said, "Know who you are." Well, I was not sure who I was, and that, in itself, caused turmoil in my mind. I had to redevelop my confidence. I had to remember. The separation was difficult because it left a void in my life. I had been in a relationship prior to meeting James, but that breakup was nothing like this. The relationship was not comparable to James's and mine. The attention and consideration were different. James and I exchanged letters; we had "our song" and places we enjoyed going together.

This was my last year at this school, and I had to concentrate on my studies and prepare for another transition—going to a four-year college and continuing my education in preparation for my future career. I had so much going on, and I struggled emotionally to follow through with everything. I managed to regain my focus and take the necessary steps to prepare for the next school year. I sent out applications so that I could transfer. Prior to graduating, I was accepted to a university. That marked the beginning of another new beginning. I was excited.

Receiving My Associate Degree

Attending this junior college was a great experience. I did so much in two years, and my learning there was social, emotional, and academic; I also learned leadership skills and learned more about myself. I made the Dean's List all four semesters. I chose not to become an exchange student, mainly because I didn't want to be separated from Mama by going to another state.

I became a member of *Who's Who among Students in American Junior Colleges*. I assisted with organizing a protest that would grant better living conditions for the students. I was an advocate for girls who might have been victimized. I had a community outreach program in which I taught dance to underprivileged children. I learned to be apart from my family while learning more about myself.

Now it was time for me to move on to another chapter of my life.

I was so excited about graduating again and having Mama attend. I wanted her to see where I was attending school. She had been so supportive of me while I was there. I was on a work study program and didn't need much while I was at school, but Mama would send me spending money occasionally. I told her not to send it because I didn't need it, but she reminded me that she was my mother, and that was her responsibility. She continued to send spending money and encouraged me to buy food so that I would stop losing weight. She checked on me to make sure that I was OK, and she made sure that I came home from time to time.

I appreciated how she kept me connected to my upbringing. I would have surely disconnected at some point if she had left things up to me. She kept me from getting lost in myself while I was away. She wanted me to keep family in the forefront, and she always reminded me to put God first. The foundation that she and Daddy built was solid; they had planted strong roots.

Graduation day was approaching, and I had my cap and gown. Students talked about the schools they would attend. I would see some of the same students at the school I would attend that coming fall. All the exams were completed, and I was proud to have made the Dean's List again. Mama was looking forward to coming to my graduation, and she drove up with Edna the morning of the graduation.

All of my things were packed. I would be heading home with them to enjoy another summer before the first semester of my junior year. When they arrived, I was elated! What a moment it was when Mrs. Jones walked them to my room. I had moved into a new dorm my sophomore year. The old dorm had been closed, so I wasn't able to show Mama the old bathroom I'd told her about during my freshman year.

Before graduation, I walked Edna and Mama around the campus and tried to show them all the places there and their purposes. The last place I showed them was the gym, where I reported for the graduation ceremony. I wanted to be sure that Mama met some of my instructors, and I was able to do that. Many remarked on how young Mama looked and how easy it was to mistake her for my sister. I was proud of my mama and so thankful that she was there for me. I was glad that Edna had driven her up and made sure that she had enough time to visit the areas on campus. It was obvious that Mama was glad to be there.

Now it was the time during the ceremony for my row to be called up for our degrees. As I stood there waiting to hear my name, I glanced over to where Mama and Edna were seated. They were both smiling and seemed as excited as I was to receive my degree. My name was finally called, and Mama and Edna clapped and clapped again when the degree was placed in my hand. It was a bittersweet moment. I was happy and relieved to have graduated, yet I was saddened that I would not see many of those classmates again. We were more than a college; we were a family away from our families.

Mama and Edna met more of my instructors and some of my classmates. After taking a few pictures with classmates, I went back to my dorm with Edna and Mama. We loaded the car with all of my belongings, and then we were on our way home.

No Turning Back

I was back home in my community, but I was not the same person. Although I had changed and had made mistakes, I was beginning to like who I was. This was home, the place where I first learned anything, where love and healing were first introduced and then again with the first teacher I'd ever known. I was back with Mama. I was able to hear those hymns and songs I had missed so much while I was away. Although the words were the same, it felt different. Mama sang, "I'm gonna lay down my burden, down by the riverside; won't study war no more." Yes, I had been there and had not known how to lay down my burden before leaving home, but I had learned to let some things go, to fix what I could fix, and to move on.

I thought about the relationship that I had put on hold because it was too difficult for me to deal with at the time. Now, for the first time since I decided to take some space, I felt OK about it. I know now that it was because I was home, and Mama was there to ease my pain. I couldn't undo what was done, but I could learn from my experience and move on. I was ready to dive into what was next for me and hopefully would make better choices. I was ready to push through any future obstacles or challenges. At least, that is what I thought at the time.

- 10 -

Decisions, Decisions, Decisions

> Forbearing one another, and forgiving one
> another, if any man have a quarrel against any:
> even as Christ forgave you, so also do ye.
> —Colossians 3:13 (KJV)

SUMMER WENT BY RATHER QUICKLY. I WORKED PART-TIME to earn some spending money and to buy things I needed for enrolling in another new school. Mama was always ready to give me what I needed, and I loved her for it, but I wanted to do for myself and ease her load a bit, although she never complained and always did everything with a smile. I had chosen a college that was closer to home, yet far enough to need transportation. The advantage of going to this school was that I could take a Greyhound or Trailways bus to school. I didn't have to rely on anyone to take me to school or pick me up. I could take the city bus to the bus station when I traveled to and from school. I was looking forward to my junior year of college because it would denote that I was getting closer to having my bachelor's degree in nursing. I was excited about this because I was still thinking about becoming a nurse at the time.

Leaving home was routine for me by the time I graduated from junior college. There was little anxiety, and it was mostly geared toward the anticipation of the type of roommate I would have. Who would she be? Where did she live? Would I get along with her? Would she like me? Would she be nice? In any case, I was going to school, and if any of those questions were answered in my favor, I would be satisfied. I didn't think they would all be answered. I thought about one of the roommates I'd had in junior college. That was a nightmare! She wasn't pleasant, was very inconsiderate, and wanted things her way and her way alone. After I complained to Mrs. Jones, I was able to move out, and another girl was assigned to my room. This was perfect! We shared the same interests, and there was mutual respect. We got along well, and I was thankful for Mrs. Jones's intervention.

I decided to remain positive. I convinced myself that I would have a great roommate and things would be fine.

Now I was preparing to leave. As usual, I had a checklist, and Mama helped to ensure that all items were packed. I was on my way to school and was looking forward to new experiences. This time, Edna drove me to school, and the goodbyes were less dramatic for me.

I went to my dorm. Since I was the first one to show up, I chose the bed I wanted. I was surprised to see three beds in that room. There were six girls in my family; by the time I was in my junior year of college, two sisters were still living at home, so I wasn't bothered that there would be three of us in that room. I only hoped that things would work out.

As I began to unpack, one of my roommates showed up, and after introducing ourselves, we assisted each other with putting away our things. After we finished organizing the room, Stella and I decided to walk around campus to see what was available. Stella had been at the school since her freshman year, so she showed me around. I had not visited this campus beforehand and was only familiar with it from the brochures I received during the summer.

It was a much bigger campus, with several dorms and other buildings for students to congregate and participate in activities. There were also several outdoor areas available for students to gather. Stella showed me where we would register for classes; we were excited about being there. After walking around, taking in all the sights, we decided to go back to the dorm, where, by this time, more students were checking in. There was luggage in the hallways and on the lawn. We rushed up to our room to relax and become better acquainted with each other. We shared information regarding where we were from, our families, and how many siblings we had. As we were chatting, the door to our room opened, and another girl entered, carrying her luggage. She was the third person to occupy the room. We greeted her and although we were okay with a third roommate, we were liking the idea of just the two of us. Now there were three of us, and it was in our best interest to get along. Olivia seemed nice but made little effort to chat or socialize with us.

Things moved smoothly on campus. It was great sharing the room with Stella. Olivia moved out of the room a few days after school started and moved into an apartment off campus. She wanted her privacy and did not want to live in the dorm. After receiving this news, Stella asked if her cousin Colleen could move in with us. Colleen was a junior, and she was granted permission to move in. This was a great arrangement—we were able to choose our third roommate.

I met Colleen during the first week of school, and she, Stella, and I spent most of our time together. We enjoyed each other's company. Colleen was a Christian, and it was really great having her in the room. She had a peaceful spirit. She made us laugh and was always reminding us of the positive side to any situation. She knew God and reminded us often of doing what was right.

About halfway through the first semester, after I'd settled in and was attending classes, I lost interest in going to that school, as well as losing interest in majoring in nursing. I changed my major to health administration and would begin taking courses for that major the following semester. When I went home for a visit, I told Mama that I didn't want to stay at that school. I really liked my roommates and would miss them, but the school didn't interest me. I wanted to transfer to another school.

"Complete this year", she said, "don't leave in the middle of a semester. After you've completed the first year, then decide if you still want to transfer. Things could change by then."

"Okay," I said, "I'll wait until the end of the year."

As much as I wanted to leave at that time, I honored Mama's recommendation and decided that I would stay for the year. I didn't like the courses I was taking and felt that I wasn't getting the information I had signed up for. I decided to make the best of it, however, and to wait it out. Still, I wasn't academically invested. In one course, the instructor taught everything but what was mentioned in the course description. I was not gaining the knowledge required to meet the objectives of that course.

That first semester of my junior year was not going as I had anticipated, and I was looking forward to seeing it end. I didn't get involved in any extracurricular activities. I was approached to pledge a sorority at one point but declined because I did not have any interest in sororities. It just wasn't something I wanted or needed to do. I did like watching some of the "step" shows presented by the sororities and fraternities and would selectively attend them. These were entertaining events. Each fraternity and sorority would do a routine with dance steps, and words pertaining to their organization. Although I wasn't interested in being a part of these organizations, I enjoyed the entertainment.

It was shortly after the beginning of school that I decided that I would get in touch with James. I'd told him prior to my graduation that I needed some space, so I figured that I would see where he was in his life. I hoped to get back together and pick up where we'd left off. I decided that I would write to him. In the first letter, I checked in to see how he was doing. I updated him on some of the things that I was doing. I sent it off and awaited a response. After a couple of days, when I hadn't heard from him, I wondered if he had left Fort Bragg and maybe had returned to

Connecticut. I figured, though, that my letter would have been returned in that case, and did not get the letter returned. I decided to write him again and then again. At one point, I thought that something might have happened to him. After several failed attempts to contact him, I decided not to send another letter. I would move on and hopefully transfer to another school.

After I sent the last letter, I decided to call Mama and tell her about my efforts to communicate with James. I told her about the letters and that he had not responded. I don't know what I was expecting her to say, but I hoped she would be supportive. I still had not gotten over the conversation I'd had with her about those girls giving me a hard time. I thought she might introduce me to another Bible verse and give me a lesson on living for God and letting it go. Maybe she would tell me that I shouldn't have written to James. That's certainly what I was thinking. I was surprised by her response.

Mama was very gentle with me. She didn't tell me that I was wrong, but she did agree with me when I told her that I would not send another letter. She very calmly said,

"Baby, don't worry about it. He isn't going anywhere, and he will be back. He's just testing you. Just wait and see; you're going to hear from him again."

At that point, I was ready to move on. If I heard from James again, so be it. If I didn't hear from him, I would be OK. I told Mama that I would just wait, and I would let her know. She seemed confident and assured me that I had nothing to worry about. After all, I'd broken it off, and, according to Mama, he needed time to decide if he wanted to see me again. She added that, as of now, it was his decision. I took that feedback and her advice and decided to move on with things I had to do at school.

About two weeks after I spoke to Mama, I received a letter from James. He was basically checking in to see how I was doing, and he updated me on information about himself. He planned to come to campus and visit me. Shortly after that, he arrived on campus, and we began to spend time together. He visited as often as he could, and we went to the movies, walked around campus, and shopped together at the local mall. We really enjoyed each other's company and stayed in touch via phone calls and letters. It wasn't always easy because he was stationed at Fort Bragg and couldn't always leave when he felt like it, but we made use of the time we had.

I informed Mama and kept her posted on his visits; I was delighted that she had been correct. She only said to me, "I told you he would call you. He was just testing you." She pointed out that when I stopped contacting him, he decided to contact me.

I was relieved that we were back together. Things seemed to be working out for us. By this time, I had gotten used to the campus but was still looking forward to transferring to another school at the end of my second semester. I had several months left before I could think about transferring but was counting the days.

I made it home more often while at this school I didn't have to rely on getting a ride home. Living closer to home made it easier for Edna to pick me up. I looked forward to going home to see Mama and to see what surprise she had waiting for me on my bed. I planned my visits home around James's visits to me. On his last visit prior to my going home, we decided that we wouldn't spend as much time apart as we had during the breakup. I knew at that moment that things were getting serious, and my original plans were no longer plans. I had news to tell Mama.

Getting Married?

James's and my relationship grew into something beyond my expectations. He told me that he wanted to get married. I agreed, but I needed to tell Mama. He and I visualized what our wedding would look like, and I was getting excited. We talked about who would be the groomsmen, bridesmaids, maid of honor, and the best man. We had everything planned in our heads, but I wanted to talk to Mama before moving forward with plans. James and I decided that after we were married, we would settle in Burlington. I didn't want to be too far from Mama. I wanted to be near her and have her remain in my life. James had no complaints because the two of them hit it off really well when he first met her. He had been very helpful, and Mama appreciated that and continued to think of him as a "nice boy."

Mama was excited to hear the news and gave me her approval. She suggested which church to contact to do the wedding and assured me that the pastor of that particular church would conduct a nice ceremony. Since Daddy wasn't there, we decided that I would ask my uncle, Mama's brother, to give me away. While I was home on Thanksgiving break, I followed through with some of the plans and kept James in the loop as we planned the wedding. With Mama's blessing, we planned to get married in April 1976. I talked to the pastor Mama had recommended and he graciously agreed to marry us. He said he wouldn't charge us to use the church, even though we were not members.

Mama seemed pleased that I was planning a wedding. She'd thought I wouldn't ever get married or have children. Now, she looked forward to my planning a wedding. She knew that there was a possibility she might see grandchildren from me. All I had to say at that point was that I would not have a lot of children. I was beginning to like the idea of Mama seeing my children.

When I returned to school, my two roommates accompanied me to a nearby bridal store to help me select wedding invitations. I found ones that I liked and couldn't wait to show them to James. I planned to show them to Mama during my next visit. I called James and told him about the invitations; he would see them the next time he returned.

He was scheduled to complete his service with the army in 1976, and I would complete the school year after our wedding. We talked about what married life would be like. James told me once that he wanted to have eight children. I quickly told him that I would not have eight children. I would commit to one and nothing more. He felt that we should have more than one because the child should have siblings. He suggested that I revisit my answer. James continued to discuss children, and I eventually gave in to having three. I stuck to that number. James came from a family of eight, which is why he felt that having a large family was a good idea. On the other hand, I also came from a family of eight, and because of that, I felt that a small family would be better.

I knew then that I couldn't be the woman or mother that Mama was. She devoted all of her time to her children. She didn't work outside of the home, and where I saw that as a benefit, I knew that I couldn't be that. I wanted a career, and if I was going to have children, I didn't want more than I felt that I was capable of parenting as well as Mama had done for us. I did not want to be a stay-at-home mom; if I was going to have children and have a career, I did not want to compromise the well-being of my children. I also didn't want to compromise my efforts to be the best that I could be on the job. We decided that we would have a maximum of three children and become a family of five. It was a plan that I was looking forward to seeing through.

Christmas vacation was approaching, and I was excited to have at least two weeks at home with Mama. I could spend that time continuing to plan for the wedding. I wasn't certain that James would be able to come for the holidays, but I was OK with that. It was an exciting time for me. In all the excitement, I almost forgot how much I wanted to transfer, but I quickly came to my senses after attending one of my classes and taking an exam that had nothing to do with the class. I was disappointed and couldn't wait to share that with Mama as evidence that I needed to transfer.

It was at the end of the semester, and I found satisfaction in completing the survey for that class. As honestly and discreetly as I could, I identified reasons why I didn't like that class. After taking the exam and completing the survey, I was on my way home to spend this holiday with my family.

- 11 -

Broken Plans, Unintentionally

> For my thoughts are not your thoughts, neither
> are your ways my ways, saith the Lord.
> —Isaiah 55:8 (KJV)

THIS VISIT WOULD BE DIFFERENT FROM ANY VISIT I'D HAD since I'd graduated from high school. I'd learned so much over the years but had so much more to learn. Mama had been a driving force in everything that I'd done. She had consoled me when I was sad, confused, or just unhappy. She applauded me when I'd accomplished anything and thanked me when I'd done anything that she considered extra. Through it all, she had loved me and made herself available whenever I needed her—as well as times when I didn't think I needed her, but she knew I did and provided for me. She never stopped giving God credit for all that she did and for all of my accomplishments. She did that when it should have been me giving God credit. This visit caused me to reflect on so much. I was to be married in a matter of months, but we still had not organized our wedding party and had not formally scheduled any meetings or arrangements for the wedding.

As always, Mama had something waiting for me on my bed. It was a large stuffed animal, an orange-and-white checkered dog with high floppy ears. It was beautiful, and I was happy to have another item to add to my welcome-home collection from Mama. It was good to be home. Mama was always glad to see me or any of her kids come home. It was always good to have such a warm and nurturing reception.

Christmas had always been my favorite time of the year, but this year there was something more to it. Mama's hugs seemed lingering; it was hard to let go. There was so much comfort just being near her, but it was not until that Christmas of 1975 that I genuinely realized how much I loved being with her.

I settled into the house and got into my usual routine at home. Mama and I were in the living room. She was reading the newspaper, as she always did. Suddenly, she said, "I didn't know that Mildred died." Mildred was an old friend of hers that she hadn't seen in years.

I looked over and saw that she was reading the obituaries. I asked, "Why do you always read the obituaries?"

"I read them because they're part of the newspaper," she explained.

"I read them for information, should I decide to pay my respects. There are times when I learn for the first time of the passing of someone I know."

"It's so morbid to read the obituaries so routinely," I said.

"We all have to die someday. Remember that it's important to live a life according to God's Word so that we're ready when death comes."

I didn't want to talk about it or hear about it, and although I did not verbalize how I felt, Mama somehow knew.

She said, "Look, gal, I'm going someday, and when it happens, you are not to be sad about it. When someone leaves this world, you are to rejoice because they're going to be with Jesus."

This time, I said, "Mama, I don't want to talk about you dying."

"Avoiding talking about it will not stop it from happening. I'm only telling you that because I want you to understand."

Mama had several talks about this over the years, but I still wasn't ready to hear this kind of talk. I wanted to focus on enjoying my vacation and spending as much time with her as

I possibly could. That conversation ended as quickly as it had begun, but we continued to talk about school, and she updated me on the community and the possibility of going to church to sing. I learned to look forward to singing at church, rather than dread it. I was not in a choir at my school, and I missed it. It had become a pleasure to sing, whenever and wherever Mama planned. It didn't matter anymore because I enjoyed the time at home with Mama.

Shortly before going back to school, I was sitting on the sofa, daydreaming. Mama came into the room and told me that she thought she had to see a doctor.

"Do you feel sick?" I asked her.

"No, but there is a lump in my abdominal area." She leaned down toward me and told me to feel an area she was touching near her side.

I immediately sat up and touched the area; it felt hard.

"You need to get it checked, Mama", I said.

"I'm going to have it checked", Mama said.

I didn't say anything, but when she walked out of the room, I felt tears flowing down my face. I just stared up at the ceiling and cried uncontrollably, not knowing why I was crying or if the tears would stop. There was an emptiness in the pit of my stomach, and I hoped that Mama's issue wasn't anything major. Mama didn't mention her stomach again before my return to school, and neither did I. I figured I would wait until she had it checked, and then I would ask.

As I waited to return to school, Mama scheduled an appointment to see a doctor about her stomach. She had always said that she would go to Duke Hospital in the event that she became ill. She was treated there years ago and believed that the doctors and staff there would attend to her medical needs more proficiently. Edna made arrangements and adjusted her schedule to take Mama to the doctor. Mama didn't seem worried. She never seemed to worry when she was sick because she always said that God was in control, and it was in God's hand.

I tried not to worry, but I couldn't shake the feeling I had. That feeling was there before Mama told me to feel what seemed to be a lump in her stomach. As I was leaving to go back to school, Mama made a point of telling me that she was going to be all right. She reminded me to complete the school year, regardless of how I felt about it. I promised her that I would indeed complete the school year and was thankful that I only had one semester left.

It was good to get back to school. I received my schedule for my new classes and was pleased with them. There was always a chance that I would not get the hours I signed up for when I registered. I was happy to see that I had all the classes and hours I registered for. I was all set to dive into my schoolwork. It was a new semester and a new year. I thought that this would be the year I'd get married, finish my bachelor's degree, and prepare for a master's degree before having kids. I wanted my career in place when I conceived my first child. I was so excited and wanted time to move as quickly as possible so that I could put my plans in gear.

My courses were more exciting than the prior semester, and I really had to focus and study. They were more challenging, and that's what I wanted. I had one instructor who would not excuse any absences. That didn't bother me because I was not one to skip class or stay out due to sickness. He made a point to tell his students that he would not excuse an absence even for family funerals. He said, "The only absence for a funeral that I will excuse is if the funeral is your own." Regardless of the situation, our assignments had to be in.

I thought he was the most inconsiderate teacher I'd ever had and wondered how the school could allow him to implement such a strong and inhuman rule. I was bothered by it, but figured there was nothing I could do but honor it and hope that I didn't need to take time off. Normally, I would have called Mama and discussed it with her, but I knew that she was following up on her condition (whatever it was), and I didn't want to bother her with it. So I let it go.

Linda Aurelia B. Blackmon

Mama's Appointment

Mama's appointment was scheduled shortly after my return to school. I learned that there was something in the area of her side, and the plan was to remove the lump. It was diagnosed as a benign tumor. Mama would need to have surgery. It was January, a few months before my wedding. I decided, when I heard her news, that I would not continue with wedding plans. I wanted to wait until Mama had her surgery and had recovered before moving forward. I wanted her there, and I wanted her to know that her presence was necessary.

I was not comfortable with Mama's having surgery, but I wanted to be there. It was to my advantage that I was attending school in the same city as the hospital, and I would be able to visit between classes and on weekends. I decided that I would not go home on the weekend while Mama was in the hospital. I would be able to see my family there, when we all would meet.

Mama was going back and forth to the hospital for her appointments until she had her surgery; Edna was driving her. I was notified of Mama's scheduled surgery, and I made sure that I was there. All of my assignments were done, and I planned it so that my classes would not clash with the bus schedules for the hospital.

The day of her surgery was a lonely day, and Mama wasn't available to assure me that everything would be all right. I knew that if she could have, she most certainly would have comforted me and reminded me that God was there with me and with her. But she couldn't say anything, and I dared not approach her with my worries about her condition beforehand. We gathered at the hospital and waited as Mama went in for her surgery. Although my sisters and I were together, it was still a lonely time. I wanted Mama to come home, whole and ready to resume her life.

That would not be the reality.

After the surgery, her surgeon came out to give us the report.

He told us that Mama had cancer, and it had spread beyond the area they noticed before the surgery. Although the doctor did not say it at first, I felt in my whole body that I could lose my mama. Edna asked the doctor how long she had.

To this day, I appreciate his answer: "I can't say how long she will live, nor can I say how long any of us will live. At any moment, we could be hit by a car and leave this world."

His answer gave me hope. I didn't have the stress of a time clock and wondering, after so many months, weeks, days, hours, or minutes, if this would be the day or time. Instead, I did what I could do, and that was to take one day at a time. Mama had always said, "God is in control," and so he was.

Going to school was very difficult for me at this point. I tried as hard as I could to maintain my average, but my As were turning into Bs. I was trying to keep my grades above a C average, but for once in my college years, I couldn't hold it together, and I did eventually receive a C. Worse than that, I didn't care. I wanted my Mama back to where she was before she became ill.

I took as many bus rides as I could to the hospital. It became routine as I went up to her room to visit her. As sick as she was, she was still beautiful, lying in bed, with her thick, long hair flowing over her shoulders. She was alert the first time I saw her in the hospital, and she smiled when I entered her room. I became familiar with the staff there, and as I approached Mama's bedside, she teased me, saying that she heard me flirting with the doctors.

I blushed a bit and said, "No, Mama, they were flirting with me."

She laughed and shook her head. It was a relief to see her actually chuckle.

On one occasion when I visited, I insisted on helping her to eat. After some resistance, she agreed to allow me to do so. As she paused between bites, she told me, "I should be feeding you, not the other way around."

I reminded her, "You did that already—and with all of us. Now it's my turn to feed you for once."

She smiled, but I could see in her eyes that she didn't like having her daughter feed her. She was so independent, and she was always doing for her children. It was hard to see her in bed and incapable of doing for herself. She was normally up daily at five o'clock in the morning, reading her Bible and doing things around the house.

Through it all, she was able to muster a smile, and I knew that was her way of saying everything would be all right.

Home from the Hospital

Mama was released from the hospital but not in the capacity I had hoped. She was wheelchair-bound, and she would be in bed while at home. We had to make arrangements at home to accommodate her needs. The dining area became a hospital room; we ordered a hospital bed so that she could incline when she needed to sit up. She was no longer able to walk upstairs to the bathroom or to do her daily cooking in the kitchen. I was still in school, and Edna was living nearby and available to step in between caring for her own children. We made arrangements for how we would participate in her care during her illness, and we all pitched in to ensure that her best interest was at the forefront of everything. It was going well.

Edna was still transporting Mama to and from the hospital. On one occasion when I was home, I went with Edna to take Mama to her appointment. On the way home, we had a flat tire and had to take Mama from the car and into her wheelchair so that we could change the tire. Mama didn't say much during this time, but it was obvious that she didn't like what we were going through; most likely, she wished that she could help. I was changing the tire that day and was struggling with it while Edna watched Mama.

A Way That's Mighty Sweet

We were blessed when two young gentlemen stopped and finished changing the tire. We were able to drive home without further incident. That was the last time we transported Mama to and from the hospital.

Mama was bedridden but still conscious and able to communicate. Her words were few, but we were able to figure out what she wanted. We continued caring for her, and it wasn't a problem. It was an honor to be able to do something for this remarkable, God-fearing woman—the woman who had always put us first, sacrificing everything for us. It was evident that she was not improving, but I refused to think that she was leaving me. That hope kept me going, and as long as I could see her, I was OK. I didn't know how to believe otherwise, although Mama had several conversations about God's will and that it wasn't a bad thing. During times that seemed difficult, I could hear Mama singing, "Lord, don't move this mountain, but give me the strength to climb." This was a huge mountain in my life, and I had no way of getting around it or over it. My strength was diminishing, and I felt weak. I kept thinking, *Why did this happen to Mama?* I had no answers.

On one occasion while I was home, it was my turn to take the night shift. I would have to stay awake downstairs to be there for Mama. I would check on her to make sure her bed linens were clean and to turn her, as she wasn't mobile. By this time, Mama wasn't doing much of anything; she was barely awake most of the time. The doctors said she was in a semi-coma, meaning that she was awake, could hear us, and could open her eyes and see us. She knew what was going on and needed no type of breathing support. That night, I checked on her before I got comfortable in her favorite recliner.

As I was sitting there, almost asleep, I felt something touch my head. I looked up and saw Mama, and I screamed loudly.

Mama looked at me and said, "Why are you screaming? Take me to the bathroom." She had not been out of that bed and had not walked since her surgery. It had been weeks, and I was stunned to see her standing over me. A few days before I came home, I'd had a dream of her asking me to take her to the bathroom. I'd thought how nice it would be to see her walking and asking to go to the bathroom. That time had come, and I was seeing just that. I got up and had her lean on me as I walked her upstairs to the bathroom. Afterward, I walked her to her bed, and she seemed pleased and went to sleep.

Before going back to school, Mama was able to talk to us as she lay in bed. As we gathered around her, she gave what seemed like her final advice for us. She and Daddy had always put God first and then family. She told us on that day to remember to be there for each other because we needed to stick together. Mama knew that, if provoked, my reactions were less than appropriate, so she also gave me some advice on controlling my temper. I believed she knew that she was responsible for keeping me in control. She always analyzed situations that I brought to her attention, and she knew that I would do as she said.

I heard all that she had to say, but I still thought that Mama was going to be with me. I couldn't think of losing her; I had lost Daddy. I said OK and promised her that I would remember what she had taught me. James got a chance to visit Mama while she was sick, and she seemed pleased to see him. Although she couldn't eat, he came bearing gifts of candy on Valentine's Day, and that made her smile.

I went back to school and tried to carry on as usual. My roommates were very supportive, and I was blessed to have them. They did what they could to make things easier for me; they would offer to bring me things from the Student Union or the store. They offered to check my mail for me, to return any library books, and anything that would help me to feel better. I liked the idea of keeping busy and needed it to distract me from thinking of losing my mother. It was too much, and I didn't talk about it much to anyone. I carried it with me and held on to it, hoping that it would resolve itself.

Little did I know at the time that Mama had given me answers to dealing with disappointments and situations that I could not control. She had always told me that God was in control, but I wasn't making that connection and couldn't deal with what I was going through. It was evident in my studies.

It was March 1976, and I had decided that I would not have a wedding. We had planned to get married in April that year, if Mama had approved. I figured if Mama couldn't be there, I didn't want the big church thing with the wedding dress, the wedding party, and the huge celebration. It wouldn't be the same without her, so I decided that I would not move forward with the wedding. I didn't have the time or patience to plan anything. I had much catching up to do with my schoolwork. I was behind, with papers due, and I had to research and study to complete the papers. I was overwhelmed for the first time in college, but I had to finish this semester; I'd promised Mama that I would. I had a final paper due from that teacher who refused to take any excuses for a failure to turn in an assignment. Although it was due at the end of the semester, I had to start the work sooner rather than later.

The Phone Call

I decided that I would complete his paper early so that I could start on some of the other work I had overlooked. I checked out several books on the topic and put them on my desk, hoping to get to it within a day or two. I wanted to submit it early to avoid penalties and possibly failing the course. I thought it was best to take a day off to collect my thoughts and focus. I couldn't visit Mama now because she was no longer at the hospital, and it was not as easy for me to go back and forth to see her at home. I decided that I would check in and get reports from my family regarding her condition.

About a week had passed, and I still had not started that final paper. I thought it was best that I take notes from the books first and then write my paper. I collected all of my note cards and was pleased that I had a plan and would start soon. I managed to catch up on the other assignments I'd missed and saved the big paper for last. I felt confident that I would get it done and was on my way to completing the assignment so that, I hoped, I could wrap up this year. It was a good school, but it wasn't working for me, and I needed to move on.

I did a final evaluation of things I needed and figured that I would start the next day. I lined up all of my books and planned to begin working on this paper after breakfast the following day. I felt a sense of relief and went to bed after a long day of organizing and making an effort to follow through. It was a struggle, but I knew that Mama would be proud.

The next morning at five o'clock, someone was knocking on the door. I tried to ignore it at first because I was exhausted from all that I was going through, and the stress of completing that paper was too much. The person kept knocking and yelled out, "There's an emergency phone call for Linda."

I yelled out, "Coming!" There was only one pay phone on that floor. I'd never received a phone call that early in the morning. I could feel my blood pressure rising as I threw on my robe and rushed out of the room. I picked up the phone; it was my uncle. He said,

"Your mama passed. You need to come home. Do you need a ride?"

"No," I said, "I will take the first bus home. I will be there in a few hours."

I felt like someone had placed a mountain on each of my shoulders, and I was numb. I slowly hung up the phone and went to my room to get a dime to call the bus station for the next bus leaving for Burlington.

I had two and a half hours before the bus would leave for

Burlington. The city buses ran every fifteen minutes, so that wasn't a concern; I would make it to the bus stop on time. As I was getting dressed, I remembered that paper, and I thought about how Mama would feel if I did not submit it and failed the course. I grabbed the books, read one paragraph from each book, combined that reading with my note cards, and typed my paper.

My roommates were awake from my scurrying around, although I had tried to get ready without disturbing them. Stella was surprised to see me typing a paper after learning that I'd lost my mother. I told her that it was for the professor who would recognize a funeral as an excuse only if I was the deceased. She shook her head and told me that she would take it to his office for me later that day. I was thankful because I had not thought about how I would get the paper to him. My bus was scheduled to leave at eight o'clock that morning and his office did not open until eight o'clock. I appreciated her willingness to help me. I thanked her, grabbed my bag, and rushed to the bus stop.

- 12 -

Where Do I Go from Here?

> The troubles of my heart are enlarged: O
> bring thou me out of my distresses.
> —Psalm 25:17 (KJV)

I WAS RELIEVED THAT THE CITY BUS ARRIVED ON TIME, AND I was able to make it to the Greyhound bus station without delay. I boarded my bus, and as it pulled off, I began to dread what was coming. Riding the bus home that day was the first time since Mama's illness that I actually sat in one place and thought about everything that was happening. It was surreal; I felt like I was dreaming or in a place where I didn't belong. I was emotionless, and I refused to believe that she was gone. I had received the phone call from my uncle, but still, I wasn't convinced. As I rode home, I thought about conversations I'd had with Mama.

It wasn't that long ago when she had reminded me that we weren't to be sad when someone leaves this world and that the day would come when she would be gone. She said that in death, she would be going home to God, and that was good. I found nothing good about it as I thought about what my life would be without her. I wasn't crying because I was angry! I knew why I was angry, but I didn't know with whom I was angry. I wasn't mad at Mama because I knew if she'd had a choice, she would have stayed with me. I wasn't angry with God because Mama had convinced me that this was a part of life that must take place. I wasn't angry with myself or anyone. I didn't know how or where to direct my feelings, but I hoped they would go away.

I had my memories of this wonderful, amazing, and loving woman who loved God and loved her family. She was selfless, and while she was ill, she continued to tell me what I needed to do. Now, what was left for me to do? How would I accomplish anything with her gone? I was devastated and lonely. An emptiness took control of my being; my body and mind were affected by Mama's leaving. Daddy was gone, and I felt I had nowhere to turn. I wondered what would happen to us as a family. Mama was the glue that held this family together, and as I thought about her, I was overcome by fear. I was really scared, hopeless, and alone.

The bus pulled into the bus depot in Burlington. I didn't want to get off, but I knew that I had to. I had reached my destination, and I was going home to face what was. Edna was at the bus station to pick me up, and when I entered the car, I could see that she had been crying. She asked about the trip as we drove toward home.

Everything reminded me of Mama. I thought about how excited she was when we moved into the apartment and how generous she was to the workers once we moved in. As Edna turned onto the street leading to the apartment, I could feel my nerves overtake me, and I could feel tears rolling down my face. As we approached the house, I envisioned Mama standing in the yard with her hands outstretched, waiting for me to get out of the car and walk into a very warm and overdue embrace. I wouldn't get a hug from her on this day. As we passed the front of the house to park in the back, I noticed the wreath on the door. The funeral home placed a wreath on the door, recognizing that a loved one had died and was to be respected. Seeing that wreath brought me into reality, and I was very emotional and didn't want to go into the house. Mama wasn't there.

We were all there, and relatives constantly stopped in to extend their condolences, to drop off food, and to reach out to help in any way. There was much planning to do with the funeral home, and we met with those people as soon as possible to go over details. The bed that Mama had slept in was still in the dining room. Mama had been rushed to the hospital prior to her passing and never returned home.

When everyone was gone, we all got together to discuss how we would take care of the details with the funeral home. Someone had to select the coffin and the items she would be buried in. I knew I couldn't go and quickly made it known to my siblings that I couldn't do it. It was too much for me, so one of my older sisters agreed to work out the details with the funeral home.

The funeral went well. We were all dressed alike in navy blue dresses that Edna made for the funeral. Mama was buried at her church cemetery, where Daddy was buried as well. As we sat through the funeral, I thought, *Maybe she is at peace. Maybe she is with God, like she said.* I never saw her appear worried or frightened when she thought that she might be sick. As always, she made sure that we knew what our responsibilities were, once she left this world. She appeared peaceful.

We agreed that we would have her wear a beautiful nightgown instead of an outfit because she was laid to rest. It was a beautiful light-blue nightgown, and it appeared that she was sleeping. The ride back to the apartment was as empty as the ride to the church. We said our farewells at the burial, and it was certain that Mama was gone. We had to continue with our lives, as we had been taught.

The Next Step

Prior to Mama's burial, we learned that Mama had taken out insurance to pay for her funeral. We weren't aware of that beforehand, but we weren't surprised. Mama believed in paying her bills. Before we began to break down the apartment, Edna suggested that we look into Mama's bills to see if there was anything unpaid. Mama was not one to acquire a lot of bills because she lived within her means and was very strategic when making purchases. We got together and visited the office of her only creditor to see how much she owed. We were planning to pay the balance because we knew that she would not want it to go unpaid.

When we met with the creditor, Edna informed him of Mama's passing and explained to him that we would pay the balance. Edna took on the responsibility of tying any loose ends. The gentleman asked us to wait while he checked her file. When he returned, he told us that Mama didn't owe anything. She had insured her loan, and he handed Edna a check. He told us that he owed us because there was money left over from the insurance, and the bill was now paid in full. We didn't expect that; Mama had not mentioned any of this to us. We were thankful but not surprised. Mama was still taking care of us. She always said that she was the mother, and she would take care of us. She never wanted it the other way around.

We stayed in the apartment for a couple of days after the funeral, and then I headed back to school. Edna was getting a new apartment, and I would stay with her when I came home for the weekend. I was told to go back to school, and they would take care of the house. It was already happening—taking care of each other. I got on the bus to head back to school. I thought about where I would live after I finished that year. School would end in two months, so I had to start planning for how I would live. When I returned, I took the city bus back to the school to finish up the semester. Life would never be the same.

I had no choice but to get back into my school routine. I couldn't call Mama anymore to discuss my concerns, and I didn't have the unrealistic hope that she would get better and everything would be back to normal. The wedding was no longer delayed, but I was not planning to get married. I was angry because during the time I was home for the funeral, James did not show up, and he didn't attend the funeral. I felt this was insensitive to my situation, and because of this, I thought it was best to forget about getting married.

My roommates had taken up a collection for me. I figured I would use the money to help with finding a place to live, once I left college. When Mama passed, I hadn't had time to talk to anyone about my situation before I'd left to go home, so Stella and Colleen notified the dorm counselor and the Office of Student Affairs of the loss of my mother.

Before the end of the semester, James showed up at school with a cast on his leg. He apologized for missing my mother's funeral and for not being there for me. He told me that on the same day Mama died, he'd broken his leg and had to stay off it for a few weeks. In addition to breaking his leg, he'd had car trouble and wasn't able to get it fixed. He'd hitchhiked to the school to visit me, wearing a cast. I told him I wanted to wait to get married. I'd really wanted Mama to be a part of this major transition in my life, and with her gone, it wasn't the same. He agreed, and we canceled the wedding. In my mind, it wasn't going to happen at all. I had given up on getting married; it wasn't something I wanted at that point in my life. I wasn't certain what I wanted. I was still numb and felt at a loss for my mama.

By early April, with the end of the school year approaching, my main focus was completing my courses and facing the next challenges of my life. I knew I wouldn't be returning home. As far as I was concerned, there was no home. Prior to returning after the funeral, I had stayed with Edna for a few days. I now thought of packing and preparing to move to the boarding house, where I planned to live until I finished school.

About a week before the school year ended, my sister presented the idea of sharing an apartment, so I agreed. As soon as I made up my mind to share an apartment, I went to my future landlord and told her about my situation. I had not told her that Mama had passed, so I shared that with her and said that I understood if she could not return my deposit. She was very understanding and told me that it was not a problem because she had a waiting list. Usually, she would not refund the deposit, but because of my situation, she gave it back. I was thankful because I was returning to Burlington without a job and with only the Social Security benefits I received from my daddy's death.

Finalizing My Loss

I returned home to share the apartment with my sister. Things were different, and it was difficult being in town without Mama. All the attention left with her—the warm greetings, the smiles of approval, and the shifted eyes and frowns whenever I did or said something ridiculous or something that I shouldn't have. I quickly realized how blessed I was when Mama was with me. I didn't have to cook because Mama made all of my meals when I was home. Now, I figured that I could live off sandwiches, and I had no trouble making those. Mama did teach me a few things about cooking. She never forced me to learn how to cook but made an effort to teach me basic cooking skills and recipes. I was only attentive to the things that I loved to eat. I learned to make her delicious banana pudding. She taught me how to roast a turkey, and I watched her make turnip greens, squash, applesauce, and simple dishes that took very little effort to make. When James had visited, she had served him a piece of her homemade applesauce cake. James asked me to get the recipe, but I'd said, "Later." I'd taken for granted that she would be available when I needed her. I was comfortable with her cooking, and she loved having food ready for us when we returned home from school, from elementary school through college. I never got that recipe.

The first apartment my sister and I lived in did not meet our standards, but it met our budget, so we moved in. We stayed there for less than a year. I began to look for work, but work didn't come easy. I was not successful at finding a job, but I didn't stop searching. Soon after we moved into this apartment, my sister found a job, and we moved to another apartment that did meet our standards. That would be our home until we were able to rent separately. Months went by, and I did not have a full-time job. I was able to substitute teach for a while. It wasn't something I wanted to do, but it provided some income for the time being. I was hesitant to take on a substitute teaching job because I didn't want to work with elementary school kids, but I found it rewarding. Kids asked innocent questions and really looked up to me to guide and direct them. It was a good experience. I had second thoughts when they placed me with the high school kids. They were pranksters and did mischievous things. It was a big adjustment and challenge to work with the high school kids, but I managed to get through it.

I applied to a college in the area so that I could start my classes in January 1977. I had not planned to start in September 1976. I needed some time to adjust to being without Mama and figured that it would be best to start the following semester. I had promised Mama that I would continue, and I was committed to finishing my senior year. It took longer than usual to hear from the school. I consistently watched the mailbox for a letter, either accepting me or rejecting me, but nothing came. Instead, I received a phone call from the school.

"Hello, Ms. Brown," a woman's voice said. "I'm looking at your transcript, and it seems that you had a 4.0 GPA for two years and a 3.0 for one semester in your junior year and during the last semester, your grades dropped. Can you explain why that happened? Usually when we see such a drop in grades, there is a major life event that causes it."

I wasn't sure at first if I should give an explanation. I didn't want to talk about it because I would start thinking about Mama and possibly break down while on the phone, but I told her I had lost my mama.

"My mother was sick during that last semester an she passed. It was difficult to focus on my courses", I said.

"I see", she said, "we will take that into consideration and you will receive and acceptance letter. You will be able to attend classes in January. You will also receive a notice to preregister for the spring semester."

I was thrilled to know that I would actually transfer to another school and hopefully finish my degree.

Life wasn't the same without Mama, although a year hadn't gone by. It was extremely hard, although I didn't talk to anyone about it except my friend Daisy. She was trying to get her tuition for the following year, so we were both feeling sorry for ourselves. I was missing Mama, and she was trying to figure out how she would pay her school tuition. She was afraid of missing the deadline and having to wait another semester in her senior year. I was sulking about not having a mother and how life just didn't seem important anymore.

She agreed that her life was changing because of the possibility of taking a semester off from school. We waddled in our sorry and realized that neither of us could control what was happening. We decided that we would just mope along and let the chips fall where they may. We had no intention of making any effort to make our life situation better.

Several days later, I was driving my nephew, Edna's son, home. Daisy and my other sister Nora were in the car with me. There was a very slow car in front of me. I waited until I reached the designated passing line in the road to pass that driver. The driver of the car looked at me and sped up. I slowed down to get behind him because it seemed as if he was staying with my vehicle to prevent me from passing in front of him or getting behind him. Suddenly, a car came toward me. I attempted to get over again, but there was no room. I told Daisy and Nora that I had to go off the road to my left to avoid getting hit head-on. I had no other choice. I missed the car heading toward me by seconds. We went off the road and down a steep hill. Daisy was talking to me the entire time. My nephew was quiet, which was a blessing in itself. The car leaned on two wheels and felt as if it was going to flip over, but it didn't. It tilted and was on all four wheels again. After it spun around a few times, the engine shut off and came to a halt. The front end of the car was pointing upward, facing the road, which was above us on a hill. I had no idea that I would go down a hill when I went off the road. I thought that it was a ditch or a narrow shoulder where we could pull off.

As we got out of the car, we noticed a lake behind us, and we were thankful because none of us could swim. It was a scary moment. We looked up and saw about fifty people standing at the top of the hill. One onlooker yelled out, "Who was driving that car?" I proudly said it was me. He told us that they'd seen the car go down the hill, and they thought we'd been killed. From their view, it appeared that the car had flipped over. He offered to help us and to take us to a phone to call our family. Nora went with him to make the call.

Things were different then; spectators tried to assist us, and we never thought—although we should have—that we were taking a risk by allowing him to take any of us to the nearest phone booth. Fortunately, it wasn't far from the accident. Nora returned shortly and informed us that she had notified Daisy's father. He arrived and directed us on how to get the car back to the road. We were able to drive my nephew home without a scratch.

The next conversation Daisy and I had was about how stupid we were to think as we did before the accident. Daisy's mother was in tears and reminded us that we were blessed to leave that accident unharmed and for me to leave without getting a traffic violation. She envisioned losing all of us to that accident and gave God thanks for saving us. I knew I had no choice, but I didn't think any officer would have believed me if I'd told him that I couldn't get in either lane. During the accident, a truckload of guys had passed by and warned us that the sheriff was headed our way. He never showed up.

Daisy and I saw that incident as a sign that she and I were being punished for saying and thinking terrible things because nothing had gone our way. We vowed that we would never say anything so ridiculous again. I remembered what Mama had said to me years ago—how dare I feel sorry for myself when Jesus Christ went through what he went through. In a moment, I felt ashamed and made a decision that I would stop having the pity parties, stop feeling sorry for myself, accept life as it was, and make the best of my situation. I was ready to move on. Daisy was ready as well. I focused on going back to school, and Daisy's brother gave her the money for her tuition. I thought I was on the right track.

Things began to move rather quickly after that summer. So much had happened in 1976. I moved on, but I would never forget Mama. I wasn't trying to forget; I was trying to live with the memories because they were good memories, and I had to hold on to them. I don't remember Christmas that year. It was the first Christmas I spent without Mama, and the excitement wasn't there. The holidays became a blank in my memory, and it would not be the first Christmas I couldn't remember. Christmas, as I knew it, was really about family. With Mama and Daddy gone, family was not as it had been. They always made Christ the center of Christmas, but I always placed them there as well. Christmas would always be my favorite time of year, but it wouldn't be the same. I had to redefine my Christmases while keeping Christ in the forefront. I learned many lessons in 1976, although at the time, those were lessons I rather would not have learned. They would prove to be lessons, however, that continued to shape and mold me into what I am today.

- 13 -

Overshadowed with Pain and Loss

> The Lord is nigh unto them that are of a broken heart; and saveth such as be of a contrite spirit.
> —Psalm 34:18 (KJV)

IN 1977, I WAS IN MY SENIOR YEAR OF COLLEGE AND LIVING off campus. I went through the motions of moving on. I did what I needed to do to get back into school and to focus on graduating the following year. Living without Mama was still new to me, and I didn't want to adjust to it. Nine months had passed since her death, and it was still like a bad dream to me that I wished would go away. It didn't seem real.

I never expressed to anyone how I felt about Mama's death. I went through many emotions but prayed about none of them. It was evident that we all missed Mama, but no one knew the depths of my loneliness. No one knew that I felt homeless, although I shared an apartment with my sister. No one knew because I kept it to myself. I lived with a void that felt like a deep hole in the pit of my stomach that would not go away. I was lost and couldn't find my way. I had no direction, and Mama wasn't there to give me direction. I did the only thing I could do, and that was to take one day at a time—minute by minute and hour by hour. I had to figure it out for myself and do the best I could.

James finished his service in the army at Fort Bragg in the same year that Mama died. He moved back to Connecticut, and we stayed in touch as much as we possibly could. His visits were not as frequent as they had been while he was in North Carolina. He managed to visit me once when he traveled to Georgia and stopped over in North Carolina on his way there. I also managed to visit him in Connecticut while visiting my older brother. We kept each other updated on what we were doing. Our relationship did not seem to be affected by the long distance between us. He planned to enroll in school for the following semester, and I hoped to graduate soon.

School was certainly different from what I had experienced in prior years. This would be the first time I lived off campus and commuted to school. I missed living on campus, but off campus had its advantages—I did not have to wait until the weekends to see family or call long distance to talk to them. At first, I missed walking to my classes without needing a ride to school, but I soon adapted, and as time went by, I liked it even more.

I quickly learned that transferring was not as simple as I'd thought it would be. I changed my major and had to take a few more courses so that I could graduate on time. I figured that I would attend summer school to avoid graduating late. I had missed one semester, and summer school would put me back on track. I was beginning to enjoy my time there and felt that I was getting back into the swing of things.

Although things seemed to be going well, I could not stop thinking about Mama. I was pleased that I had gotten her advice about transferring to another school. I was thankful that I had chosen to decline the offer, while in junior college, to be an exchange student in a different state. Had I accepted that offer, I would have missed out on spending the time I had with her. She was proud that I was selected and told me to go, but as I thought about it, I somehow knew that I needed to be near her. I needed to hear her last words of advice for me, and I needed to be there to let her know that I would listen to her.

I needed to see her face and feel the comfort that radiated

from her. It was no different when she was ill; her expressions sent messages as they always had. I knew she was saying that she cared, and if she could have done it differently, she would have. I could see her telling me that it was her time and that we would be all right. I heard her words through her eyes and through her faint whispers as she talked to me for the last time. I wanted her to know that I was there for her.

I managed to function in school as if things were OK with me, but I never stopped thinking about Mama and how much I missed her. I thought home would never be the same because she was not there. I was convinced of it, and it wasn't. Mama often said that none of us is here to stay in this world forever and that death is a part of life. "It's in God's hands," she always said. "You must move on, and don't give up when someone dies. Rejoice because they are with God."

I was beginning to see what she meant. I knew there was nothing I could do about it but to move forward. I just could not find a place in my heart to rejoice. I would not celebrate her leaving this world. I really could not! I didn't know how to pray.

Taking one day at a time had a different meaning for me. One day at a time was all there was, simply just getting through. I had always loved reading, writing, studying, and learning new things. I went to school each day, and I did well, but it was a struggle. It did not feel natural, as it had before. I felt cheated because Mama wasn't there, and there was no more advice for me. I reminded myself of all the things she'd said to me, and that fueled me at times to get through some of my challenges. I still had family, but there seemed to be a disconnect on my part. Again, I went through the motions and appeared to be OK, but there was inner pain stagnated in what seemed like the core of my soul. I needed relief and couldn't find a way out. Despite everything that had happened—the loss of Mama and the wedding cancellation—I did have my family. They were there for me, but I wasn't available for them. I had to find a place to call home—not just a building but a place in my heart where home would exist again.

Silent Decisions

James continued to stay in touch with me. We wrote letters and talked on the phone as much as possible. I was engrossed with my schoolwork, but my extracurricular activities were few to none. I met with friends as much as possible, including Daisy and her brothers. I wasn't working full time, but I did substitute teach from time to time, and that little income helped a lot. By the time I attended summer school, I had moved to another location with my sister. Although the amenities included with this apartment were improved, it had no positive impact on my life. Since Mama passed, I had moved three times in only a year.

After I finished my last summer class, I received a phone call from James. He asked if I would go to Connecticut with him. I could finish school there, and we could get married there. It wasn't a decision that I could make instantly. I needed to talk to someone—but who? My original plans had been to get married and stay in town with Mama, but now she was gone, and I didn't want to discuss it with anyone.

As I look back, I know that during the time, I wasn't ready to hear advice that would not have favored what I wanted to do or what I thought I wanted to do. I told James that I would get back to him. I had no extra money to pay for the trip, and I didn't want to ask my family for it. Before I could say anything about the bus fare to Connecticut, James said that if I decided to go there with him, he would wire me the money.

I thought about it and I wanted to go, but had moments when I felt like I needed to stay. I wasn't certain what I wanted to do. I decided not to discuss it with anyone. Like me, my siblings were getting their lives together and adjusting to being without Mama.

I thought about the pros and cons of staying and going. Neither outweighed the other.

I called James and told him that I would go with him. We chose a date, and he gave me instructions regarding picking up the MoneyGram for the bus ride. I made up my mind that I would leave and would have a one-way ticket because I would relocate and live there. I made one of the toughest decisions I had ever made, as I had much doubt regarding moving. The only thing I was sure of was that I wasn't sure.

Moving in with James without being married went against everything I was taught by both my parents. There was an understanding that I must be married before moving into someone's residence, and it certainly was wrong to live together as a married couple when single. I gave it very little thought and decided that it was best to move. I needed a new environment, a new start now that Mama was gone, and a new way of seeing things. As I justified my reasoning for leaving, I convinced myself that leaving was the right thing to do. James and I agreed on a date for my arrival, and I then notified my family that I was leaving.

Leaving wasn't as easy as I had imagined. My young niece and nephews were very tearful on the day of my departure. I had not thought about them when I convinced myself that I needed to leave. Not once did I think of how others might be affected by my leaving. Edna drove me to the bus station. She had also driven Mama to attend my graduation. Now, this goodbye was different. I had no idea when I would be back to visit. I was hurt to see the little ones in tears, and for the first time, I wished I had not decided to leave. I knew, in that moment, that I would miss them as much as they missed me, but my decision was made, and I was following through with it.

When I arrived at the Greyhound bus station, my bus was there, and I boarded immediately. It would be a long ride from North Carolina to Connecticut. As I boarded the bus, I felt doubt rising within me. I thought about my family and was so thankful for the parents with whom I had been blessed. I had two God-fearing parents who loved God enough to love me. They gave me the most valuable and precious gift possible—the love of God, loving parents, and knowing who I was and whose I was. I always felt valued and loved by my parents. I felt safe and protected. They were my safe place, and my home was my haven.

There was always joy and laughter in our home, as well as times when I was redirected to change my behavior and to act right. Sibling rivalry was there, but it was under control. I argued with my siblings, but it came with a price. There were lectures regarding disrespect and not following God's command. To seal the understanding of treating each other with love and respect, my parents always ended with a lecture and making me hug the person I'd argued with. Often, I thought it would have been easier to just get a whipping and be done! I know now why this was so important. As the bus pulled away from the station, I knew that our sibling bond would always be there. For the first time since Mama's death, I felt as if I was turning my back on my family and thought that I might be losing them forever.

Nothing was really clear, and my decisions were not sound, as I wasn't sure of anything at that time. I was on the bus with a trunk of my belongings and without any solid plans for my life. All I could do was think about what I had lost—first Daddy and now Mama. It just didn't seem fair, but I couldn't harp on that thought. Mama made it clear that someday she (like Daddy) would leave us, and we would have to move on. Well, I was doing just that—moving on to uncertainty and more confusion. I thought about leaving school without finishing that last semester of my senior year of college. Mama would have wanted me to finish. I told myself that I would finish once I was in Connecticut. I would continue with my career goals. I thought about the conversations Mama and I had over the years. I already missed her guidance and her encouraging words. She was the backbone of the family, and she certainly held us together after Daddy died.

As I passed by many towns and states, I remembered some sights I'd seen a year ago. After James was released from the army in 1976, I went to visit my oldest brother, Hulon, who also lived in Connecticut. I was able to visit James a couple of times while I was there.

The bus stopped in New York, and I had a short layover. Once I boarded my bus to New Haven, I was on my way, and although I didn't have to change buses, the bus made stops in nearby towns, and I was able to see parts of a state where I would reside. It was a totally different world. I wasn't sure if I would be able to settle down there. Again, I gave it little thought and, instead, focused on making a home, whether it was temporary or permanent. It was a new beginning.

After riding for hours, I had fallen asleep, but was I startled awake when the bus wheels squealed into the bus depot in New Haven. The driver called out over his intercom, "Last stop, New Haven, Connecticut." I sat up and wondered where James was.

- 14 -

A New Future; Perseverance and Hope

> Fear thou not; for I am with thee: be not dismayed; for I am thy God: I will strengthen thee; yea, I will help thee; yea, I will uphold thee with the right hand of my righteousness.
> —Isaiah 1:10 (KJV)

JAMES LIVED IN A THREE-BEDROOM TOWNHOUSE THAT HE shared with his friend and fraternity brother. I had no idea what I was moving into but was pleased that it was a decent, livable space. It was most certainly a bachelor pad, and I became instantly nervous upon learning that there was another person sharing the apartment with us—something I had not known when I made the decision to move. I stayed as close to James as possible because I didn't know his roommate. I would later learn that this roommate would treat me like his little sister, and the living conditions weren't as bad as I'd thought. James told me that we would move to our own place the following semester. He was still in school and wanted to get through that fall semester before moving. I was in agreement and was excited to learn that we would get our own place soon.

Here I was, living in sin and shame! Neither James nor I was working, and he was still in school. I decided to look for a job. I planned to wait until the following semester, starting in January 1978, to complete my senior year. I wasn't there long before I delayed my return to school. I went through classified ads, searching for a job—no luck. James's friends suggested that I apply for positions, but finding work wasn't that easy. I was still a student and needed something sooner rather than later. I had an associate's degree, but I found nothing that would land me a job where I could continue to work while in school. I decided that I would look for work as a certified nurse's aide. I had experience working as a nurse's aide, and it would provide an income. I applied at several nursing homes and hospitals but had no luck.

I was starting to miss home, my family, and my friends. When I called my family to report that I had arrived in Connecticut safely, they all reminded me that I still had a home in North Carolina. At the time, I didn't think so because Mama was no longer there. I have since realized that my family is my home. I missed them but thought that it was best to stay in Connecticut and start a new life there.

After several weeks in Connecticut, I began to feel really sick. I thought that it had to do with the change of climate. It was August, and the weather was cooler in Connecticut than it had been in North Carolina. I couldn't keep food down and was tired and sleepy most of the time. James took me to a doctor, and after several questions that I didn't want to answer and tests, he concluded that I was pregnant. This was not the news I expected to hear. I was numb and had no concrete feelings.

James didn't seem bothered by the news. He was surprisingly excited. He assured me that everything would be all right. I was inclined to believe almost anything at that point. The bottom line was that I was pregnant. I couldn't do anything but have the baby and hope for the best. The doctor advised James to take me to an ob-gyn for my prenatal care. We made that appointment immediately, and I was on my way to motherhood. After seeing that doctor the first time, we had a due date, and I was told that I could work if I wanted to. The baby seemed to be OK and was only a few weeks developed. I was still in the first trimester. So my job search continued.

About a week after my first prenatal checkup, I received a call from a nursing home, offering me a job. They had an opening for a nurse's aide and asked me to come in for an interview. James drove me to the interview, where they offered me the job and gave me a start date. I was happy to have found work, as we needed the income. I realized, the second I learned that I was pregnant, that I would not be able to go to school that next semester. James was receiving an income from his veterans' benefits, and the money I would make from the nursing home would help with bills and household expenses. We would need it, once James and I moved into our own place. For now, I could save and prepare for the baby and a new apartment.

I was living with a man who was not my husband. We were still planning to marry but had not taken that step yet. I was overcome with shame and embarrassment! Mama would be disappointed because I'd gone against her and Daddy's teaching. Even more important, I was not acting like the Christian they had raised me to be. They would both say that I was "shacking up" and would insist that I marry.

Getting married, however, was the last thing on my mind. I wanted to start working and to think about the type of mother I would be to my child. I bought a couple of uniforms for work and a few maternity clothes prior to starting my new job. James's mother was excited about the pregnancy, and his family hoped for a girl. They had mostly boys in his family, and at the time of my pregnancy, his parents had no granddaughters.

I was neither excited nor disappointed about having a baby. I was nervous, scared, and lonely for the person I needed most in my life during a time such as this. I needed Mama! I'd seen her become excited when my married sisters were expecting. She made sure we all understood the importance of having babies and said that God saw us as mothers or parents when taking care of his special gifts. She would always say that children were gifts from God, and they were to be "chastised," not whipped or harmed. She loved children and never was too tired to give any child her attention. Now, I was about to have her grandchild, and she wasn't here to enjoy this birth or be a part of it. I was sick with grief, thinking about having this child without Mama, but there was nothing I could do but have it. Although I knew that Mama would have been disappointed in my behavior and having a child out of wedlock, she would have rejoiced at the birth of another grandchild. I often thought, *What have I done?*

Although I felt sick, I had to go to work. I needed this job. James told me that I didn't have to go to work and that he would take care of me and the baby. He would make things work. I insisted on working, so he went along with me and took me to work. I notified my job of my pregnancy prior to my first day at work, and they told me that it was OK. I said that pregnancy would not stop me from doing my job. They understood and told me to let them know if I needed time off if I felt too sick to work or if there were complications. They were willing to work with me and would allow me to take an early leave, if it came to that.

My first day of work was orientation. I got to know the patients on my caseload and the staff I was assigned to work with. Learning the routines of the work was a two-day process. I was oriented to the schedules for basic care, such as baths, mealtimes, recreation, medications, visits, and the policies and procedures of the facility. It was an easy training period that was brief and to the point. I got acquainted with several coworkers and had lined up a carpooling situation to assist James with getting me back and forth to work. I felt as if I was well on my way to setting up house and becoming a mother to my unborn child. I couldn't help but think of all of those times I'd declared that I would never have children. Now, here I was, not only ready to have a child but actually looking forward to it.

On the third day of my job, I was on my own. James dropped me off, but I planned to ride back with a coworker. This was a relief that James wouldn't have to pick me up because I was working the second shift, from three o'clock until eleven at night. That workday started off well. I got my assignment and was confident as I started to visit my patients, alerting them that I would be their nurse's aide for the evening. I only had a couple of hours to prepare them for dinner. Mealtimes was one of my favorite times of the shift. It gave me a chance to greet each patient individually and assist them with eating. Some of them needed help, but others did not. Some of them asked if I had children. I always said no and never revealed that I was expecting one; I wasn't sharing my pregnancy with the patients at the time. I figured that I would wait until I began showing before I made them aware of it. It was good to be working and starting a new life in Connecticut.

I had worked for almost half of the shift when I started feeling cramps in my stomach. I didn't know what to expect but decided to ask the head nurse if I could step off the floor briefly, thinking that I would go to the bathroom to freshen up. As I went to the bathroom, I saw little spots of blood. I dismissed it because I'd been told that spotting was normal in pregnancy. I saw this as a good sign and went back to the floor to continue my work.

An hour later, I felt uncomfortable. I went to the bathroom and noticed that there was more blood. I was bleeding again, but this time it was worse. I called James immediately and told him that I was bleeding. He said he would be there as soon as he could. I then told the head nurse that I had to leave and I told her why. She had me sit down immediately and assigned my patients to my coworkers. I felt bad that they had to take on my caseload, and I apologized to them over and over. They assured me that it was OK and wished me well.

Getting to the Hospital

James arrived rather quickly; I was convinced that he'd been speeding. He rushed into the room where I was sitting and had me lean on him as he escorted me to the car. We were about thirty minutes from the hospital. He was careful not to go too fast, but he had to hurry because the bleeding was not decreasing. I was bleeding nonstop and the cramping was worsening. As we were driving, James kept me posted on how far away we were from the hospital. I wasn't yet familiar with the route to the hospital—or anywhere for that matter; I was still learning my way around.

We were about three blocks from the hospital when the car stopped running—it slowed down and then came to a complete stop. We didn't know why. There was gas in it. It was an old car, but it had been faithful to us up until this point. Now, it was dead, and we had to walk to the hospital.

It was a scary night. Again, James held me up as I leaned on him while we walked to the hospital. We had no cell phones at that time, and there was no pay phone nearby. It took us approximately twenty minutes to walk to the emergency room. It was difficult for me to walk, and I walked slowly.

When James told them what was happening, they put me on a stretcher immediately and wheeled me to the examining room. I was a nervous wreck. James was calm but very talkative; he asked many questions while entering the emergency room. The doctors examined me and said nothing during the examination, but I knew there was something wrong, based on their expressions toward each other. They communicated without words, and I was anxious to hear what was going on. I knew that it couldn't be good, so I waited silently for them to give us the results.

After they finished examining me, they called James into the room. The examining physician looked at us both and said, "I'm sorry, but you're not going to have this baby. Who examined you?"

"Doctor Madison examined me", I said, "he said everything looked okay.

He shook his head and said, "He should have told you that you have a high-risk pregnancy, and you should not have been working. You're not having this baby. I'm going to put you on two months of bed rest. You are to go home, lie down, and put your feet up when you can. Do not get up except to go to the bathroom. Someone will need to cook and bring your food. When you go to the bathroom, you will discharge tissue. This is an indicator that the baby is aborting. You are to take that tissue, wrap it, and bring it to us so that we can analyze the tissue."

He turned to James and said,

"get her home and have her lay down. She has to be on bed rest for two months."

James assured the doctor that he would do just that, and we left that examining room, knowing that we would need to get a ride home—walking would take at least half an hour, and I was feeling weak.

Once we were in the lobby, James made several phone calls to friends and family. No one was able to pick us up. Some of them appeared not to be home, as they did not answer the phone. Others told James that they couldn't pick us up for various reasons. In any case, we were in the same predicament as we were when trying to get to the hospital—except this time, we had a farther walk. We didn't have enough money to call a cab, so we had no choice but to walk. It was after midnight, and that may have been a blessing because there weren't too many people hanging out.

I felt weak and tired because I had lost a lot of blood. I'm certain that had the hospital known that we didn't have transportation, they might have kept me. They instructed me to stay off my feet, but we could do nothing but walk home. We made it home safe and sound, and, surprisingly, the bleeding was very light. It decreased through all of the stress I'd endured while walking. James held me up all the way home and reminded me that everything would be all right. I just wanted to lie down.

- 15 -

It's Me, It's Me, It's Me, Oh Lord

> And all things, whatsoever ye shall ask in prayer, believing, ye shall receive.
> —Matthew 21:22 (KJV)

THINKING ABOUT LOSING MY BABY WAS VERY HARD ON ME. Each time I made a trip to the bathroom, I would stop and look at my maternity clothes, realizing that I may never wear them, and I would start crying. I wanted to have this baby now more than ever. It was difficult to think that I had said, at one time, that I would never have children. Again, I felt ashamed, but this time it was because I had not wanted children, and now that I was pregnant, I was faced losing this child.

I felt trapped, as if I had nowhere to turn. Everything was being done for me. James was doing my laundry; his mother made trips over to the apartment on a daily basis to make sure I had enough food, and she checked on me while James was in school. She was very attentive to me and would tidy up the place when she could. We had the support of his mother and his roommate during this time, but I felt alone because I didn't have my family with me. Hulon was a truck driver at the time and couldn't stop by much. I cried a lot when I was alone; I didn't want anyone to know about my crying for fear that they would feel sorry for me. I was angry with myself and also upset because I couldn't ask Mama to forgive me. I had defied all that I was taught, and I thought that maybe I was paying the price for my wrongdoings.

At times when I cried, I would think, *Why should God give me a chance to be a mother?* I was not following his commandments, nor was I following the rules I was taught growing up. I felt guilty and ashamed for wanting to have this child when I wasn't married. I thought, *How can I celebrate something that is a sin against God?* I was having a different kind of pity party. I didn't think that I deserved God's forgiveness because of what I'd done. I had a dream during the time I was confined to the house for those two months. Mama appeared and scolded me for living with James, unmarried, and having a child. In the dream, she said, "Child, you ought to be ashamed of yourself." She had that expression on her face that she had when my behavior did not meet her expectations. Then she said, "But don't worry; everything is going to be all right."

As I continued to cry over my situation, I was suddenly reminded that God was *still* in control. I pulled myself together and started praying to God. Although I was not saved at that time, I'd seen how God had made a difference in Mama's life when she struggled with illnesses and uncontrollable situations. I asked for his forgiveness and asked him to please let my baby come into this world. I acknowledged that I hadn't been faithful in my walk with him. I realized that I had not walked with God at all. I was more focused on being obedient to my parents, to Mama. I couldn't call on Mama now, and somewhere in my spirit, I knew that I had to call on God. I asked over and over again to let my baby live. I remembered Mama saying to me that God is in control, and it is God who makes the decision if anyone lives or dies. The doctors had told me that my baby would not enter this world, but I'd seen miracles in my family firsthand.

The doctors had told Mama and Daddy that Mama would not live after she had her stroke. When she had surgery, they said she would not walk again and that she would not live more than five years after her stroke. Mama never gave up. She couldn't walk at first, and all of her hair was shaved for the surgery. It was her faith in the Lord that brought her through it all. She refused to wear a wig because she believed, in her heart and in her soul, that she would have hair again. She knew that she would walk again and did not allow the doctors' diagnosis to influence her will and efforts to get stronger. She knew this because she had faith. She walked with the braces on her legs until she was able to stand alone, and she was able to take them off and walk without them. She was back to where she was before she had that surgery.

Then there was the miracle of giving birth to my baby brother. When Mama was carrying him, she was told again that either she or my brother would not live through the birthing process. She was advised to allow them to abort the baby. Mama would not hear of it. They told her that it might reach a point of saving only her or the baby. Mama told the doctors to save the baby. I cried and thought that Mama might die in order to save the baby. I felt that Mama would leave us "just" to save the baby. Mama heard me crying, and she said,

"Doctors cannot decide who lives or dies. Only God knows that, and I'm not worried." She knew that God would protect them both, but she had to give the doctors an answer. She prayed and knew that God would protect them both. She was right. She went into labor, and she and my baby brother came through it.

Mama had the normal concerns that most women have after delivery, but she went home on time and had no complications after leaving the hospital. My brother was a healthy boy with no deformities or birth defects. God took care of them both, and the doctors' prediction was incorrect. Mama's strong faith in God got her through this.

I truly believed that God would spare my baby. Then I thought, *But I'm not the God-fearing woman that Mama was.* I continued to pray. I had never prayed as I did when I realized that God would certainly pull me and my baby through this. I'd only prayed in the past when I was blessing my food or saying my prayers before bedtime, and those were ritual prayers I prayed as a young girl. Now, it was my time to really talk to God. I didn't feel that my prayers were enough at the time and wondered how I could ask for anything. I didn't think that I was deserving of God's grace and mercy.

Here I was, in a situation that defied all that I'd been taught by my parents and the church! I was torn between wondering how I had gotten myself in such a situation and if I deserved God's mercy. Of course, I didn't! I quickly learned that praying is talking to God. There were times when I realized that God was (and is) the only one to whom I could truly talk and say how I felt. Although he already knew before I asked, I needed to have a conversation with God.

Calling on God was the only way out. I prayed daily, and as the time approached for my follow-up appointment, the bleeding had ceased. I stayed in bed for the duration of the two months. I had not seen any tissue that I was told would certainly discharge. I was not feeling any physical pain or discomfort, although my nerves were rattled. I was walking on eggshells as I continued to be on bed rest until my next appointment.

At the end of my first trimester, I was doing better but not quite out of the woods. I had to remain cautious, and I could not go back to work during this pregnancy. My job ended, and that made things all the more difficult. James was still in school, and we were making it at a bare minimum. His mother filled in the gaps for us and made sure there were groceries available. I was mindful of climbing stairs and being on my feet for long periods of time; I stayed in the bedroom. It was best that I stay upstairs in the apartment, and I did no cooking or cleaning during that time.

I was able to adjust to these requirements and by the end of the second trimester, I was up and about and doing things I'd been unable to do a month ago. Although I was more mobile than previously, I was still considered high risk, as having a miscarriage was not ruled out completely. I was also wearing my maternity clothes and was so thankful that I was finally showing. I looked pregnant and felt good about it. I wanted to experience all that happened during pregnancy.

The one thing I would not experience was having my mother with me to witness the birth of her grandchild. I remembered how happy she was when my nieces and nephews were born. I knew that she would be pleased to see my child enter this world. Not having her here was a reality that would not change. I was thankful for the experience I had with her, and I would tell my baby about the grandmother he or she would never know.

I would also be able to tell my baby about the movement inside of me, the new life inside of me, and the kicking I felt from time to time. I had heard so much about pregnancy—the pain of childbirth, the morning sickness, and the inability to walk at times. I heard all about the negative things that could happen with pregnancy.

I remember Mama telling me that I was breastfed, and because of that, I decided that I would nurse my child. I knew that I wanted to be a good mother, even though I didn't know how I would manage with the limited funds we had. I wanted to provide the love and nourishing home that my parents had given me. I believed and hoped that James would be the father who would complement what I wanted for our child. I was scared and nervous about being pregnant and becoming a mother. I questioned myself often, and being away from home and from my family didn't make it any easier.

Nonetheless, I was excited about feeling a life inside of me, a miracle from God inside of me, preparing to come out. An infant who God knew before it was conceived. I felt nothing but joy while carrying this child, and I believed that once it was born, the joy would multiply, and I would thank God as often as I could for his wondrous works. I was thankful for his miracles and blessings. Carrying this child was a major milestone in my life because I was able to witness the birth of another human being. I was so thankful for God and for his mercy and grace. All of the years that Mama and Daddy had talked about God, about knowing who I was, putting God first, and listening to God as well as talking to him, had met me head-on. For the first time in my life, I came to God, asking for help. I asked him to save my baby, and I hoped that my child would be with me for years. But only God could make this happen; only God knew for sure if my baby would live. I kept praying and found peace in prayer alone.

Out of the Woods

My third trimester was as close to normal as possible. As I awaited the birth of my child, I went to the doctor for follow-up exams and tests needed for prenatal care. I was informed that things appeared to be normal. I was growing, and I was happy about it because I knew that the larger my stomach became, the more my child was growing. I experienced all the signs I'd heard about and probably more.

I was sick of vomiting, especially when I ate things I really loved and regurgitated. I ate a large portion of a pizza in one sitting and often craved steak. James would run out to get pizza whenever I craved it, and he would often surprise me with a nice-sized steak. I was delighted to be the recipient of such delicacies. On one occasion, I had a strong urge for a pizza. James stopped what he was doing and went across town to get a pizza, just as I liked it, with everything. He ate a couple of slices and figured that he would have some later. Well, I finished the pizza, and shortly after he noticed that there was no more, I vomited, and it splattered all over the bedroom floor. I thought that James would be upset over the mess, but he simply said, "I'll clean this up." As he was cleaning, he remarked, "All of that pizza went to waste."

I was hungry shortly afterward, and, again, James satisfied my craving and obliged me with what I wanted to eat.

Months prior to my due date, we decided to move into our own apartment. I was out of the woods at this point but was reminded to take it easy. James and I successfully moved, and I was able to set up house as I preferred. This was truly our new beginning. We knew prior to moving that this apartment would be temporary because there was only one bedroom. We would need a second bedroom for the baby, but this would have to do for now. James was still in school, and I was focused on my pregnancy, hoping that everything would go well, but I thought about how things might have been, had I finished school.

It was in my plans to enroll in school as soon as I could after the baby was born. Little did I know that it wouldn't be that easy, especially with my family being so far away. It was early spring, and this would be my first home with James and our child. James was working part-time while going to school; I couldn't work due to my pregnancy. I did what I could to make our small apartment a home and fell completely into the role of wife and mother-to-be. It was a challenge, with many responsibilities and adjustments that frightened me when I thought about it. James was there with me, but I was emotionally and mentally alone. I stayed in touch with my family as much as I possibly could.

By April 1978, I was counting my days to delivery. The date was approaching quickly, and I was excited but nervous about the baby coming. We had not purchased any baby items, but we had plans to start doing that toward the end of April and early May. We had yet to figure out where the child would sleep. Although there were no concrete plans, I figured that we could always put a small dresser in our room. We would have to place the basinet in our room as well, temporarily.

I hadn't been in Connecticut for a long time, but I was beginning to get homesick. I missed my family, and as much as I wanted to go back to North Carolina to visit, I didn't want to use any funds that might compromise the debts we had to pay to keep things afloat. I was getting bigger, and it was more difficult to move around because of the strain the baby was putting on my back. I decided to focus on avoiding stress (as much as possible) and pray for a safe and healthy delivery.

We had been in our apartment a couple of months when Connecticut had a huge snowstorm. The amount of snow was significant, and people were urged to stay indoors. I had experienced the heavy snow in the short period I'd lived in Connecticut, but prior snowfalls were quickly removed, and life continued as normal. It was different this time. It was the most snow I had ever seen! James managed to leave the apartment to pick up some things we needed. He left with a friend of ours and ended up stuck across town. We both thought he would be able to get there and return before things worsened. That wasn't the case. He was not able to return to the apartment and had to stay until people were cleared to travel at any distance.

Messages flashed across the television screen, telling viewers that no one was allowed on the streets—walking or driving. In the meantime, I was home with a close friend. She stayed with me while her fiancé had gone with James to pick up the things we needed. The car was stuck, and there was no information regarding how long it would take before they could get help.

I was concerned about being there without James. The baby was due the next month, May 19, 1978, but I was concerned that it might come during the storm. Days had gone by, and there was no news regarding when James and his buddy would return. He kept in touch as much as he could to see how I was doing. We were able to watch news and were informed that the snow had stopped and removal would be underway as soon as possible. The snow was difficult to clean up, and soldiers from Fort Bragg were called to Connecticut to assist with the cleanup. I prayed often while James was away and asked the Lord to please allow my baby to reach full term before its birth. I didn't want the baby to come early, and I was so relieved when it didn't.

A couple of days later, James and his friend were able to return. It was a joyful moment, but the time I'd spent during that week reminded me of the need to see my family. I told James I wanted to go visit, and he said he would help me get there. Once the snow was cleared and the travel ban was lifted, I decided to visit my family in North Carolina. I had not gone home since I moved to Connecticut, and I was overdue for a visit. I missed my family, and after almost nine months, I realized that my family was *home*—both those in North Carolina and James in Connecticut.

A new level of excitement overtook me. I began to pack and could think of nothing except the familiar places I would see when I got back to North Carolina, the people I would visit, and the joy of having my family connected with me while I was pregnant. Mama wasn't there, but her friends, siblings (my aunts), and close neighbors who knew her and loved her would be available to see me. The thought of that comforted me because I knew how Mama loved her family and friends. I was ready to take that trip back, pregnant or not.

I had moved to Connecticut by bus and was convinced that I did not want to take the bus to North Carolina, especially in my condition. I was approved by my physician to travel; I was told that it would be OK. I was relieved to know that taking this trip would not put the safety of my child at risk. I would not have gone if I had been advised to stay home. Although I had never flown before and I was a little skeptical, I decided to fly because the bus ride would be too much. As nervous as I was, my need to be with my family outweighed my nervousness. I wasn't afraid and was looking forward to going home. I was thankful that the weather was clear, and travel was deemed safe by local governments.

I anxiously informed my siblings that I would be coming home. They had not seen me pregnant, but I wasn't concerned with what anyone might think. I owned the decisions I made, and

God saw fit to allow me to carry this baby after doctors assured me that I would not have it. I wasn't going to worry about it. I was OK at this point and, as he stated, "out of the woods."

I was beginning to see what Mama had tried to tell me for years—God is in control. I packed a few things to take along. I didn't need much clothing because I planned to return before my due date. The baby was due on May 19. I was certain that it would come on time, and I was ready. I had planned to return to Connecticut between the first and second week of May. That would give me enough time to visit everyone and spend some quality time with my relatives.

James drove me to the airport and encouraged me by telling me that I would be all right. He had flown several times and had much positive advice for me. I listened and told him that I would call when I arrived in North Carolina. After I checked in at the airport, I had a brief wait and then was able to board the plane. I was carefully attended to by the flight attendants. They briefed me on their responsibilities to assure me that I would have a safe and stress-free flight. That's just what I needed to hear. All I could think about were the what-ifs, and I would fill in the blanks with many negative statements. What if my water breaks and I deliver on the plane? What if the plane crashes and I never see my baby or family? What if, what if, what if? I suddenly snapped out of it and remembered that God was still in control. It was then that I decided to say a prayer before the plane took off to deliver me and my unborn child to North Carolina. I was at peace.

- 16 -

Familiar Faces and Familiar Places

A man's heart deviseth his way: but the Lord directeth his steps.
—Proverbs 16: 17 (KJV)

THE FLIGHT TO NORTH CAROLINA WAS PLEASANT, although I had a layover in Raleigh. As much as I wanted to get to my family, I had no complaints about the layover. The flight had proven to be much better than the bus ride. I still couldn't believe that I was flying; I always had a fear of flying and had vowed to myself that I would never fly. There was something about this pregnancy that gave me hope, a new direction, and insight toward life. I knew that I was already changed. I was no longer the person I was a year ago or even two years ago. I had new goals and had put my prior goals on hold. I was about to take on a role I'd had no intention of doing; I was going to be a mom. For the first time, my family would see me differently. It was frightening, challenging, exciting, and totally unknown.

I had convinced myself that I was having a boy. I decided that I wanted all boys and talked myself into believing that I would. Although I knew that I had no control over the gender of my child, I thought it would be nice to have a boy. I had also decided that my boy would have his father's name; he would be the third—James Wilton Blackmon the third. James suggested numerous times that we needed to choose some girl names. I didn't think it was necessary, but I went along with him and picked girl names. When

I went through the book of baby names, I didn't see any names that I really liked. I believed that a name must have meaning and must be taken seriously, which is why I wanted my boy to be "the third." He would be the third generation with the name James W. Blackmon.

James agreed with me about having a name with meaning. He was OK naming him James the third, if it should be a boy, but he asked, "What if it's a girl?"

"Its not going to be a girl, its going to be a boy", I said, "I can't think of any girl names, but you can"

Although I'd agreed to consider some girl names, I couldn't come up with any. My heart was set on boys only, so James provided possible girl names. I had reservations about some of the names he chose and refused each name he selected.

James then told me, "I have an idea. I will create a name for the baby, if it's a girl. I'll put our names together"—James and Linda—"and create a name for her. I'd like to name the baby *Jaminda* if it's a girl."

I liked that and agreed to the name Jaminda. I thought about this during the plane ride to North Carolina and then decided, *No, it won't be a girl*, and I continued to wait for the birth of my baby boy.

After about an hour layover, I boarded the plane again for Greensboro, North Carolina. I was carefully escorted to my seat on the plane before the other passengers boarded. It was such a treat to be perceived as special; I was certain that I was getting the royal treatment. This would be a special story to tell my child. For a moment, I thought about being back in Connecticut and delivering this child. I was so thankful that I could make the trip safely after that heavy snowfall and being shut in for several days. Before taking off, I remembered to thank God for watching over me and allowing me to reach my destination safely. The plane took off with a little turbulence, but I wasn't worried. I had a sense of relief when the plane leveled and quickly transported me to Greensboro.

After exiting the plane, I was escorted to a waiting area, ready to meet my family. As I walked toward the baggage area, I was met by my sister Renee, with open arms and a very welcoming smile. I immediately had a flashback to when I would return home, and Mama waited for me with open arms. It was so surreal, and the warmth that transcended from Mama to me was present at that time. I was truly home.

After the greeting, I was whisked to the nearest fast-food restaurant to get food before riding to Burlington. Renee had two children of her own and understood the importance of feeding a pregnant woman. That was a blessing because I was starving! The food at the airport was good but not nearly enough for a growing baby and mommy.

It was great to be home. Riding through the familiar places and seeing things I once loved was heartwarming. We made a few stops before going to Renee's house and paid a visit to Daisy and her mother. They said little, but it was apparent that seeing me pregnant was a surprise for Daisy's mother, Mrs. Geneva, who said, "Well, look at you! When is this happening?"

I reluctantly told her that I had at least a month before my due date, and I would be back in Connecticut in due time.

"Be careful," she told me. "Don't do anything to make it come earlier."

"I'll be careful," I told her, thankful that she didn't ask any more questions.

I realized that this was my time to cue my sister that I wanted to leave. I told her that I was tired from the trip and wanted to settle in. She drove me to her house, and we chatted on the way there. Renee was excited to have me stay with her while I was there. I planned to stay two weeks and was happy to be there with her and her two children. I missed them and still felt bad about leaving and not having much time with them. This would be a time to give them quality time and to make up for all that I'd missed over the months. We reached her house, and I quickly settled in, unpacked, and tried to figure out how I would make the best of my time while I was there.

A Warm Welcome

It was great being back. I looked forward to visiting old friends and picking up where I'd left off, but in very little time, I learned that it was difficult to do. Many of my friends were preparing to graduate from college and moving on to new lives. They were meeting their career goals and living up to their senior superlatives. It would be a while before I returned to school, but I was content with my situation. I was surrounded by my family and friends. After I finished unpacking and got a little rest, I was whisked off to meet with my other siblings. I moved slowly and with every intention of being careful so I wouldn't do anything that would cause an early delivery. I used this time to consult with my sisters who were mothers and could answer questions about childbirth.

I asked the usual questions—will it hurt? How long will it take to deliver the baby? Will I get stitches? How long before I can wear my normal clothing after the birth? I was told that having a baby hurt less than a toothache. At that time, I had not had a toothache and could not make that comparison. I was told that the baby had his or her own mind and would enter this world when he or she was ready. Time varies, and I would have to wait for months before I could fit into my normal clothing. Listening to the possible things that could happen made me anxious. I was OK because I knew that I would be back in Connecticut in time for my child to be delivered.

I dived into a routine for the two weeks I planned to be there. I spent time with my siblings and was so glad to see my nieces and nephews again. In the short time I had been away, they had grown so much and had not forgotten their auntie. I spent time with them as much as I possibly could. My time was limited during the day because they were in school. I spent my days catching up with Daisy. She filled me in on old classmates and where they were at this time. She was preparing for her college graduation and was excited that she was finishing her four-year program and receiving her bachelor of science degree. She was on her way to fulfilling her dream and starting a career in teaching. I was happy for her and honored when she agreed to be the godmother of my child.

Daisy was nonjudgmental, although she knew that my situation was completely the opposite of what I'd been taught. We both had been taught the same thing, and because of our upbringing, we took it upon ourselves to focus on nothing but pursuing our careers and reaching our academic goals. She was supportive and assured me that she would be there for me, and we would stay in touch. Daisy was home for the weekend and promised me that she would check in on me while I was in town. She planned to see me again before going back to Connecticut. It was a good reunion for both of us; we were able to catch up, share stories, and laugh about the good times we had prior to my leaving.

I made my rounds, visiting relatives when I could. It was difficult for me because I did not have my own transportation and had to wait for someone to drive me to see everyone. My sisters were working but drove me as much as they could. Everyone was excited that I was home; many of these relatives had not seen me prior to my leaving. I hadn't said goodbye or told them where I was going. I was just gone!

I wasn't planning to offer explanations for why I'd left. It was irrelevant at this point and simply no one's business. They could see that I was pregnant, but they never remarked about it. I wasn't seeking approval; I expected ridicule, gossip, and a few "shame on you," but didn't get any of it—at least not directly. It was good to see everyone; they appeared to have changed to some degree.

I spent most of the time in North Carolina resting, and that soon became boring. Although it was a vacation for me, everyone else was working and saw me when they were free. My sister got me out of the house and took me with her to work on a couple of days. Soon, I felt useful, but my activities were at a minimum. I was so big that I found it difficult to move around. My back was bothering me, and I felt uncomfortable most of the time. I stayed in touch with James as much as I possibly could and updated him on my condition without communicating the physical discomfort I was having. I was sick, and the discomfort was short-lived. I didn't think it was necessary to report.

Shortly after I arrived, I was talking to a relative about baby names and shared the names on which James and I had agreed. Although we had decided on Jaminda, we had not decided on a middle name. We were stuck on names that would go well with Jaminda. I figured that I would come up with a middle name for her, but again, it would have to be meaningful. I decided to resort to the baby-names book but still was not successful in finding a middle name. I thought of names of some of my elderly relatives but none of those names sounded right. I couldn't come up with anything, but I still had time to think of a middle name. I would wait until I returned to have James help me with this.

The following week, Daisy came home from school to visit with me. I was feeling down by then and was glad to see her again. I went with her to the laundromat. As we waited for the clothes to complete the rinse cycle, she and I caught up. I shared my experience of living in Connecticut and made comparisons between North Carolina and Connecticut. I was adjusting to the culture there but missed North Carolina.

We were reminiscing about old times and trying to figure out which classmates were in town, when I suddenly interrupted her, saying, "I think my water has broken. I'm not sure, but think I should go to the nearest hospital."

Daisy had brought one of her brothers with us to the

laundromat and asked him to watch the clothes while she drove me to the hospital. It wasn't time for this child to be born, and I was nervous because all of my prenatal care had taken place in Connecticut. I was early and concerned about delivering this baby with different doctors, who had no medical records for me and knew nothing about the bleeding I'd experienced in the first trimester of my pregnancy.

As Daisy carefully drove to the hospital, she said inspiring words all the way there. She told me that everything was going to be all right and not to worry. She was always a calm person, and I appreciated her more now than ever to maintain a calm demeanor as she transported me.

It was April 24, 1978, and my baby was due on May 19. I was afraid but prayed on my way there that my child would be all right and free of medical issues. It was now a matter of time. My baby was on the way.

- 17 -

A Life Forever Changed

> A woman when she is in travail hath sorrow, because
> her hour is come: but as soon as she is delivered of
> the child. She remembereth no more the anguish
> for joy that a man is born into the world.
> —John 16:21 (KJV)

I DIDN'T HAVE TIME TO NOTIFY MY FAMILY THAT I WAS ON MY way to the hospital. At that time, we didn't have cell phones, and I did not take the time to make a call on a pay phone to my siblings or James. My priority was getting to the hospital. I arrived at the hospital around 12:15 in the afternoon and was greeted by unfamiliar faces.

I thought, *I wish my doctors were with me during this time.* Daisy parked in front of the emergency room and ran through the doors. She was followed back to the car by a nurse and a wheelchair. As the nurse rolled me into the emergency department, she asked my name, date of birth, when was my baby expected, and how I was feeling. I wasn't feeling any pain at that time. I calmly answered her questions.

We were greeted by other hospital personnel as they took me into the examining room and had me lie down. After examining me, they took me to a delivery room and told me that the doctor was on his way to deliver my baby. They were very attentive and continued to check on me to see how far I had dilated. They told me that the baby was definitely on its way and assured me that I would be OK.

Here I was, a pregnant woman they had never seen, but they treated me as if I had been a long-term patient. I have always appreciated the kindness from the medical team assigned to attend to me on that day. The staff at Alamance County Hospital in Burlington made me feel safe, and I truly believed that my baby and I would be OK.

It seemed like an hour had gone by before the doctor came in, but it was only about fifteen minutes after I was registered and prepared for delivery. The doctor entered the room, introduced himself, and told me that the baby would be here soon. He said that test results were in, and everything looked good. He checked me to see if the baby had moved down and told me to get ready for delivery. He didn't seem concerned that the baby was coming early.

All I could think about was how I would manage the early birth of my child while I was visiting in North Carolina. My visit quickly changed from a visit to parenting on my own. I was instantly a single parent, and I began to wonder if I was ready for this. I thought about how I would travel back to Connecticut with the baby.

Suddenly, I began to feel pain and was informed that I was having contractions. I had not taken Lamaze classes and did not know what to expect during the delivery. The nurses coached me as I went through the process of childbirth. There was a huge mirror over my bed, and the doctor asked if I wanted the mirror adjusted so that I could see the baby's birth. I didn't want to watch because the pain was unbearable, and I didn't think that I could focus on the mirror while I was in pain.

In between pushing and breathing, my baby exited my body and entered this world. I felt so many emotions at that time—I was frightened, anxious, happy, excited, and nervous, and I thought, *My baby and I got through this.*

I heard the baby cry, and the doctor informed me that I had a healthy baby girl, five pounds and one ounce, sixteen inches long. Her time of birth was 1:25 p.m. The kicking around inside of me was over, and now I would be able to hold my little girl and feel her move around in my arms. I was exhausted but wanted to tell my family as soon as I could that Jaminda was here. The nurses wrapped her up and laid her on my chest so that I could hold her. She was snuggly wrapped in a pink blanket and was wearing a little pink cap on her head to keep her warm.

I looked at her and realized that this little human being actually had grown inside of me; it was a miracle. At the beginning of my pregnancy, I'd been told that she wouldn't make it. I thought about how I'd prayed, and God answered my prayers, although I didn't deserve it. I was not saved, but I believed in miracles because I had witnessed them through my mother. Now, I was a mother—something I had declared that I would never be.

That birthing process was more than I could have ever imagined. I knew in that moment that things would change. I felt as if I had changed and was looking forward to growing as a mother.

Once back in my room, I completed the birth certificate and officially named her Jaminda. I still had not taken the time to select a middle name. Family was important to me, so I decided that I would honor my sister Renee by giving Jaminda her middle name, which was Faye. After completing the birth certificate for Jaminda Faye, I was told that I would be in the hospital for a few days. They wanted to make sure that I was comfortable when nursing her.

I had chosen not to use formula because I wanted to nurse her with my milk as my mother had done for me. I didn't like the idea of being in the hospital for six days, but I didn't complain because I was so thankful that little Jaminda was healthy. I called my family and informed them of Jaminda's birth. I assured them that we were both OK. They couldn't believe that I had given birth in such a short time. Soon, they were in the hospital, visiting; they couldn't wait to see their niece. I informed James and his mother of Jaminda's birth, and they both hoped that I would return soon.

After three days, I felt that I was ready to leave, but the doctors did not agree. I learned how to breastfeed her, and, in my opinion, I was pretty good at changing diapers and burping her. I was doing well and had learned a lot about taking care of her from the nurses who visited my room daily. Nurses would check in on me between rounds. On one occasion, the nurse brought Jaminda to my room.

She said, "Ms. Brown, Jaminda is the only baby in the nursery and we have been playing music for her. Don't be surprised if she grows up loving music."

"Music is a part of our household", I explained, "She will love music."

I appreciated the attention they gave her. When I held her and talked to her, she watched and listened as if she was familiar with the interaction.

On my fifth day in the hospital, I was told that I could go home. Jaminda was nursing well, and I was comfortable feeding her. Then I was told that I needed to wait six weeks before returning to Connecticut. The doctor wanted to check me and the baby to make sure that we were ready for travel. This was not the news I'd expected, but I understood why it had to be. I gave my sister the news, and she was excited that I would be around longer so that she could help me with the baby.

Leaving the hospital was exactly what I wanted. I did not know the depth of my situation until I went home with Renee. I was a mother; I actually had a child and was responsible for her well-being! I was changing diapers, bathing her, changing her clothes, and wondering how I would survive this new role. I wondered how Mama did it with eight children and I knew that I would not have eight children. Regardless of the pain and adjustments I was going through, I still wanted to have at least two more. Looking at my little sparkling-eyed baby girl was a reminder that it was worth it. I just needed to be more prepared if it happened again.

As I thought about my role, I also thought about James not being able to experience Jaminda's first moments, hours, days, or weeks. I wanted the six weeks to pass as quickly as possible so that we could head back to Connecticut.

I was tired, but I adapted to my new role and loved it. Jaminda was eating well and squirming when lying down, as if she was trying to move about in just a couple of weeks. I was feeling great and was back in my normal clothes. This was a good sign that we would make our trip home as planned.

Returning to Connecticut

The six-week stay in North Carolina was actually two months before I was given clearance to return to Connecticut. I was excited for James to see his daughter for the first time and for his parents to see their first and only granddaughter. I had an extra bag with me to bring the new clothes and baby items I'd received from my family. Saying goodbye was difficult again; it reminded me of separating from my family the year before.

I decided to take the bus back, although it would take longer. I would have a short transfer in Bridgeport and avoid waiting in New York. James was aware of our return schedule and was looking forward to meeting Jaminda.

As I was planning to return, I did not factor in how I would change Jaminda's diapers on the bus ride. The bus ride was very uncomfortable, and it didn't take long before I realized that I had to change Jaminda's diaper in the bathroom of the bus or on my lap. It was an all-day trip; we left in the morning and arrived in the late evening, but James was at the station, waiting to pick us up. Upon our arrival at the apartment, James played with Jaminda for a while, and then we were all off to sleep.

The next day, I learned that James had found a church to attend while I was away. We all began attending the church as a family. It was good to be back in church again, and it felt like the right thing to do as a parent. I had been in church all of my childhood. Daddy drove us there every Sunday and made sure that we behaved properly. I couldn't help but think how I would be as a parent with my own child in church. I hoped that it would be like it was when I was growing up. I used to love dressing up in my patent leather shoes and wear the pretty dresses Mama made for me.

I remembered the church associations we attended, where everyone would bring food. Daddy would open the trunk of the car once we arrived and display all of the delicious food Mama had prepared for the associations. Everyone would share what they brought with each other. It was like a big family reunion. I hoped that I would be able to provide my child with that experience.

We attended that church routinely. I was really into God's Word and evaluating my life. After attending the church for a few weeks, I knew that my life had to change. I thought about it but did nothing about it. Then one Sunday in July 1978, I got saved while in church. I felt free for the first time; it was like all of my burdens were lifted, and the weight of what I'd gone through was lifted from my shoulders. To this day, it was the most fulfilling feeling I've ever had.

I accepted Christ as my Savior, and for the first time, I understood what Mama was preaching to me all those years. I knew that Christ died for my sin, and I was not deserving of it. I realized that I had not experienced anything on earth compared to what he had gone through. I knew that I had to change how I lived because I was now a new creature, saved by grace. I was reborn and a child of God.

I had always been God's creation, but now I was his child. I

felt honored and privileged but still undeserving. I thanked God for saving a wretch like me and for saving my child and protecting her when the doctors told me that she would not live. I thanked God for hearing my prayers, despite the way I was living. I now possessed that "little light," and I was going to let it shine!

I was going to make a change and live for God. I remembered that Mama had required me to memorize the Twenty-Third Psalm:

> The Lord is my Shephard; I shall not want. He maketh me to lie down in green pastures: he leadeth me beside the still waters. He restoreth my soul: he leadeth me in the paths of righteousness for his name's sake. Yea, though I walk through the shadow of death, I will fear no evil: for thou art with me; thy rod and thy staff they comfort me. Thou preparest a table before me in the presence of mine enemies: thou anointest my head with oil; my cup runneth over. Surely goodness and mercy shall follow me all the days of my life: and I will dwell in the house of the Lord forever. (KJV)

Yes, God protected me when I didn't know that I needed protecting.

My first step to living by God's Word was to stop fornicating. I was still living with James and wasn't married. I had no desire to continue living that way, but I was anxious to find a place to live. I wasn't working and had no money of my own to secure a place for me to live. I sought the assistance of the pastor of the church I was attending. He introduced me to the church "mother," Mother Whitworth.

The first time I met her, I could feel the warmth and love radiating from her. She embraced me on the spot and told me to come live with her, get myself together, and stay there until I got on my feet. She welcomed Jaminda and me into her home with open arms and invited James to come visit whenever he wanted. She believed that we should continue to be available for Jaminda. She told me that God had sent me to her. She was living alone and could use the company.

I was grateful to God for sending her to me, and I was thankful that fornication had become a thing of the past for me. I vowed that I would live upright and not practice marital behavior until I was married. I made this clear to James, and he seemed to understand; at least, that's what he told me.

I was able to find a part-time job to make ends meet for Jaminda and me. I made enough to pay rent to Mother Whitworth. She never pressured me but talked to me constantly about God and some of the mistakes she'd made in her younger years. She often coached me about parenting and allowing James to be a major part of Jaminda's life. She babysat for me while I worked and treated me like family. She encouraged me when I needed it, corrected me lovingly when I needed it, and helped me with Jaminda when I returned home after a hard day's work.

She also made sure that James felt welcome to visit his daughter. James and I were not really dating at the time. I was focused on God, work, and Jaminda. I was beginning to feel the impact of being a single working mother. It was tiring, but I enjoyed coming home to my daughter each day. She was growing and starting to eat solid food. She had a fun-loving personality, and she was a playful child who knew what she wanted. I talked to her often and sang to her. The hospital staff had been right—Jaminda loved music. She wasn't speaking words, but she made sounds to the music and sang in her own language.

Although James and I were not intimate once I moved out, we did begin to see each other again, but most of our time together involved talking and spending time with Jaminda. James would keep her overnight at times to get to know her. We grew closer, but it was a different closeness. God was now included in our relationship, and there was no turning back to old ways. We no longer behaved like a married couple because we were not married.

I learned how to pray and talk to God about my life and my situations. I was a baby in Christ, and I needed and wanted to grow. Growing continued with God—there will never be a time when I've finished learning or have reached a place where I no longer need God. It's ongoing and forever.

I wanted to live by God's Word, and when I fell, I knew God would pick me up so that I didn't falter or continue to fall. I was ready to move forward and make a home for my daughter and me.

Several months had passed, and James had spent a lot of time with Jaminda and me. On one occasion, when I returned from work, James was at the house, waiting for me. I couldn't understand why because I had given him specific hours to visit with Jaminda—hours while I was at work. Mother Whitworth had invited him to stay until I got home. Mother Whitworth was a very wise woman with a strong faith in God. On that occasion, James proposed to me, and I accepted. We were married in November that year, and we set up house with our daughter.

James had gotten a larger apartment where Jaminda would have her own room. He bought a new crib for her and surprised me by setting up her bedroom so it was ready for her. He had completed her room after I accepted his proposal. I was pleasantly surprised, and Jaminda enjoyed her room. James had positioned her bed so that she could see him when he passed by her door. He would blow kisses at her, and it didn't take much time for her to learn to blow them back at him.

It was a new life for all of us. James and I, for the first time, would parent together, and Jaminda would have her parents under the same roof.

- 18 -

Obstacles and Disappointments

> These things I have spoken unto you, that in me ye
> might have peace. In the world ye shall have tribulation:
> but be of good cheer; I have overcome the world.
> —John 16:33 (KJV)

MY LIFE WAS NEW TO ME AND FOR ME. JAMES ASKED that I not work the first year but stay home with Jaminda. The idea sounded ideal at first, but as time went by, I realized that I wanted and needed to work. We were making ends meet but not as well as I would have liked. I was nervous about putting her into a day care. Mama had been a stay-at-home mom and took care of us while Daddy worked. I admired her, respected her, and honored her for such dedication, but I couldn't do it. I wanted a career, and I wanted to be a mom at the same time.

After several months went by, we decided to put Jaminda in day care. Although I had reservations over separating from my child, I was at peace in sending her to the day care, which was owned and operated by family. I was relieved and felt that she would be cared for. They were excited that she would be a part of their day care family, and by the time Jaminda attended the center, she was familiar with her relatives.

I settled into married life with ease and was thankful that I had the experience I had growing up in a household where my parents demonstrated respect and love for each other. I only hoped that I could be the mother my mama was to me and that Jaminda would have the father/daughter relationship with her dad as I had with Daddy. I was content having a family of my own and looked forward to the years ahead.

I was able to find another temporary job and contributed to maintaining our household. My new roles as a wife and mother were tiring after a day's work. Mama made motherhood look easy. My becoming a mother made me respect her even more. She never complained about having too much to do and was always excited to have us home when school closed. Daddy always appeared excited to see us when he returned home from work. This was my prayer—to have that everlasting excitement of having my child around me. As tired as I was, I was always looked forward to picking up Jaminda from day care, especially when she was trying to talk. My wonderful days of motherhood were just beginning.

Jaminda was a sweet, inquisitive child who loved to explore. She was eating solid food early, and she quickly identified her favorite snack as apples. She loved apples and managed to bite them with the few teeth she had. I enjoyed watching her eat them.

She tried to walk by holding on to any piece of furniture she could reach. She never crawled forward but always backward; amazingly, she learned to walk her own way. She held on to the furniture until she was able to let go and walk. She wasn't quite a year old when she was walking independently.

She was indeed a blessing, and I thanked God for her every day. I knew that things would get better, and I trusted God to give me what I needed—I only asked for what I needed. I knew that I wanted to finish school, but I wasn't concerned about school at that time. I wanted to provide a safe and secure home for my daughter and knew that it involved my doing my part to reach that goal. I was grateful that I knew God because I had less doubt of my abilities. I knew what God could do. I had to work on my patience, be still, and know that God was and is in control.

Linda Aurelia B. Blackmon

Increasing Our Family

After Jaminda's first birthday, James and I discussed having a second child. We decided that we would have a second child when Jaminda reached the age of three. We would have a third child when the second child reached the age of three, having each of our children three years apart. This was an exciting plan, as we hoped that our financial situation would have improved by then, and we would be ready to move on. I was ready and couldn't wait to execute this plan. Watching Jaminda grow and develop during those three years was rewarding. She already loved books and could have a reasonable conversation. I felt confident that she was ready for a sibling.

By the time she turned three, James and I had started new jobs. We were hoping that at any time, I would be pregnant with a second child. It wasn't that easy! I was getting frustrated because nothing was happening. My friends were having babies; some were having a second child, and I couldn't help but wonder why I wasn't. I became even more frustrated when one of my friends went into labor, and during the delivery, they found out that they were blessed with twins. I was happy for her but again wondered why I wasn't having another one. It was heartbreaking, and I wondered, *What could I have done wrong*? Was I being punished for something I did but forgot about? Could it be because I had never wanted children?

I quickly reminded myself to stop feeling sorry for myself and remembered that God doesn't work that way. I was forgiven the moment I received salvation. I thought, *It's best that I just wait and see what God has in store for me*. I prayed and talked to some friends about what I was feeling. Prior to my pregnancy with Jaminda, I talked often about wanting all boys. I was so thankful for the little girl God blessed me with, and I vowed that it didn't matter whether I had a boy or a girl; I just wanted the baby to be healthy. I prayed and prayed that God would allow me to have a second and third child, if that was his will. If it was not his will, I would be hurt, but I would still rejoice, knowing that he gave me one.

By the time Jaminda was five years old, I had enrolled in school and was working on my bachelor of science degree. I would finally complete what I had started years ago. I became pregnant at this time as well. I was ecstatic and immediately started to envision what that child would be like. I thought about how Jaminda would react, knowing that she had a sibling on the way. We had never discussed with her about having another child. We felt that it was best to wait before we told her about the pregnancy—she might not have understood, and quite frankly, I wasn't up to explaining to her what it all meant. So we waited. I shared the news with a few of my very close friends and family. We were all excited, and the excitement increased as weeks went by.

I was still in my first trimester when I went for a checkup and learned that I had miscarried. This was devastating, and I immediately shifted from a happy mode to tears. My doctor informed me that I would need a D&C procedure. I didn't want to have it, thinking that there was still hope. She explained that they would clean out the uterus to remove the contents of the pregnancy to avoid infection. She assured me that it would not be painful, but I would experience some discomfort.

At the time, I thought that it couldn't feel any worse than the emotional pain I was feeling. I didn't understand why I was going through this, but I was determined to persevere and leave it up to God. I thought about my pregnancy with Jaminda; that pregnancy had beaten all odds, and I had delivered a small but healthy baby.

I knew about miracles. I saw it with my mother, and I witnessed it in my own life. I knew that God would not put on me anything that I could not bear. It strengthened me to keep trying and trust that God would get me through it. I was told to wait a couple of months before trying again, so we waited.

After a year, I became pregnant again, and I had another

miscarriage. I kept praying and asking God to send me a second child, if that was his will. I asked him tell me if I should stop trying, and I would. At this point, only two close friends knew about my pregnancies. I told them that I was praying to God and asked if they would pray for me as well. I had to be led by God to stop trying for a baby before I gave up.

Jaminda was now seven years old, and I still was not pregnant. I made appointments to see if I could actually become pregnant again. I met with several doctors at different locations, and they assured me that I could *not* get pregnant. I'd given birth and had two miscarriages, yet they were telling me that I couldn't get pregnant. I went through several tests at Yale New Haven Hospital. This had become a project for me. They gave me a dye test to see if my fallopian tubes were functioning properly. I took several tests and repeated tests. After my final appointment, they confirmed that I could not have any more kids. I refused to believe them. Deep in my spirit, in my soul, I knew that I could have more kids. I needed someone to tell me why I could not have kids, but I wasn't getting any answers.

When Jaminda was eight years old, she began developing as a young girl—physically, emotionally, and cognitively. She was very articulate and could express herself very well. She had attended a friend's birthday party, and when I picked her up from the party, she began crying in the car. I thought something had happened at the party and was prepared to call the parent and ask questions. Jaminda was crying, however, because while she was at the party, she noticed a lot of the kids there had siblings. She was crying because she wanted a sister.

I assured her that her father and I wanted another child, and we were hoping that someday we would have one. I told her that she would have to wait and see because it was a decision that God would make for us. She was OK with that answer and hoped that it would happen. We didn't share any information with Jaminda about the miscarriages and would not share any medical issues of that nature with her.

I continued to pray and ask God if I could have another child. I wasn't comfortable with the diagnosis that I could no longer have children. It didn't sit well with my spirit, and I had little faith in human perspective but much faith in God. He had not shown me that I would not have more children. I had faith in God and God alone, and I knew what miracles he could perform. My daughter was a miracle, as was my mother, after doctors told her that she wouldn't live long after her stroke. God is omnipotent; all power is in his hand.

I prayed and I prayed. Two to three months after I was told that I couldn't have children, I was pregnant again, Like before, I was excited. It was evident that I *could* get pregnant. I didn't know what the outcome would be, but I was prepared for whatever would come. I hoped and I prayed that this third time, I would carry this child full term, but that wasn't the case. This was my third miscarriage. We had not told anyone about this pregnancy, and although it was hard, it was easier because no one else knew. James and I decided that we would not share any news regarding pregnancy until we were out of the first trimester. I was glad to have kept this news to ourselves.

After that, I still was not ready to throw in the towel and walk away from the miracle that I felt was coming. I had to keep the faith because only God knew what was going on. He had all the answers, and no one could reveal those answers until God allowed it.

Jaminda was nine years old when I became pregnant a fourth time. I was out of the first trimester with this pregnancy, and I thought that this would be the one; I was going to have this baby. I went to the doctor after I entered my second trimester to get my routine prenatal checkup. After my doctor examined me, she told me that she had some bad news. She gently told me that the baby I was carrying was no longer alive. I refused to believe her. She said that they would need to clean my uterus to avoid infections. I told her no! I wasn't ready to remove the fetus at that point. A part of me believed that it wasn't true, and I didn't think that I could bear a fourth miscarriage.

I decided to get a second opinion and chose to no longer use that doctor for my prenatal care. It was too much for me at that point, and I didn't want to waver because I knew that God was in control. I didn't trust that diagnosis, so I parted with that doctor—with the fetus still inside of me. I couldn't let go.

- 19 -

Let Go and Let God

Know ye that the Lord he is God: it is he that hath made us, and not we ourselves; we are his people, and the sheep of his pasture.
—Psalm 100:3

I WAS AN EMOTIONAL AND PHYSICAL WRECK. I WAS HURT AND confused and didn't want to part with the baby inside of me. The few people with whom we shared the information were concerned about me because I refused to have a D&C. I couldn't do it! I was not going to risk anyone taking that baby from my body until I had some answers. I went to work as if nothing had happened. I informed my administrator that I might have to take some time off for another procedure for a miscarriage.

I felt I had to tell him something to avoid the risk of losing my job. I had secured a good state job that provided me with excellent benefits. James and I informed our family of what was going on, but we chose not to tell too many people. We had not shared the pregnancy with close friends, other than a few very close friends of mine.

It was a depressing time for me. I appeared to be functioning well because I wouldn't believe that it was true. To me, it was another misdiagnosis, and I needed a second opinion, although I wasn't doing anything to get that second opinion. I was just waiting but wasn't sure of what I was waiting for. I thought that I'd been misdiagnosed, and the baby would be born. As I was waiting for answers. A friend advised me to get the D&C.

"Linda, you need to get this done", she said. You can cause medical complications for yourself. Let it go and get the D&C. Keeping the baby inside of you can be fatal."

others told me to let it go and to get the D&C because keeping a baby inside of me could be fatal.

I said, "When God tells me to give up, I'll give up. He hasn't told me to quit, so I won't." Then I said "I will think about it."

The tone in my remark was rude, and I had to apologize for my behavior. I really wasn't myself, but I didn't want to give up my baby. Thinking about losing the baby would have made things worse for me. I didn't know if I could continue to keep up a brave face and convince myself that there was no problem.

Without my knowing it, James was searching for a place for me to get a checkup and a second opinion. He didn't tell me he was doing it; that was a wise decision because I wouldn't have heard him and probably would have lashed out at him, thinking that he had given up. A few days had passed since I received the news, and James had talked to people he worked with regarding my situation. At the time, he was working in a hospital and shared with me what had happened. His coworkers directed him to a place that might be able to help.

James came home from work and told me, "I know of a place that will be able to help you with your situation"—meaning that they would check me to see if the fetus was alive, and they would find the problem that was keeping me from carrying the baby to full term. The way he explained it to me was convincing and believable. I was ready to give it a try. James made an appointment within the week with the health center that was recommended.

The following day at work, I planned to inform my administrator that I would need some time off. Before I did so, however, he came to my assigned unit and told me that he had researched and found a place for me to go get help. Apparently, he wasn't convinced that I was OK and did what he could to help.

"I know of a health center with expertise in this field and they may be able to help you," he said. "Contact them and take the time you need to find solutions for your condition."

I thanked him and told him that James had acquired the same information and that I had an appointment. I told him the date of my appointment, and he told me to take it off. I would take the following day off to visit the health center. A day off was granted before I asked for it, and I was so relieved. I knew God was looking out for me, and this was my blessed assurance. Things started to feel right again.

Finding Answers

The health center was over an hour's drive from our house. I was tired and still felt pregnant, although there was no movement inside of me. My body was just tired from the stress of not knowing what was going on with me. I needed answers. James was calm and thought positively. He kept saying things would be all right, and I believed that as well. I knew, deep within my being, that things would be all right, regardless of the outcome. I just wanted the outcome to be favorable for me, but God was in control, and he made no mistakes.

I had never gone to this health center before and had no idea what to expect. I figured that it couldn't be any worse than what I'd gone through already. I decided to be prepared, regardless of the outcome. I truly believed in my heart that I would have another child. I could feel God's presence in all of this.

We entered the building, and James did most of the talking; he made the appointment. I was drained from anticipating what might happen and didn't have the strength for conversation. After he explained why we were there, they took us to the office of the attending physician. He talked to us and decided to check me to see where I was with the pregnancy.

"The doctor told me that the baby wasn't alive," I said.

"I'll examine you and do an ultrasound of the baby as well," he said.

I went through a complete examination and finished it with an ultrasound. The doctor asked that we wait in his office while he reviewed the test. We waited there for several minutes. I hoped that he would bring good news. I didn't want to hear that my baby was dead inside of me. I prayed silently in my head and asked God to give me the strength to be open to whatever news he delivered. At that point I wanted peace. I wanted to be accepting of whatever came, and I wanted to be a whole mom for Jaminda. I felt that I had slacked in some areas of my parenting throughout all of this, and she didn't deserve that.

The doctor came into the room and said, "Mrs. Blackmon, we have to abort the babies because they are not alive."

My heart sank. He'd said *babies*. I'd had no idea there was more than one. I asked him, "What babies? How many are there?

"You had twins. One of them aborted, but there is still evidence that there were two."

I felt sick knowing that I was pregnant with twins. I thought about the beauty of having two babies at once, and that would have completed my goal of having three children. I sat there in shock, not knowing what to say. It felt as if I was there but wasn't really.

Then he said, "The babies are not alive, and you can't keep them in there. It could cause an unhealthy situation. You could get an infection that could possibly get into your bloodstream."

I interpreted that as a fatal situation, and I couldn't do that to Jaminda. I agreed to proceed with the D&C. They did the procedure there and told me that they would figure out why I was having miscarriages. They made another appointment for me to come up to their office and start that process. I felt that there was hope that someone would come to a conclusion and provide me with answers about my miscarriages. I went home feeling relieved.

The following week, we went back, and they put me on a schedule to determine the best time for me to get pregnant. They felt that it would be best, from that point on, to communicate by phone so that I would not be stressed by the long ride to their office while participating in the process. They were trying to determine why I was not carrying the pregnancy to full term. They instructed me to call them daily and report my temperature. With that information, they would be able to tell me the best time to conceive. They instructed us not to get pregnant in the meantime.

I never gave up hope that I would have another child, but now I was really convinced that Jaminda would have a sibling. I had instructions and a better understanding regarding my situation. I was excited and nervous at the same time. I had to stay focused on God. I had to be still and listen to him and know that he was still with me. So that's what I did.

A couple of weeks after this process started, we received news of a death in the family. We had to go to North Carolina to visit with my family. We arrived after the funeral but were able to spend two weeks there before returning home. Once we were home, I called the health center and reported my temperature. I had followed through with the process while in North Carolina and continued once we returned.

They made another appointment with us for the following week—another follow-up appointment and consult. They examined me, and afterward, they told me that I was pregnant and had been for thirteen days. My immediate response was to cry because they had told us to avoid getting pregnant. Neither the doctor nor James could console me; I cried uncontrollably.

The doctor said to me, "I thought this was what you wanted."

"It is what I wanted", I said, "but I don't want to lose another baby."

He looked at me and said, "You're not going to lose this one. We found the reason why it keeps happening." Your condition can be treated with an antibiotic. You have a condition where any time you catch a cold during pregnancy, the cold virus settles in the sac where the baby was growing. This would then cause the baby to abort, and you miscarry.

"There may have been times when you caught a cold, but it didn't affect you—meaning that you didn't know you had a cold—but it affected the baby. It had to be there when you were carrying your first child, but somehow, she got through it."

Then he said to me, "You don't need us anymore. I've written a letter explaining your condition, and I've recommended a high-risk specialist to attend to you. You can choose another one near you, if you like, or see the one we're referring."

He gave me the letter and a number to call to request a high-risk specialist in my area.

I couldn't believe that I actually had reassurance that I would have this baby. I decided to see a high-risk specialist in my area to avoid long rides for appointments. I called the number as soon as I got home and made an appointment. I also thanked God!

-20-

And Baby Makes Four

> And this is the confidence that we have in him, that, if we ask any thing according to his will, he heareth us.
> —1 John 5:14 (KJV)

WE BEGAN TELLING ANYONE WHO WOULD LISTEN THAT we were having a second child. We told Jaminda during the first trimester. I genuinely felt like it was going to happen. I was overwhelmed with excitement, and Jaminda was happy to learn that she would have a sibling. She was hoping for a sister, but it was too early to know.

I would do things differently with this pregnancy. It was recommended that James and I take Lamaze classes, and we agreed without hesitation. This was never offered when Jaminda was born ten years ago, so I thought it would be interesting. Although I was not a first-time mom, we thought the Lamaze classes would be helpful. I was so grateful that my odds were better this time.

I was successful in finding a doctor close to where I lived to attend to my pregnancy and was very pleased with the doctor who was referred to me. On the first visit, Dr. Patterson read the letter from the health center and assured me that he was familiar with my condition and that everything was going to be fine. He prescribed an antibiotic for my condition, and—amazingly—that was all I needed to carry this baby full term.

The baby's due date was November 12, 1988. I thought, *It'll* be here before Thanksgiving, another reason to give thanks to God. I gave thanks to God daily as I carried this child. It would just be another topic during the meal to thank God for our new arrival.

Jaminda wanted to start selecting names for the baby, so I told her that she could make suggestions. We had decided that if it was a boy, his name would be James the third, but we would need to think of some girl names. I wanted to name her Jamie Lynn, but Jaminda suggested that I give her my mother's middle name and name her Jamie Elizabeth.

I wanted Jaminda to be involved to validate her position as a big sister. I liked that name and told James that was what I wanted to name her. He didn't seem too pleased with it at first, but I figured that I had enough time to persuade him. We had months to think about it. We both had been through a lot with the pregnancies and the miscarriages, but I felt that I should be able to name her and that he would come around. It was just a matter of time.

I was excited to share the news with my colleagues and the administration. I informed them as soon as I could, so that they were aware, in the event that I needed to take some time off. I was hoping that would not be the case, but I needed to plan ahead. Some colleagues assured me that they would fill in for me if there was a problem with scheduling.

Mozelle, had always been there for me when I needed time off. I couldn't wait to tell her.

"Mozelle," I said, "I'm pregnant again and this time I'm going to give birth!"

"You're kidding me", she said, "You know that if you need time off, I'll work your shifts for you. Just let me know!"

Everything was going well. I could really rest easy knowing that I had back up when I wanted to take time off.

I wanted to make Jaminda a part of this process. I knew it would be easy because she was such a loving and considerate child. She always thought about others and never demonstrated selfishness. She was happy to share her thoughts and wanted to know what she should call the baby until we found out if it was a girl or boy. I let her decide.

"Well, mom", she said, "the baby's first name has to begin with a J and since we don't know if it's a boy or girl, can we call the baby *Jaye*?"

So, Jaminda decided that we would call the baby *Jaye*. I agreed and that's what we decided to call the baby until he or she was born.

Jaminda would talk to the baby daily before it was born. She would read the baby bedtime stories and sing to her sibling. She became really excited when she felt the baby kicking, and I shared that excitement.

Dr. Patterson assured me that I could continue to work, so I decided that I would work as long as I possibly could. I was an emotional wreck during this pregnancy; my hormones were scattered, and I couldn't get comfortable. It was an extremely hot summer that year, and there were times when I dreaded facing my moods.

James was very patient with me, considering my behavior. I was miserable but still grateful because I knew it would be worth it. God had given me another child, so there was no room for complaining. I had to get through it, and I knew I would. I just didn't know what I would do to get there.

My appetite was uncontrollable, and it bothered me to walk. My back hurt all the time. The people I worked with had concerns about working alongside me because I was working with at-risk children. They were afraid that I would go into labor on the job. One of my coworkers said that he was afraid to work with me because I might get hurt and cause problems for the baby. I worked in an environment where kids would become physically aggressive and, at times, combative. Other coworkers were very cautious, and if they anticipated that a child would give me problems, they would intervene for me. I knew that I was fine doing my job as expected, but I wasn't going to stop them from being protective.

After a while, the kids I worked with began to be protective as well. Everyone was cautious because I was so big during this time. Other than an occasional backache, I was fine, and I was not concerned about anything going wrong.

During my eight month, my doctor pulled me out of work. He was concerned because I'd been accidently pushed by one of the kids on my job. Two girls had a physical altercation, and as I walked past them, one of them fell against me, and I fell against the wall. At the time, I thought my water had broken, and my administrator insisted that I call my doctor. Dr. Patterson was in surgery when I called, but he directed me to go to the hospital where he was performing the surgery. He had me admitted there so that he would be nearby if the baby came early.

Soon after I was admitted, Dr. Patterson examined me and said that my water had not broken, but I was having some contractions. He had me stay there for four hours. He then told me, "I'm giving you a doctor's note and taking you out of work until the baby is born."

It was the second week in October, and the baby was due on November 12. I didn't want to be out of work that long, but I knew that it was best for the baby. James had rushed to the hospital, thinking that the baby was coming. We were both relieved that the baby was not born that day, and I was discharged from the hospital.

Now, I was home alone during the day. Jaminda was in school, and James was at work during part of the day. He was working second shift at the time, so once he went to work, I sat at home, waiting for Jaminda to get home from school. Although I was not able to work, I was glad to still be able to pick her up from school. It was always a pleasure to see her and catch up on what her school day was like. No matter how well her day went, she was always excited to come home and talk to little "Jaye" and read stories.

Jaminda was already a wonderful big sister, and I knew that she would be a great helper once Jaye arrived.

I spent a lot of time thinking about the blessing I was receiving. I had carried this child without any complications, and I was so thankful that God allowed me to carry this child. I had remained steadfast in believing that God would get me through my trials. I consistently prayed for a normal delivery, and I took nothing for granted. I often wondered what I had done to be so blessed. God was with me throughout this process, and none of it happened because of anything I had done. It was all God!

The results of an ultrasound earlier revealed that we were having a girl. I thought how Mama would feel, knowing that her granddaughter would carry her middle name. I felt so proud and so accomplished, and I had no one to thank but God. He was and is my all in all.

To God Be the Glory!

It had been a little over a week since I was placed on maternity leave. My friends and colleagues had given me a baby shower. I collected many gifts, and a friend passed down her baby's crib to me for Jaye. My home was beginning to look as if a baby lived there. Jaminda moved into a larger room so that Jaye could have the smaller one.

The daughter of a very close friend was pregnant at the same time. She went into labor on October 22, and my friend asked me to babysit her other granddaughter because she had to go to the hospital. Of course, that was perfect. Jaminda could help with the four-year-old granddaughter. I didn't anticipate any problems. James was at work.

Her granddaughter, Nadine, was preoccupied with Jaminda as I watched TV. All was going well until later that evening. It was a little after eight o'clock when my water broke. This was not expected! I had to get to my friend, who was in the delivery room with her daughter. I thought, *How can I call her?* I called the hospital, identified myself, and informed the nurse who answered the phone that I was pregnant and needed to get in touch with my friend Cathy. "Please go into the delivery room, and tell Cathy that my water broke. I need someone to pick up her granddaughter and my daughter because my water broke!"

I had called my doctor prior to calling the hospital, and he told me to get to the hospital. Cathy came to the phone and couldn't believe what I was saying. She said she would send her son-in-law over to pick up the girls. He apparently had fainted during the birth of his baby, and he welcomed the break to babysit the girls.

James and I had a backup plan for transporting me to the hospital—his friend Jack—in the event that the baby came while he was at work. I called Jack and his wife to tell them that I needed to get to the hospital.

I heard her yelling, "Jack, you have to go get Linda now and take her to the hospital!"

As I heard him scurrying in the background, Toni, said, "Don't worry Linda, he's on his way. He will be there soon." As she was hanging up the phone, I heard her yell out to him, "hurry up!" As soon as I hung up, I called James. He was on his way too and would be there soon. I didn't think that he would make it as soon as he thought. He worked about forty minutes away. I waited for my ride to the hospital but had not packed a bag to bring with me. I figured that James could bring the bag before I left the hospital.

Jack arrived shortly. He was a funny guy, always telling jokes and making me laugh. He carefully assisted me down the stairwell of my apartment and walked me to the car. He had spread out and layered huge black garbage bags across the back seat. I couldn't help but laugh when I saw that and hoped that I wouldn't slide from one end of the seat to the other. It was such an experience, sitting on those bags, drenched with discharge and praying that I'd get there before Jaye decided to come. At the time, I wasn't feeling any contractions and wasn't in any pain. I was just thankful

A Way That's Mighty Sweet

that things had gone as planned. We arrived at the hospital in a matter of minutes. I had survived the slippery ride, thanks to the seat belts.

While I was getting checked in, James rushed into the hospital. He had sped all the way there, and I was again thankful that he had not gotten into an accident. He did get a speeding ticket, but he said he would deal with that after the birth of his daughter. He got there in time to go with me into the delivery room. Jack accompanied us to provide moral support for James. I was glad Jack was there for James.

I was wheeled to a delivery room and prepped for delivery; it was a waiting game from that point on. Dr. Patterson was there, and as we waited while I was in position to deliver, James and the doctor discussed the football game that was on. I was not happy with them talking about sports because I was getting closer to delivering our child. I also wondered how Jaminda was doing. James called Cathy's house to check on her, and he learned that Cathy's daughter had had a girl around eleven thirty that night. James would pick Jaminda up the following morning.

We now proceeded with the delivery, and James and Dr. Patterson turned off the TV.

The delivery was going well until the doctor noticed on the heart monitor that the baby's heart rate didn't appear normal. He assured me that there wasn't a problem with her heart because he had monitored her heart throughout the pregnancy, and there weren't any issues. He proposed that the umbilical cord was either around her neck, or she was squeezing it. He asked me to stop pushing so that he could check.

Jaye was not squeezing it; it was around her neck. When I stopped pushing, James was amazed at how the doctor was able to remove the cord from around her neck as quickly as he did and without injury. After giving a couple of good pushes, she came and without any oxygen loss. At 2:03 in the morning on October 23, 1988, the baby was born. The ultrasound was correct; it was a girl! I heard her cry, and the doctor laid her on my chest. Oh, what a glorious moment. My little blessing had entered this world weighting seven pounds, fourteen ounces at nineteen inches long. She was a healthy baby girl.

Once back in my room, James still wasn't sure about the name I had chosen. I was convinced that her name would be Jamie Elizabeth. Nonetheless, I delayed naming her officially until the next day. I was just relieved that she was here. I now had two beautiful daughters, two blessings. Before James returned the next morning, a nurse brought Jamie into the room to spend some time with me. As she handed her to me, she said, "Here's little Jamie Elizabeth." I was shocked and asked her to repeat what she had just said, and she repeated it. She told me that before James had left yesterday, he had informed the nurses that we were planning to name her Jamie Elizabeth, and we would sign the birth certificate when he returned. I was so pleased that he had not given it as much thought as he could have. I was holding my little Jaime, and soon her name would be official.

James returned shortly after the nurse brought Jamie into the room. I told him about my conversation with the nurse. He said that he had no problem with naming her Jamie Elizabeth, but he wanted to spell her name differently from the traditional J-a-m-i-e. He would spell it J-a-i-m-e. We were in agreement with the spelling of her name; I liked his spelling much better than the traditional way. So my second baby girl was named Jaime Elizabeth.

After spending a few hours with me that morning, James went home to give Jaminda the news about the birth of her little sister and to bring her in to see Jaime. I anticipated that Jaminda would feel a little left out after being the only child for ten years, but I planned to include her in everything so that she wasn't. When Jaminda came to visit Jaime, she seemed very excited and remarked over and over about how cute Jaime was. She wanted us to come home soon.

I was relieved the moment Jaime was born and couldn't wait

to get home. We were now a family of four, and my children were healthy and well. I was ready to be a mother of two.

- 21 -

I Won't Complain

> For every thing give thanks: for this is the will
> of God in Christ Jesus concerning you.
> —1 Thessalonians 5:18 (KJV)

JAIME WAS A SNUGGLER AS AN INFANT AND ALWAYS WANTED to stay close to me. She would rub her little head into my neck as if it was her way of hugging. She was very responsive and loved being around her sister. She was a joyous addition to the family, and I was again so thankful to have that little girl. Jaminda was a blessing to her sister and to us. She did whatever she could, within her capability, to help out. She never complained about being left out or not being able to have what she needed because of Jaime. Instead, she reveled in knowing that she finally had the little sister she always had wanted. That was reassuring, as we had taught Jaminda to express herself freely and respectfully with us. She could always tell us if something was bothering her, and she had done so on many occasions.

In Jaminda's mind, that was the end of having siblings. She got what she wanted, and she was content. But it wasn't that simple for James and me. We originally had wanted three children—well, I wanted three children; James wanted more. I also wanted all boys when I was planning. I was delighted to have the girls and made it a point to include in my prayers that the gender of my children didn't matter; I just wanted three.

Now that I had two, there were times when I thought that I shouldn't ask for that third child. God had answered my prayers and allowed me to have two. Maybe I shouldn't ask for another one. That thought was short-lived! Not only did I ask for another one, but I planned to have that third child as soon as I could. I thought that it was OK if they were a year apart instead of three years, as we had originally planned. James and I had decided that we should not wait to have the third child. My doctor had assured me that I was OK, and I shouldn't have any problems having a third child. Our minds were made up, and the process of conceiving a third child was in place. It could be any gender, and that would be OK.

As time went by, I was able to put Jaime in day care. Jaminda continued to be the proud big sister, and James enjoyed his girls. My health was good at the time, and my doctor did not foresee any complications with my carrying the baby to full term and delivering a healthy baby. He did warn me that because both of my babies were born early, there was the possibility that a third child also could come early. We were OK with that. We informed family and friends that we were trying to have one more. We were so thankful for the two we had, but a third child would complete our family.

Our lives continued as normal. Jaime enjoyed going to day care, as I was back at work full time. Jaminda was in school participating in her extra curriculum activities and nothing was interrupted. It worked out well. We worked opposite schedules so that one of us would be home with the children to avoid babysitters, and we also didn't want to make Jaminda responsible for Jaime. She was only ten and not ready to take on the responsibility of babysitting her younger sibling.

Jaime (like Jaminda) talked early. She tried to have conversations and responded when anyone talked to her. At the time of her birth, I was not attending church as much as I wanted to. I worked weekends and attended church when I could. I knew that church and knowing God was pertinent, and I had to bring God into my children's lives. I sang songs about God and talked to them about God so that they would know of him. I missed going to church and was concerned that my children were not in church enough. I remained prayerful and taught them how to say their prayers. I prayed that I would be released from weekend work.

When Jaime was about a year old, I thought that I was pregnant. I was nauseated—I had morning sickness and felt sick most of the time. I couldn't wait to make an appointment with my doctor. My hopes were high, as I thought that I would be a third-time mom soon. I told a few close friends that I thought that I might be pregnant.

Dr. Patterson, however, told me that I was not pregnant. Tests indicated that I actually had a hormone imbalance, and that was corrected with an injection. I was disappointed, but I couldn't complain. I had too much to be thankful for. I decided that I would continue to try. I knew that if it was God's will, it would happen, and I believed that with all my heart. I was again thankful that there was no major problem prohibiting me from conceiving. It was simply up to God because he was in control and had never left me. I was OK.

Jaime was now a little over a year old, walking and talking. She was into everything, as she was inquisitive and very observant. When people saw her, they would always say, "That baby is growing so fast! She's getting out of the way for another baby." I'd heard that saying before, but hearing it at that time was a sign to me that I was going to have that third baby. I just didn't know when because my plan was not working.

When Jaime was about sixteen months old, I started to feel ill again. I was feeling the same way I'd felt when I had the hormone imbalance. I didn't think I was pregnant; I thought that I would need another hormone injection. I dreaded calling the doctor but to overcome my sickness, I had no choice. I needed to see what was wrong. So I made the appointment.

Test Results

I went to the appointment and went through what had become a ritual for me—blood work, urine samples, palpations, and answering numerous questions. I felt sick, but I knew that it was another hormone issue. I sat in the doctor's office after the examination and waited for him to return with the results.

Dr. Patterson entered the room and seemed very serious. "It is not a hormone issue like before," he said, "but it is a hormone issue."

What now? I thought.

He said, "You're pregnant," and he congratulated me. I was stunned!

Then he said, "Your baby's due date is December 25 or the twenty-sixth. You're going to have a Christmas baby."

I was elated, and I talked to God all the way home, saying that I couldn't believe he was allowing me to have a third child. I thanked him over and over again. I couldn't wait to tell Jaminda and James. Jaime was too young to understand, but she would be there when I told Jaminda and James. I couldn't wait to call up my friends and family to share the news.

When I returned home, I shared the news with James and Jaminda. James was excited, and he and I both agreed that we didn't care about the gender. We would be thankful for a healthy baby and a healthy delivery. We were so blessed to have the opportunity to have a third child. I told Jaminda we were having another baby and that she would know the gender as soon as we heard. Jaminda did not seem as excited as she had when I was pregnant with Jaime; she said very little when I told her about the pregnancy. I thought that she might react differently when she learned the baby's gender.

Now we were planning for a third child. In the meantime, we set up an extra bed in Jaime's room for the baby. It was important that Jaminda's room was not disrupted. My baby would arrive in December, if I was able to carry to full term. I was looking forward to a Christmas baby—another gift and blessing from God. I knew then that if it didn't come as scheduled, I wouldn't complain because God was in control.

- 22 -

Concerning Issues

> For I the Lord thy God will hold thy right hand,
> saying unto thee, Fear not; I will help thee.
> —Isaiah 41:13

THIS PREGNANCY WAS DIFFERENT FROM MY PREGNANCY with Jaime. My prayer was that I would not become as emotional. My prenatal checkups were going well, other than my weight gain. I had gained quite a bit of weight with Jaime, but I was packing it on much faster now and at an earlier stage. During the first trimester, I gained more than Dr. Patterson felt was normal weight gain. He recommended that I change my diet and cut back on sweets and unhealthy foods and snacks. I realized that I had not eaten like this during my other pregnancies. I tried my best to avoid eating sweets and unhealthy snacks and overeating. I was concerned but not enough to modify my diet, as recommended by my doctor. Those cravings were strong, and I was weak!

Everyone was feeding me, especially at work. Everyone brought me snacks and "special treats," all of which I should have avoided. It was extremely difficult to say no, and it was so satisfying to consume the treats. I thought it would be rude to say no when people were trying to help. My morning sickness was not as bad as it had been with my second pregnancy. I had developed a love for lemons that helped me with the accumulation of salvia throughout the day. I had this condition with Jaime, but it was worse with this pregnancy. I couldn't stop eating lemons. Not only was I eating the lemon inside the peel, but I was eating the entire lemon, peel and all. I began to worry about eating lemons, but I'd been told during the last pregnancy that it wouldn't hurt the baby, and it was OK if I continued to eat them. So, I did!

I had reached my second trimester and had not encountered any complications. My blood work was normal, but I was still gaining too much weight. The doctor told me that I was getting too big, and my weight could cause complications with delivery. That connected with my will power! I didn't want to jeopardize the health of this child and decided that I would cut back on my portions and my sweets. Sweets always were my weakness, but I had to attend to the baby's health as well as my own. I would have sweets once a week, rather than daily. I gave up coffee for all of my pregnancies but struggled to give up anything else—but I did.

Jaime was not quite two years old during this pregnancy and wasn't asking questions; she would just rest her little head on my stomach when I held her, as if it was a pillow. On the other hand, Jaminda did what she did when I was pregnant with Jaime—she would feel my stomach and wait for the baby to kick. She would also place Jaime's hand on my stomach and let her feel the kick. She told Jaime that there was a baby inside.

Throughout my pregnancy, I did everything I could to keep things as normal for Jaminda and Jaime as I possibly could. We continued to let them go to the park, Jaminda still visited her friends, and we took them both to amusement parks and traveled with them. I quickly learned that being pregnant with one child was less complicated than having two children while pregnant. The age gap between Jaminda and Jaime was a benefit because Jaminda could run around with Jaime while I watched.

As I reached the end of my second trimester, I decided that I would find out the gender of the baby. James couldn't attend this appointment with me, although he'd come to all the others. I told him that I would not tell anyone—including him—the gender when I found out. But of course, I wasn't able to keep it to myself once I found out. After the ultrasound and my usual physical examination, I was informed that I was having a boy. I could clearly see his little body on the monitor!

I was excited that I was having a boy. During the early weeks of my pregnancy with this child, I heard so many comments about it being a boy or girl. A friend told me that I was having another girl because I had two already. I had no reason to believe this and just said, "I'll have to wait and see."

Now it was confirmed that I was having a boy. We had already decided that if it was a boy, his name would be James Wilton Blackmon III. We had not thought of any girl names for this pregnancy, for whatever reason. So, little James was on his way. I was ready to buy some blue clothes.

I tried as hard as I could not to reveal the gender of our child to James. That was a complete flop!

"Is it a girl or a boy?', he asked.

I responded, "I don't know." The minute I told him that I didn't know the gender of the baby, he said, "You don't lie well."

So I told him. We were excited to know that we had a son on the way.

When Jaminda returned from school that day, I told her that she had a baby brother coming, and his name would be James. I was looking for some excitement, but what I got was tears and a sad twelve-year-old. It wasn't until that moment that I learned that she thought she was getting another sister. As she cried, face full of tears, she said,

"I didn't ask for a brother." I want another sister; I don't want a brother!"

"Jaminda", I said, "We don't always have things the way we want them. You did not get a sister because you wanted a sister. You have a sister because God decided that you would have a sister.

Now, God has decided that we will have a son, and you will have a brother."

I reminded her that she had no say regarding getting a brother or sister, but we wanted her to know that she had a baby brother coming, and she would still be his big sister.

I was glad to know how she felt, and she was able to move on without any further disappointment. She continued to feel him kicking and moving around in my stomach, and each time, she would call Jaime over to feel it as well. She sang to him and called him by name. It was pleasant to watch; she had such an angelic voice at such a young age, and it was evident that singing was something she would love for years to come. She never complained again about having a brother.

Complications

I was feeling really good about things going as well as they were. I had limited the number of sweets I was eating, but I continued to enjoy them. I visited the doctor's office often and had more blood work done. He was monitoring more closely because I was approaching my due date. Everyone at work was looking out for me; even the cook, Marie, enjoyed making some of her favorite recipes for me. She would make them at home and bring me a dessert occasionally. She made the best Mud Pie, which consisted of cake mixed with rich, dark chocolate pudding and crumbled cookies, topped with whipped cream. It was my favorite recipe, and it wasn't overly sweet.

I was sitting at the desk when Marie entered the office.

"How are you doing?" she asked.

"I'm a little tired. I'm taking my break."

"I have something that I know will cheer you up."

That's when she handed me the bowl of Mud Pie that was hidden behind her back.

A Way That's Mighty Sweet

"Enjoy. It won't be long now before your son is born."

"Thanks Marie", I said, "You just made my day!"

It was early October; I had a little over two months before my due date. I couldn't wait to dive into that Mud Pie; it was the perfect way to take my break. I settled back in my chair in the quiet of the office and prepared to eat that dessert. The spoon was almost in my mouth when I heard my name paged over the speaker. I panicked, thinking that something must have happened at home. It was a rule at my house that in the event of an emergency, I should be paged rather than called at the office. It was easier to reach me with a page, and we could avoid delays getting me to the phone.

I put the spoon down, thinking, *I'll have that bite when I'm off the phone*. I picked up the phone and said,

"Hello, this is Linda. How may I help you?"

"Linda, this is Joan, Dr. Patterson's nurse. He asked me to call you and let you know that he needs to see you tomorrow morning at eleven o'clock. He also asked me to tell you that you are not to eat any sweets until you see him."

I was perplexed and at a loss for words for a few seconds. "Why", I asked.

"Well", Joan said, "he said he will talk to you tomorrow. You are not to eat anything sweet until you meet with him."

I immediately called the supervisor and made him aware of the phone call. I would need the following day off, and he would need to look for someone to cover for me. To ensure that I had the day off, I called a colleague and made her aware of my circumstances. I asked if she would take my shift if the supervisor could not find someone to fill in. She called the supervisor to say that she would fill in if he couldn't get anybody to work the shift.

I called James and made him aware of the phone call, and he decided to go with me to the meeting. I sadly looked at that Mud Pie and wished that I had taken that one bite before answering the phone, but now it was too late. I gave it to a coworker, who was more than willing to take it off my hands.

I was beginning to worry about the conversation that I was going to have with Dr. Patterson. I was feeling good, other than getting tired easily. I thought it must be my weight; maybe that's why I was so tired. I had not gotten on the scale, and although I thought about it, I decided to wait until I saw the doctor.

I was able to complete my day at work without complications and was very anxious to leave and go home. It was difficult to focus on work when I was wondering if my baby was OK. I picked Jaime up from day care, and Jaminda was home from school when I got there. Once I was home, it was evident that it would be a long night. James was working that evening, and I had to make dinner. As Jaminda, Jaime, and I sat down to eat dinner, Jaminda filled me in on her school day, and Jaime nodded when I asked her about playing at the day care and having fun. Her conversation was limited, but she communicated nonetheless. That was one restless night, but I knew that I would have answers soon.

The next morning, Jaminda did her daily routine to prepare for school—she got dressed, had her breakfast, and headed to the school bus stop. Later, I got Jaime ready for day care, dropped her off, returned home, and prepared for my visit to the doctor's office. I decided that I wouldn't worry because the stress from worrying wasn't good for the baby or me. I prayed about it and left it in the hands of the Lord. There was nothing I could do, and I knew that if it was really bad, I would have been in the hospital by now. I let go of my anxiety and decided to wait until I heard the news instead of jumping to conclusions. James came downstairs and told me that he was ready to go.

Dr. Patterson's office was a ten-minute drive from our house, but it seemed as if we had driven an hour by the time we arrived. After checking in, the nurse said Dr. Patterson would see us in his office. He was waiting for us. I was getting nervous again and didn't want to hear any bad news about the condition of my baby.

Dr. Patterson stood up when we entered and asked that we sit. He then closed the door. I sat there quietly, waiting for him to start the conversation, but James wasn't waiting.

"Is there something wrong with the baby?" James asked.

Dr. Patterson assured him that there wasn't anything wrong.

"But there is a complication that can be corrected," he told me, "if you follow instructions. I have the results of the blood work, and it came back positive for diabetes. You have gestational diabetes; it's caused by the pregnancy."

I had never had diabetes, and I was concerned that I had been diagnosed with it now.

"I believe that the baby is pressing down on your pancreas and is affecting the production of insulin," Dr. Patterson said. "You will have to change your diet, stop eating sweets, and lose weight. If you do that, everything should be OK, and the diabetes will go away once the baby is born."

He placed me on a low-fat, high–complex-carbohydrate diet. He then said, "If you don't follow the plan, you will have to inject yourself with insulin daily."

That got my attention! I couldn't see myself sticking a needle into my leg on a daily basis. I knew that it would be difficult for me to do that, so I had to follow those instructions.

I didn't know anything about complex-carbohydrate diets, so I called a family friend, who was a diabetic, to assist me with a diet plan. She told me that avoiding sweets was a must and that I should avoid bread as much as I could. She gave me a list of items that would help. My diet would consist of fruit, grains, vegetables, yogurt, fish, and healthy foods. I made up my mind that I would follow through with the plan. I now understood why I was tired and dragging most of the time. My weight was affecting my sleep, and I didn't feel well most of the time overall. I wasn't worried about losing my son because God had shown me that I didn't need to worry. I now understood that it was the diabetes, and I could control it. I did not want to be in a position where I needed insulin, especially during my pregnancy. Unlike before, I was not told that I would not have this child; I was told that I could actually do something about my condition.

As I was getting closer to my due date, I figured that it was time to go shopping for little James. I had not done any baby shopping because I wanted to wait to learn the gender, and I had delayed it because I was so tired. Now that I had my diet under control, I was feeling better and ready to shop until I dropped.

It was the beginning of November 1990, and there was much campaigning for local and state government officials. I had not missed an election day in any category and was looking forward to casting my vote. I involved Jaminda when I went to vote to familiarize her with the voting process. Although Jaime wasn't ready to absorb the concept of voting, I took her with me. It was a busy time out, but because of my healthier eating, I had more energy; I wasn't as tired. I was able to purchase much-needed items for little James, thanks to the generosity of friends' and family's gift cards. I placed the items in James's room, hoping to organize everything later.

The following week was work as usual. On November 5, 1990, my day at work seemed longer than most. I was moving a little slower than before and thought that I might have overdone it on that shopping excursion.

I picked up Jaime at day care. She was two years old and had become quite talkative. She was learning how to count and somehow was adding numbers on her little hands as we drove home. Jaminda arrived home from school shortly after we got home. She eagerly shared her day at school. It was routine to share a daily summary of our days—her school day and my work day. I only shared the positive aspects of my day.

I decided that I would decorate James's room and let my girls help with it. Jaminda, again, was a big help; she assigned little deeds for Jaime to help out. She gave Jaime small items to hold for her, and when she needed them, she would ask Jaime to pass them to her. Then she would praise Jaime for being a great helper, and Jaime would giggle uncontrollably.

We completed the room decorations to welcome James home, although he would not be there for another month. I planned to get my Christmas shopping finished early because James's due date was on Christmas Day or the day after. I shared with Jaminda how we might put the tree up the day after Thanksgiving so that everything would be ready for James. We usually decorated the tree the week before Christmas at the latest, but this year it would be different. This created much excitement for Jaminda, and it was something else to look forward to. Our work was done for the day. After taking a break from such a long day, I prepared dinner.

I was exhausted and thought that I might have overdone it with the decorating before preparing dinner. I could have picked up something for dinner, but I did not like feeding my children fast food unless I absolutely had no choice. Now that dinner was over, Jaminda was doing her homework, and James had Jaime with him while I finished in the kitchen. I had no aches or pain and was really glad that I was taking the following day off to vote early; I was going to bring Jaminda and Jaime with me. School was closed, and this would be a perfect time to be with the girls alone. It would be a girls' day out.

I finished cleaning up and took some "mommy time" alone and rested on the sofa. After resting for a short period, I noticed the time—it was bedtime for Jaime. I got up off the sofa and called out to James to let him know that I needed to give Jaime her bath and put her to bed. Jaminda still had some time before she would go to bed.

I decided to move forward with my plans hoping that I would go to bed early once I put Jaime to bed. I would need the extra rest to prepare for my day with Jaminda the following day. I was slowly walking from the living room and toward the bedroom when my water broke. I couldn't believe it! A few weeks ago, I'd had my checkup, and everything was going well. I'd lost the weight Dr.

Patterson had suggested that I lose, and my blood sugar was under control. He praised me for doing such a good job monitoring my diet, and I was pleased to hear that I wouldn't need the insulin. He also reminded me that the diabetes would most likely go away once the baby was born.

I decided to go to the bathroom before giving Jaime her bath. I was hoping that maybe I was mistaken, and it was a false alarm. I immediately began to trace my day, wondering if I had done something to cause this. I was tired, and maybe I'd been on my feet too long, but I hadn't been on my feet as much as I usually was at work. Maybe I'd done too much when I got home, but Jaminda had been a tremendous help. She even took Jaime under her wing and kept her occupied for a while.

I was careful and had done everything in my power to avoid another early birth. I wasn't sure what had happened and decided to just wait and see. I dared not panic. I convinced myself that even if my water had broken, that wouldn't necessarily mean that something was wrong with my son. After all, both of my girls had come early, and they were completely healthy.

James called out to me to remind me that Jaime was ready for bed. He had tired her out, keeping her busy, and she had fallen asleep. I didn't want to tell him that I thought my water had broken until I was certain that it had. I told him that I needed to go to the bathroom first. That called for no explanation because I was constantly going to the bathroom, so off to the bathroom I went.

- 23 -

He Blesses Me Over and Over

> In my distress I called upon the Lord, and cried unto
> my God: he heard my voice out of his temple and
> my cry came before him, even into his ears.
> —Psalm 18:6 (KJV)

MY WATER HAD BROKEN! I IMMEDIATELY WENT TO James and asked him to get the girls up and ready. My water broke and I called the doctor who instructed me to get to the hospital and he would meet us there. As I was getting dressed to go, James called his mother to notify her that we were dropping the girls off before going to the hospital.

Things seemed to be moving pretty quickly, and although I was uncomfortable, I was not worried about the delivery. I thought that there was always the possibility that it might not be the water, but I was pretty sure that it was, and I had a peace over this situation. I was not nervous, and I was not in any pain. It didn't seem as if I was having any contractions. I knew that God was with me and that my baby would make it into this world. We reached James's mother's house, which was about five minutes away from our house. Jaminda had questions, some of which we could not answer, but we promised her that we would let her know as soon as we could after the baby was born.

We arrived at the hospital shortly after dropping the girls off. We completed the registration, and they immediately sent us to the delivery floor. We were greeted by nurses who escorted us into the delivery room. This would be the first pregnancy for which James accompanied me to the hospital and was there for every step of the birth. Shortly after we were in the delivery room, my doctor showed up and assured us that he had his pajamas and planned to spend the night at the hospital; he would not leave until the baby was born. I was glad to hear this.

I felt really good until a nurse blurted out, "Oh no, she's early! We may not be able to deliver the baby here." As calm as I had been, it was in this moment that I began to panic, and I felt there might be problems with my child. Dr. Patterson heard her and immediately asked her to step outside of the room with him.

While he was out there, I felt like I was having contractions. My body and mind were overcome with fear of losing my baby. Nurses were attending to me, and they worked diligently to keep me calm. They were encouraging and supportive as they assured me that everything would be all right.

Dr. Patterson returned to the room and apologized for the nurse's comment.

"I'm sorry that the nurse spoke the way she did", he said, "she was out of line and she has been removed from this case."

He then examined me and told me that I was having contractions, but he needed to consult with doctors who specialized in premature births.

Again, I began to stress a bit. James's due date was December 25 or 26, and it was November 5. I was in the delivery room, about to deliver my child—prematurely. I had a silent talk with the Lord, asking him to please allow my child to enter this world. I didn't know if I could bear another miscarriage or worse. I started thinking about the lifeless twins I'd carried for a while, and because I was farther along with James, I prayed that he would be stillborn. I dreaded the idea of having to bury a little infant that had not fully developed. At that time, I couldn't remember the last time I'd felt movement.

As I had these thoughts, I was in pain, and James tried his best to console me. I was not easily comforted at this point and, unfortunately, lashed out at James. The pain was unbearable.

The doctor reentered the room and said,

"I will have to send a sample of the amniotic fluid for testing to see if the baby's lungs are developed enough for him to be born. If not, I will inject you with a medication that will expedite the development of his lungs." It could possibly add another week of development in a few hours. I will have to stop the contractions in order to get the fluid.

I was stressed out at this point; I was angry and felt helpless because there was nothing that I could do to help the process. Dr. Patterson left my bedside and returned with a very long needle that he would insert into my abdomen to obtain the fluid. I was too tired and drained to react. He explained what he was doing as he proceeded to insert the needle. He talked me through the process and soon told me that it was done and that I was an excellent patient. He quickly gave the fluid to the nurse and requested that it get to the lab as soon as possible.

I didn't feel anything. I just wanted answers regarding my situation, and I wanted to know if my son was going to be OK. All I could do was wait until the results were in and hopefully continue with the birth of my son. Dr. Patterson stayed with me as he waited for the test results.

James W. Blackmon III Is on His Way

The minutes we waited seemed like hours. James and Dr. Patterson traded stories about their high school days. They had discovered that they had attended the same high school at the same time. While they were reminiscing about old times, I was hoping that we would hear something soon.

When Dr. Patterson received a beep from his beeper, he

excused himself and said he would be right back. He was out of the room for about five minutes and returned with the test results—James's lungs were well developed, actually developed beyond the stage of his prenatal development. I was then prepared for delivery.

Dr. Patterson had stopped the delivery to check on the development of James's lungs; now, he had to induce labor to restart the contractions, and that was unbearable—or I thought. I had originally told Dr. Patterson that I wanted to deliver the baby naturally, as I had my other two children. Now, I asked for an epidural; I wanted the pain to stop. He asked me several times if I was certain that I wanted it. Of course I was, and I made sure to clearly communicate that! I couldn't bear the pain.

He reluctantly administered the injection, and shortly afterward, the pain subsided.

At 1:25 that Tuesday morning on November 6, 1990, James Wilton Blackmon III entered this world. My son was here, weighting four pounds, thirteen ounces and twenty-one inches long. He was the smallest of my babies in pounds but the longest baby in inches. We had a son, our only boy, and he was the third child that we had wanted.

I was ready to go home, but I had to be there at least two or three days after he was born. I was happy to hear that the gestational diabetes was gone, as Dr. Patterson had expected. James went home to let the girls know that they had a brother; he planned to bring them to the hospital to see the baby.

After James left, I had a visit from Dr. Patterson and the pediatrician. The Pediatrician said to me,

'James will not be able to go home with you. He was in the Intensive Care Unit and will need to remain there until he developed a little more. He was born with the inability to suck, and because of that, they will have to feed him through a tube. You can visit him after you're discharged, and you can visit him while you're in the hospital."

I wanted to see him, and I wanted to hold him again. I hadn't held him since his birth, and although it was only a few hours after he was born, I felt that it was too long.

They recommended that I rest a little longer, saying that I could visit with him later that day. When James called to let me know that he would be leaving soon to bring the girls to the hospital, I informed him of the situation; the girls could not visit him in the ICU.

It was election day, and I couldn't vote or take the girls to vote. James would have to take them to his mother's house before coming to visit James. It was disappointing for them and for me, but we assured them that James would be home soon, and they would be able to see him as much as they wanted.

Later that day, James joined me to visit with little James for the first time. He was in an incubator. He had a feeding tube in his nose; he looked so small, lying there, but his eyes were open, and he gazed at me as if he knew that I was his mom. They allowed me to hold him, and they taught me how to feed him while I was there. I wanted to nurse him but could not because he wasn't able to suck. They started him on soy milk after birth and asked me to start expressing my milk so that he could have that instead. While I was in the hospital, I wanted to provide his care as much as possible, and I did.

After three days, they released me to go home and told me that I could visit with James as much as I wanted. I was relieved to hear that. I wanted him to experience my touch—nursing him, changing his diaper, and cuddling. I asked for a feeding schedule so that I could come to the hospital in time to feed him.

I went home, heartbroken because I couldn't bring my baby home to his family. My girls were excited that I had returned but disappointed that their brother was not with me. Jaime was only two years old and would often ask, "Where is the baby?" Jaminda had more questions, and she understood when we told her that he had to stay in the hospital so that he could finishing growing.

They carried on as usual, and each day, I gave them a report on their brother's progress; we hoped he would come home soon.

Each day became more taxing for me. I would go to the hospital while Jaminda was in school and Jaime was in day care. James took a few weeks off from work to help me juggle my schedule. It was overwhelming, and I was losing sleep.

After I'd been home for two or three days, the nurses said that little James was losing weight. This was not acceptable; he couldn't lose weight. Discharging him from the hospital was based on his gaining weight. When I'd seen his feeding schedule at the hospital, I noticed that there were scheduled times to wake him during the third shift to feed him. He was still being fed through the tube. I asked if he would be put on a bottle soon, but they wanted to wait a few more days. I wanted to make sure that he was being fed as scheduled during the third shift, so I decided to call the hospital during the hours that I could not be there. I still had two other kids at home. Jaime was still young and wanted time with her mom. Jaminda was now twelve years old and in middle school. She was busy with extracurricular activities, and I needed to be there for her.

James was in his sixth day in ICU, and still there was no definite day when he would come home. He was beginning to suck, though, and I brought my milk to the hospital to feed him. He was now nursing from the bottle only in my absence and getting better at sucking. I nursed him during my visits. He was getting used to me holding him and was feeding well on my milk.

After visiting with him, I went through my day, as usual—picking up Jaminda from school and Jaime from day care, preparing dinner, checking homework, and preparing for the next day. I'd gotten used to being tired; it became my norm. I went to bed on the night of November 15, 1990, and woke up prior to James's feeding time. I called the hospital to see if he was being fed, as scheduled.

"Hello," I said, "This is Mrs. Blackmon. I'm calling to see how James did with his first feeding tonight"

"He didn't have his first feeding", the nurse said, "We didn't want to awake him."

"Will you please wake him and feed him because he can't skip a feeding and he can't lose any more weight."

That night, I broke down and cried. I was concerned that he might be skipping feeding times, and that could increase his time in the hospital. I went from a silent sniffle to a roaring wail! I woke up James. I was concerned that my baby was not getting the nourishment he needed to get home. James assured me that he would look into it the next day.

The next day, before James went to work, he called the pediatrician and expressed his concern for me. I was not sleeping well, and he told him how many hours a day I was spending at the hospital. The pediatrician, Dr. West, told him that he would get back to him. About two hours later, Dr. West called and told me that I could bring James home.

Dr. West had gone to the hospital and examined James. He also checked his records and saw that I had done most of his care during the day, and he felt that my son would be better off at home with his family. Dr. West waited at the hospital until I got there, and when I arrived, he handed James to me and said, "If you can provide this much care in the hospital, you can do it at home. Take him home, and see me in two weeks."

I was elated and couldn't wait to get him home. It was a great day for all of us! Little James was coming home to meet his sisters for the first time.

James Is Home

Bringing James home was the answer to my prayers. Jaminda was glad to see him and began to sing to him immediately. Jaime stared at him and placed her little finger in his hand, and he held on to it. He was only ten days old, but appeared to be as alert as my girls were when they came home for the first time, if not more alert. There were times when I visited him in the hospital and he would be upside down in his crib. The doctors called him a little squirmer and assured me that he would grow up to be a nice-size young man. Being a premature birth would not stop him from being a big man. I could tell by his ability to move around that his prematurity would not get in the way of his growth and development. We were all so excited that he was home.

Two weeks after he was home, we went to visit Dr. West for his checkup, and Dr. West gave him his seal of approval for good health. James was no longer on bottle formula, and he was gaining weight. He continued to gain weight and to grow as he should for his age.

James quickly claimed his position in the family. He enjoyed the attention he received from his sisters. Jaminda was an excellent big sister to both of her siblings, always wanting to help with James and Jaime. James was her "doodle bug," a nickname she gave him, and Jaime was "Jaime girl." Jaime became James's protector and wanted to be wherever her brother was. She talked to him all the time, and she seemed to understand that his cooing meant words he never said. He seemed to like having her around. He was a fussy baby, but it didn't matter. He was home, and our family of five was complete.

- 24 -

Those Special Moments

*Every good gift and every perfect gift is from above,
and cometh down from the Father of lights, with whom
is no variableness, neither shadow of turning.*
—James 1:17 (KJV)

EACH DAY, I THANK GOD FOR MY CHILDREN, AS WELL AS everything he has done for me. I have always referred to my children as "my three miracles." They are my living testaments of what God can do! They are my special gifts, and I celebrate each day for them—my three miracles, my blessings. It was such a joy to see my family grow from three members to five members. The one thing we wanted for our children was that they would develop into respectful citizens who loved God and people, and, like my upbringing, it had to start at home. They learned very quickly and early in life that they must love one another and that the love they demonstrated at home would follow them each time they left home. James and I were their first teachers. It was important that we build a foundation of strength, nourished by the love of God and the love of family.

It was a blessing and a pleasure having three children. I had reached the number of children I wanted, but considering what I had gone through, I would not complain if God saw fit to give us a fourth one. James and I had an agreement and understanding regarding how we would raise our children. Jaminda was the only child for ten years, and she had grown accustomed to having one-on-one attention all the time. As parents, we met challenges in all areas that we had not anticipated, but those challenges were necessary for us to parent in a way that was pleasing to God. Jaminda was a well-behaved child. She didn't have problems at school and was always mannerly and respectful. She loved school and never wanted to miss a day. She was a pleasure to be around. As tired as I would become from time to time, any moments spent with her were pleasurable. She did love to talk, and I would later learn that all of my children were talkers.

Jaminda loved to sing, and at times, she would find whatever she could use as a microphone and sing without cues. She would just sing and rock to her own singing, as if she had music. She would develop this talent and sing at events and at church. She was a loyal friend to her friends and enjoyed things that most kids enjoyed. She loved going to amusement parks and festivals, as well as school events and visiting her friends and family.

We had much quality time with her, and I wanted to give each of my children one-to-one time with me. I wanted them to have what Jaminda had; even though I knew that I would have to do some juggling, I would make it happen. God had blessed me with these children, and I wanted to show them that they were loved. We had gotten through many obstacles with Jaminda, and we felt prepared.

By the time James was three years old, we learned that he had hearing loss in one of his ears. He had demonstrated difficulty hearing, and Jaime was the only one who clearly understood what he was saying. She would translate his speech for us, and at times, when he spoke, he would look at Jaime to tell us what he was saying. His hearing was not restored; after testing him numerous times, it was concluded that he was born with that hearing loss.

With the help of speech therapy, his speech improved tremendously, and he was able to function without complications. We wanted him to accept his norm and not use it as a crutch that would limit his efforts to achieve whatever he wanted to accomplish. His speech therapy was a part of the school system, and because of that, James attended school two hours a day at the age of three. He felt good about this because it allowed him to go to school during the time that Jaime was going.

School was important to our family. The kids knew that we expected them to do well; that meant doing their best. Jaime loved school. Like Jaminda, she loved to read and wanted to be involved in everything. She was an overachiever and looked forward to going to school daily. On one occasion, Jaime was allowed to check out twenty-eight books from the school library. When she brought home all of those books, I had to have a talk with her teacher. I felt that it was too much. The teacher explained to me that Jaime wanted them so badly that she didn't have the heart to tell her no. Jaime promised her that she would read them all and return them as scheduled. Jaime did finish those books and had time to spare. She read them every free moment she had so she could get more. I gave her a limit of how many she could check out, and I also gave that limit to her teacher.

James was not as eager to go to school as his sisters had been. He created his own kind of fun by choosing to do what he wanted, instead of the expectations of the teacher. When he took speech class before he was actually enrolled as a student, he had no problems charming the teachers into doing what he wanted. On one occasion, he refused to participate, telling the teacher that he wasn't feeling well. On hearing this, the teacher allowed him to skip one of his lessons, and he was able to play with Legos instead. When I heard about this, I insisted that James apologize to his teacher and admit that he had lied to her and just wanted to play. Disrespect was not tolerated in our household, and neither was lying.

I was reminded of the time when Jaminda refused to put her toys away in day care, and she was allowed to get away with it.

When I found out, she lost many privileges at home. She was very cooperative with her day care teacher throughout her time there.

Jaime did not demonstrate any oppositional behavior, but she decided to take on a leadership role in the third grade. She decided on her own that she would monitor the lunch period, although there were adults assigned for that duty. The kids reported to her for directions while eating their lunches—when to eat, what to eat, when to talk, and asking permission to talk. Finally, one kid became tired of this process and reported her to her teacher. Jaime apologized to her class and felt remorseful toward her peers. This never happened again. We were proud and relieved that she recognized her wrong and took it upon herself to apologize and admit her wrong in front of her class without prompting. She learned her lesson, but nonetheless, we followed up with conversation at home. We raised good kids, but that's not to say that we didn't have headaches at times. We had many headaches, but it was worth it.

We taught them to believe in God and to believe in themselves, meaning that they did not allow anyone to put limits on what they could do. We made it a practice in our household to allow them to soar as far and as high as they could. We didn't force them into any activities or tell them what they should become, other than people who treat others with respect and dignity. Although we emphasized and expected education, the message we wanted them to get was that true success involved knowing God and living as God would have them live.

Jaminda exercised not allowing others to limit her capabilities when she was in elementary school. She loved to sing and always had a beautiful voice. She tried out for the choir, but a teacher told her that she couldn't sing. She was upset about it, but I assured her that she could sing, and we would get her into a choir; it was a matter of time. A year later, she was going to a different school because we had moved to a new district. The music teacher at her new school heard her singing and approached me during a

PTA meeting. He told me, "Jaminda needs to join the choir." His recommendation got her started in a community choir, where she would sing at events and receive voice lessons. The experiences she had in choirs, talent competitions, and singing engagements motivated her even more to enrich her knowledge and skill for music and voice. She would make this her life commitment.

Jaime was interested in playing the saxophone at her school. Jaminda had learned to play the flute and continued to play it until she graduated from high school. Jaime's music teacher approached me during a parent conference, saying that she had to apologize to Jaime. She had told Jaime that she couldn't play the saxophone because she did not test well on that instrument. Jaime politely had told the teacher that if she couldn't play the saxophone, she did not want to be in the band. The teacher allowed her to play the saxophone, and Jaime had first chair in her school band, as well as a seat in the town-wide band. She was a top saxophone player and continues to play in her adult life. Jaime exercised her ability to not allow anyone to dictate what she could or could not do. She did it respectfully and was able to pursue her interest of playing the saxophone.

James learned to play the trumpet with his school's music program, but he didn't stop there. He taught himself to play the piano as well—he taught himself before he played the trumpet. The hearing loss did not affect his ability to play, and he did not allow this to stop him from enjoying playing music. He never allowed his hearing loss to prohibit him from doing anything.

When he was three years old, James's grandmother gave him a small piano with about eight keys. I was always walking around the house singing something, as my mama had done when I was small. I loved singing "Little Drummer Boy." One day, I noticed James playing with his toy piano. As I was about to go upstairs, he said,

"Mommy, I can play your favorite song."

"Really, I said, "go ahead and play it."

I told him to play, thinking that he was making up something. Then he started playing "Little Drummer Boy"! I was amazed and proud at the same time. He had learned the song from just listening to me sing it and had figured out the notes. He would grow into a young man who played his instruments and told me when I sang off-key. We knew that we had strong children, and they were unstoppable at an early age.

At the age of four, James showed remarkable strength beyond his age. During his birthday celebration, he suddenly shut down and didn't want to participate. He didn't want to open gifts or have any of his birthday cake. He decided to go to his room. Shortly afterward, he came downstairs and when I looked at him, he remarked,

"Mommy, my smile is gone."

"Come here", I said, "Let me look at that."

I looked at him and became numb—the right side of his face had drooped, and he had no control of that side. When he smiled, only the left side of his face smiled. He quickly noticed my expression and said,

"Mommy, please don't look at me like that."

I immediately gained some strength to ask him questions about how he was feeling.

"Does it hurt when I touch it?", I asked,

"No", he said, "It doesn't hurt, but my smile is gone."

I was thankful that he wasn't in pain and he was able to go to bed without any difficulty. The next morning, I took him to see his doctor, and he was diagnosed with Bell's palsy. We were told that it would be temporary and was caused by his numerous ear infections. At the end of two months, as the doctor had predicted, James's condition had cleared up. He came downstairs smiling and demonstrated how his smile had returned. He smiled over and over again to make sure his smile was there to stay.

Going to church was required; we wanted our children to know God and to attend church. We started them going when

A Way That's Mighty Sweet

they were small, but my job required me to work on weekends, and my churchgoing was put on hold when I worked on Sundays. I made an effort to go as often as I could, and, at times, I had the kids go with a friend of mine, when James or I couldn't go, as a means to keep them going. That didn't work so well, but I was concerned about them not attending.

I heard my mama's words playing over and over in my head: "If you ever have children, you're responsible for getting them to church." She often reminded me that God would hold me accountable if my children were not in church. Now the time had come when I was faced with this responsibility. I tried to teach them about God and hoped that they would understand. They had ways of letting me know that they knew God in their own little minds.

I remember one day when Jaminda was about five years old. She and I were shopping. I could tell that she wanted something on the shelf at the cash register. She was told not to touch anything without asking first. As I was waiting to place my items on the counter, she looked as if she wanted something. She had not touched anything, but I could see what she seemed to be thinking about, as she was staring at an item and looking up at me.

I said, "Jaminda, don't you think about it."

She fixed her little arm next to her side, looked up at me, and said,

"Did God give you my mind too?"

I seized the moment and said, "Yes." I knew, at that moment, that although she was young, she knew that God knew what she was thinking. She was surprised to know that I knew as well.

Once I was riding in the car with Jaime. She was about nine years old; she and I were discussing why kids need to listen and be obedient—a conversation topic that she initiated. We talked about the Ten Commandments, and Jaime was moved to tell me about a situation in school where her peers were discussing that they didn't like what their parents said. Jaime said,

"I don't know why kids don't listen to their parents and obey them.

Don't they know that parents know everything?"

"You are right Jaime", I said, "I don't know why either."

In that moment, I wasn't about to tell her that I didn't know everything. I allowed her to hold on to that thought. She was able to relate her comment to the Bible by saying that was why God gave children parents. I was relieved that God remained a priority in our household, and my children let me know.

Our Christmases

Christmas has always been my favorite time of the year. I loved it because my parents made it a special time for us. Although they taught me the meaning behind Christmas, as a child I loved everything else that came with it—the gifts, the food, the fun of decorating, and the joy of knowing that after I went to bed on Christmas Eve, I would wake the next morning to new toys. I always knew that Christmas was about Jesus, and Mama and Daddy would not let me lose sight of that.

Daddy had always come home with a tree he had chopped down for us to decorate. After he passed, we had artificial trees. For the first Christmas James and I had together as husband and wife, we had a real tree, and it was a tradition that we continued throughout the years. My children were able to experience the pleasure of having a real tree, and it became a family outing to go together and participate in chopping the tree down at a tree farm. It became an activity, as we would buy hot chocolate after purchasing the tree and sip it on the way home. As we rode along, we would evaluate the trip, allowing the kids to say their favorite part of getting the tree.

We wanted the kids to understand what Christmas was about—the celebration of the birth of Jesus Christ. Prior to

Jaminda's birth, I mentioned to James that I did not want to teach our kids that Santa Claus brought their gifts. We would let them know that we purchased gifts for them and that it symbolized how gifts were brought to Mary and Joseph for their baby, Jesus Christ. James was OK with not teaching them that Santa Claus was coming. We did explain to them that other children might believe that Santa Claus brought them gifts, and it was not their place to tell them otherwise.

James's mother always wanted to take our kids to the mall or to a department store to take pictures with Santa. We didn't oppose that because that was her time with her grandchildren. We just explained to them that someone dressed as Santa was a way of showing the importance of giving to one another and to support the parents who wanted their children to believe as such. They understood and assured us that they would not spoil it for other children.

When James was about three years old, he let me know that he was interested in decorating the tree. I had a tradition of using only white lights on the tree because it reminded me of candles. One Christmas, after I had placed the white lights on the tree, James asked if we could have mixed-color lights. He wanted the majority of the lights to be colored. We stopped decorating the tree and purchased colored lights to add to the white lights. He was ecstatic! He gazed at the tree for minutes at a time when the lights were on. Decorating the tree was an activity in our house. Each ornament was strategically placed in the same place each year. The kids memorized the placings and hung them accordingly. They all enjoyed taking pictures in front of the tree to denote that they were a part of the process of decorating.

That same Christmas, James started another tradition. I was going over the menu for Christmas dinner with the three of them. The girls and James were in agreement that we would have our original menu, and for dessert, they wanted to stay with apple pie and banana pudding. James blurted out, "Make a cake."

The girls and I looked at him, and I said, "You want a cake?" He said, "Yes, a birthday cake for Jesus!"

I was glad to know that he remembered that this was all about Jesus! I made the cake as he wished, and on Christmas Day, we joined him in singing happy birthday to Jesus. It was a tradition we carried for several years.

I always shared the special Christmases I had with my parents. I told them that I learned to ride a bike without any coaching or help to stay on the bike. I then shared with them how my daddy was so proud of me for learning to ride that bike independently and had planned to buy me a bike, but, unfortunately, he had died before he could follow through with that plan. I had never owned a bike, but I made sure that each of my children had a bike. On one Christmas day when James and Jaime were teenagers, I noticed that there weren't any presents under the tree to me from the two of them. I was a little relieved because I often told them that I wasn't expecting gifts from them. I would be satisfied with a hug and Christmas greetings. On this particular Christmas, after the gifts were opened, Jaime and her brother left the living room and returned with a bike for me!

They had approached their father with a Christmas gift idea that they wanted to give me, and he obliged them. We always purchased the gifts they chose to give to me and James. Jaime was the spokesperson for the two of them.

"Mommy", she said, "James and I wanted to get you a bike because your daddy didn't get a chance to buy you one. We wanted you to have this bike because you didn't have one when you were a little girl."

James nodded as she spoke as a sign of approval. I had forgotten that I had told them that story. I don't know who was happier, them or me. It's the thoughtful things they did and still do to make Christmas a special time of the year. I never asked them what they wanted for Christmas because I wanted them to learn to be thankful for what they got. As a parent, I know my children and was pretty good about selecting things they liked. James would ask them for a list and would choose an item or two and surprise them with it.

They shared so many special moments with us and enriched our lives as parents. My experiences as a mom were more than I could have ever expected because of them. They made parenting fun and exciting, as well as overwhelming and exhausting at times. Nonetheless, they were and will always be my three miracles. To this day, although they are grown, they still amaze me. They are my precious children sent to me by God, my three miracles, and they are my gifts.

- 25 -

An Ongoing Journey

For I know the thoughts that I think toward you, saith the Lord, thoughts of peace, and not of evil, to give you and expected end.
—Jeremiah 29:11 (KJV)

When I think of the roads I've traveled in my lifetime, I thank God for holding on to me during those times when I'd let go; I've fallen more times than I can count. I look back, and I know that my life would have been a mess—maybe over—had I not accepted God into my life. I'm thankful for those times when I was lost and made decisions that were not in my best interest. He kept me safe from all harm and danger, including myself.

I am blessed to have the parents God gave me, ones who were God-fearing and instilled the love from God in me from their actions. I was in church routinely while under their care and knew about God. Those years of teaching were lost at times, as I swayed from my teachings and behaved based on my own understanding and ways of going about my life.

I look back at the life I planned for myself. It was a life without substance and without following my Lord and Savior. I was fixated on believing that I was destined to do what was best for me, and that plan did not include much of anyone else. I felt alone when I no longer had either of my parents. I was numb, lost, and unbalanced. I wasn't certain of very much. I continued to make choices that were not of God but didn't realize it at the time. I thought things were going well until I started having problems with the birth of my first child. I was saved a few months after her birth, and that's when I began to see things more clearly.

For the first time in my life, I felt that I had some direction. I knew where my help was coming from. I knew that I couldn't do things as I had planned and that I had to keep God in the forefront. I had a relationship with God, and I knew that there was more to being a child of God than attending church each Sunday morning. I had to talk to him daily and keep his words in my heart. During those times, people asked me if my family was cursed because I had so many losses. They wondered why I was going through so much when I was supposed to be a child of God. They were misguided, thinking that because I was a child of God, I should not have gone through the miscarriages and the loss of family members. I knew that trials and tribulations were a part of being God's child. I knew firsthand that I was stronger during those times than I was when everything was going my way. It was those times that kept me—and continue to keep me—close to God.

I've learned to thank God for what he has given me and to appreciate them even more when I've lost them. He gave me parents who kept me safe and provided me with the love and attention I needed as a child. The loss of the children I could have had made me appreciate my children even more. As much as I didn't understand my losses and didn't like the fact that I lost them, I appreciate the fact that I had them. They are a major part of who I am today, and I thank God for that. The conversations I had with my daddy remain clear in my head. He taught me to not worry about what people were saying as long as I was doing what's right. I have mastered that concept. I can't function as a child of God if I worry about who likes or dislikes me. I know that God loves me, and my sisters and brothers in Christ see what I see. I learned to let go and let God. This is a lesson I've passed down to my children.

Giving birth to my children has been my greatest gift. My role as a mother has been rewarding, and I thank God for that. Growing up, I wondered how Mama could be in such a good mood most of the time with all of her children. There were eight of us, and she always was glad to see us when we came home from school. She was like that with me until the day she died.

I had no plans to become a mother because I saw all the work she did, and I also saw how it didn't seem to bother her. I was adamant that I wouldn't have children, but it didn't happen as I'd thought. My plans were changed, and I found myself wondering why I was gifted with such a miracle. Why was I chosen to have little human beings grow inside of me? Why would God allow me to be a part of something as miraculous as bringing a human being into this world? And he allowed me to do it three times! This is truly an example of God's grace; I didn't deserve the wonders he has bestowed upon me.

Somebody Prayed for Me

Two and a half years after my son was born, I was faced with yet another medical issue. Each month, I would lose time from work due to hemorrhaging. I was bleeding profusely, and when treatment didn't work, I was told that I needed a hysterectomy. Although that news might be devastating for some, I didn't find it heartbreaking at all. Dr. Patterson counseled me on some feelings of loss that I might have after I had the surgery, and the hospital staff offered much support to help me deal with any feelings of loss. They offered one-on-one counseling while I was in the hospital, and they offered group sessions to help me cope with the thought of not being able to have any more children. They didn't know that God had prepared me for this and he had kept me during all of my trials.

I wasn't feeling any loss. I didn't need counseling because the true Counselor had given me all the answers to my problems. I had gone through losses of miscarriages and the feeling of not having kids, as well as not having a second or third child. I rejoiced when I was told that I wouldn't have more kids because God had blessed me with three! I knew that this problem could have surfaced years ago, and I would not have had any children. I had the greatest gifts that I could possibly have here on earth. He saw fit to give me three children when he could have said no in the beginning. The surgery did not impose any loss but reminded me of what I had.

I know now why my mama felt as she did about us. A mother is a blessing because of her children. It is an act of God! Mama always said that parents are responsible for their children knowing God. She and Daddy set a great example for that, although I didn't know it at the time. Mama also said that children should be chastised, and she and Daddy did that through lecturing when I did something against their teaching and the Word of God. Those lectures felt like sermons, and I used to think that I would rather get a whipping. But I grew to appreciate the lectures. They always processed the situations—why it happened, how I could avoid doing it again, and—most importantly—if someone was offended by my behavior. They taught me to ask for forgiveness. I understood why I had to forgive. It started at home when I had an argument or dispute with a sibling. The altercation always ended with a big hug, while Mama watched and smiled with approval that the situation was over. Knowing this made me more anxious when I thought about having children because it seemed like a lot of work. Mama intervened often to keep the respect and appreciation for one another present in our home. I've learned, over time, that it is a valuable process, and it's what God commanded us to do—to forgive.

I've taken those principles and passed them down to my

children. They did not know their maternal grandparents, but I hope that they were able to get a glimpse of them through me. I have shared so many memories of them over the years. They know how my father was protective of his daughters and the endearing things he did for us. They know that they were God-fearing people and that we were taught that God is always first in our lives. Although my children never knew them, they speak of them as if they did.

My parents taught me through the lens of the Bible; they integrated God's words with their parenting and teaching. They taught me that I could live without their being here on this earth because God will forever be with me. I would learn that I have to have a relationship with God. I have them in my memory; they're in my spirit and in the loving foundation they built for me.

I know that they prayed for me! It is their love for God and their prayers that kept me when I was too preoccupied with myself to really know what I needed and didn't know how to go to God myself. Their prayers kept me from many traps and danger that I could have easily fallen into. I didn't always have faith or even know what it was, but I had parents who did, and I believe their love for God protected me in ways I have yet to discover. My learning from their teachings was delayed, but I did learn to lay down by burdens and give my problems to the Lord. I finally realized that I was my own stumbling block, and only God could lead me around it. I fell often but learned to get up more.

My prayer is that my children pass the love for God and the love for family to their children and teach about the generations before them. They already know that they are blessed with a legacy of love and that God will be with them, whether I'm in this world or not. I thank God for my parents and for their teachings. They demonstrated the strength needed to endure or overlook the snares and arrows of the world that will come my way. I've experienced that firsthand, and I thank my heavenly Father for the teachings of my earthly father.

The arrows of this world will continue to be hurled at me, and I will continue to be struck by many of them. Then, there are those arrows that are intercepted by God and will never reach me. The ones that make contact with me are the ones that will place me in situations that will make me stronger and strengthen my faith. I know that there is no plan when God has not been involved in that plan. Planning without talking to God is a setup to fail because I can't do anything without Him.

Mama always said that only God knows what will happen, and we should never say never. I think she knew that I would have children someday. She often reminded me that there's a reason for everything. She was right! As the arrows of the world continue to come at me, I don't duck to get out of the way because God intervenes. Mama always said when those things happen, it's out of our control, but we know that God is in control, and we don't need to worry. Mama also said, "God has a way that's mighty sweet."